INTRODUCTION

Why do some entrepreneurs succeed and live the life they have always dreamed of? It is simple—they overcome failure and instill the habits of the most successful founders while taking relentless action on an idea. It is these habits and strategies I will share with you in this book from my more than 25 years of *failing and learning*. Failure is best learned (and a heck of a lot cheaper) through a *secondhand* story, so start reading and learn from my mishaps as well some amazing victories.

I will distill everything I could teach you over one year in these 365 daily lessons. This book is written as if each morning you and I would sit and share a coffee together where I will bring forth a brief insight that will reveal a more direct path to the success you are setting out to achieve. This past year I have had the privilege of mentoring my son—who just graduated high school—on his entrepreneurial journey, and this book is the fruit of what I have shared with him.

My mission is to equip, encourage, and educate entrepreneurs from every part of the globe, as it is entrepreneurship that serves as the one vehicle that allows anyone the opportunity to achieve the life they always dreamed of. Entrepreneurship will demand you bring a profitable idea to the marketplace, as well as be the founder others want to team up with and help build this audacious dream.

My hope is that this book will assist you on that journey.

—*Sean Castrina*

ACKNOWLEDGEMENTS

This book is a culmination of more than 25 years of business successes and a few humbling failures. The successes are shared with the many business partners I have had over the years who would read like a football team introduction. To each of you I say thanks Keith, Kurt, George, Steve, John, Tony, James, Charles and the list keeps growing.

My family has continue to fuel my early morning rises to put words into my computer that result in these finished works so that my countless readers can learn and be encouraged by the hundreds of axioms shared in this book.

I have a tremendous assistant Michael who has been so helpful over the last year in organizing this and other books so they become finished works. Anyone who works with me must have the gift of patience and longsuffering so thank you.

JANUARY

FEBRUARY

MARCH

APRIL

MAY

JUNE

1. Air Traffic Controller
2. Desire Zone
3. What If?
4. Addition Through Subtraction
5. Compelling Character
6. Big Hairy Audacious Goal ("BHAG")
7. The Law of Talent
8. The Law of Development
9. The Law of Greatness
10. The Law of Execution
11. The Law of Growth
12. The Law of Branding
13. The Law of Culture
14. The Law of Profit
15. The Law of Systems
16. The Law of Change
17. The Law of Should, Not Could
18. Marketing 101
19. Innovation
20. Delivery
21. Speed
22. Price
23. Filling a Need
24. Wow Factor
25. Experience
26. Obtain Competitive Intelligence
27. One Bite at a Time
28. Teachable Moments
29. Infrastructure
30. Guardrails

JULY

AUGUST

STEPTEMBER

OCTOBER

NOVEMBER

DECEMBER

JANUARY 1
ENTREPRENEURS

An entrepreneur is someone who starts a business, creates employment, and keeps doing it. I have altered the standard definition, as I do not believe becoming an entrepreneur is a one-time event. Instead, it is part of their DNA. They can't stop themselves. Though great entrepreneurs may be identified with one company—Bill Gates with Microsoft, and Jeff Bezos with Amazon, for example—they are aggressive entrepreneurs, and that's reflected in the entrepreneurial nature of their companies. Microsoft currently has acquired over 2,225 companies and purchased stakes in sixty-four others.

Sometimes a person owns a business, and it is a great business. This person may not be an entrepreneur but instead had an entrepreneurial hiccup. Years ago, he or she had a good idea and somehow also had a touch of risk tolerance and moved forward with the business. As the saying goes, "Even a blind squirrel finds a nut once in a while." They moved forward with something because there was such an obvious and big opening in the marketplace. That's great. I'm not taking anything away from that person, but they had a brief spark of entrepreneurship and became a business owner.

So, are you an entrepreneur?

Richard Branson starts one business after another. So does Mark Cuban. Maybe you watch Shark Tank and listen to people who are entrepreneurs. What they have in common is that they can't stop themselves from getting in on the ground floor of start-up businesses. It is like candy being waved in front of them.

Again, some people started one business that they are holding on to for dear life. These are people who have very little risk tolerance, so they purchase a franchise. They are protected in the same way that children are protected from throwing a gutter ball when they go bowling and have bumpers on the sides to keep them from the disappointment of throwing a gutter ball.

Entrepreneurs don't have any of those rails because we create the system, and we want to test the system that we have created. If we want to own a franchise, we want to create it. That is how entrepreneurs think.

ARE YOU REALLY AN ENTREPRENEUR?

JANUARY 2

QUESTIONS TO ASK YOURSELF
BEFORE STARTING A BUSINESS

Today's lesson will be formatted like a doctor's visit in that I am just going to list questions you want to ask yourself before starting your first business, or if you are coming off a failed business. Each question has a purpose that will reveal something valuable in the start-up journey.

Venture Capitalists bet on people more than they bet on business plans and ambitious ideas. Why? Because plans and ideas in the hands of someone with no drive, perseverance, and leadership are doomed to fail every time. However, you put an average idea in the hands of someone with these traits, and I am still willing to bet all my chips they will figure it out.

Let's begin your entrepreneurial exam:

Why do you think (show me proof) that your idea is profitable and will work?

What experience or expertise do you have with the business idea you have?

Who is going to buy your products or services and why? (Show me proof.)

What makes your business different or better than your competition?

Are you planning to quit your job to start this business? (Think that through.)

Do you lack something critical (capital, expertise, time)? Consider Partnering

What will motivate you to succeed at this? What is the payoff?

What have you ever started before? (Neighborhood watch, softball team, etc.)

Are you competitive with high energy, perseverance, and great people skills?

Are you a problem solver and able to make decisions fast?

How much capital do you need to start and where will it come from?

This questionnaire is a simple fitness test like they give you to determine if you are able to serve in the military. Each question has an answer that if positive gives you a greater likelihood of success.

HOW DID YOUR FITNESS TEST GO?

JANUARY 3
CORE VALUE STATEMENT

A core value statement defines the company's culture and states what is permitted and what is not, essentially what behavior is permitted within the company.

I'm going to share with you our value statement within Advantage. It's very simple: "To treat every customer the way we want to be treated."

What does the company stand for? That's how you build your value statement. What values do its employees embody? What does it produce and contribute to the world? Answering these questions succinctly, but meaningfully, is a challenge that is worth pursuing.

Too many companies craft a core value statement to anchor every aspect of their businesses, but they don't really ask themselves, "Is this really what I believe?"

You need to craft your value statement because that's going to dictate your behavior and how your employees act.

Example of a Great Core Value Statement

L.L. Bean: "Sell good merchandise at a reasonable profit, treat your customers like human beings, and they will always come back for more."

In their core value statement, the company is telling its customers that they're going to sell affordable products and treat them humanely, so they'll want to keep shopping there. This is a version of The Golden Rule, and it's posted prominently in its retail stores and manufacturing and shipping facilities.

A business plan should have a mission statement. It should be one that you look at regularly. It should be something that's posted. It should guide your company.

DOES YOUR CORE VALUE STATEMENT REPRESENT WHAT YOU ARE OFFERING?

JANUARY 4
VISION STATEMENT

Vision portrays the ultimate version of what the company can be. Your vision statement is based on the question, "If your company was everything you wanted it to be twenty years from now, what would it look like?" It's a long-term, perfect view of what you could turn this company into.

If your entire focus is only on trying to survive or on trying to get started, then once you get through that point, there's no direction. You don't want to be in survival mode. You want to be in thrive mode.

I'm going to share with you the vision statement of our company Advantage: "To be the most sought-after home contracting company in our area because we have the most respected reputation, providing exceptional service and quality work."

> To be the most sought-after contracting company ... To be the most sought-after contracting company requires advertising, aggressive marketing, messaging our ideal customers, and creating repeat customers and referral business.

> With the most respected reputation ... In our industry, reputations typically are not always that good, but ours is very good. We have an A+ rating with the Better Business Bureau, and we've won every possible local award. Our reputation is important!

> Providing exceptional service ... When you call our office, you do not speak with an answering service. We do not put people on hold. We allow you to tell us in full what you're thinking about your project that you want to be done. We want to completely understand it, without interruption, so we don't put anybody on hold.

> Providing quality work ... To provide quality work, you need to have exceptionally talented people. As a general rule, we don't hire anybody with less than fifteen years of experience.

HAVE A VISION STATEMENT FOR YOUR COMPANY AND WORK TO ATTAIN IT.

JANUARY 5
THREE MUSTS IN YOUR START-UP

In your small business, do you have a budget? If you don't have a budget for these three things, you will not be a business owner for long.

Have you budgeted a salary for yourself?

You must start getting paid. Your business will only last for so long if none of the owners are getting paid. The excitement will drain quickly, and there are only so many sacrifices that can be made. People will start abandoning ship, or the raw energy of growing the business will disappear.

In your start-up plan, you must have a time frame to get you to a point where everyone is making some money. If you don't budget for that money, or you don't have time to review and revise your budget, then you could find yourself one year in, and no one is making money. That is a tough situation to be in.

Have you budgeted for reserve money?

If you are not putting money in reserve, the first rainstorm or problem will cripple your business. You have to put money away systematically from every dollar of income toward reserve funds. Consistently put money into a separate reserve account, and do not touch it. Treat it the same way that you would a tax liability. It is untouchable.

Have you budgeted for marketing and advertising?

Small-business owners have told me that they love their repeat and word-of-mouth customers. All business owners love them, but it is difficult to build a business off just those two types of customers. You need to have a marketing plan in place at all times in order to gather new customers.

You can't open a second location if you don't know how to advertise or market a message that goes with the company. You have to budget for this because, at the end of every year, there are going to be clients you want to get rid of. If you don't have the budget to bring on new customers, you can't fire aggravating ones.

LOOK AT YOUR BUDGET
BEFORE STARTING A COMPANY.

JANUARY 6
BUSINESS CONSTITUTION

A business constitution is a guiding document for your business that should not be altered, only interpreted. It is similar to an irrevocable trust. If you've ever written a will, these are the guidelines that cannot be altered or changed by your estate or your loved ones upon your death. For an entrepreneur, a business constitution will lay out the guardrails and pillars that exist within your organization.

Mission Statement

A business constitution starts with a mission statement. I own a very high-end, successful home repair/home remodeling company. It has eight divisions and brings in millions of dollars in revenue per year, but it started out as a very small handyman company twenty years ago. "Our mission is to provide craftsmanship that exceeds our customer's expectations, in a timely and professional manner." That's our mission statement.

We know what our core business is: it's construction with craftsmanship. Within that, we know that we need to exceed customers' expectations. To do that, we know we need to have a talented staff and complete the work in a timely and professional manner. Having a mission statement will allow you to make decisions easily in your business.

Tagline or Branding Position

Our tagline is, "We are the leader in home repairs and projects." That tagline was put in before we ever opened on our first day. We wanted to make a bold, audacious promise from day one that we were going to be *the best*. Taking it further, our tagline establishes who our profile customer is: homeowners. That's within our constitution so we don't get distracted.

A BUSINESS CONSTITUTION WILL HELP YOUR BUSINESS MAKE BETTER AND FASTER DECISIONS.

JANUARY 7

SEVEN LAWS OF BUSINESS PARTNERSHIP

History has shown that two people with a shared goal can accomplish exponentially more than one person can. Moving forward with a partnership, there are seven laws that you should follow.

Within your partnership, one needs to be a visionary and one needs to be a manager. Having two visionaries is like a never-ending tug of war. One needs to provide the vision, and one needs to be a detail person who provides your checks and balances.

Your "reasons why" need to be critical. After starting your business, it should be clear that without your partner and their skill, resources, time, etc., the business could never have existed. With big "reasons why," it is impossible to regret a partnership.

Define responsibilities before starting the business. You have to drill down on responsibilities, job descriptions, and the time and results expected. Otherwise, you may find that the person you brought in as a partner is unable to do the job.

Losses should be jointly shared. We are not splitting the profit 50–50 if you are not taking a beating when I take a beating. We should cosign for vehicles, property, and everything else.

Payouts should be clearly defined before starting the business. Partnerships do not necessarily have to be 50–50. If two people start the business together, I think 50–50 payouts work the best. However, if someone put up 60 or 70 percent of start-up costs, the payout should most likely be equal to that share.

You should have a prenuptial agreement. A business partnership is like a marriage. All the laws need to be written out: the shares, voting shares, payouts, and share of losses. You also want to define responsibilities and what the consequences of failing to fulfill those responsibilities will be.

Decide who has the deciding vote if you are 50–50 owners. How do you break a tie when you have a two-person partnership and cannot agree on something? Determine this up front.

GREAT PARTNERSHIPS REQUIRE ADHERING TO THE 7 LAWS OF PARTNERSHIPS.

JANUARY 8

BUILDING A DURABLE COMPANY

You must build a defense system around your company because if you think your company's going to survive no matter what, you're foolish. How do you build a defense system? By using the following simple steps:

Have a defense against the competition. What happens if somebody comes into your market and does the same thing you do? What are you going to do? You need to have a plan so if competition comes into your area, you know how you are going to beat them. You need to go back to your business plan and start looking at your competitive advantages. Do you have a way you can provide better quality? Could you do things faster?

Have a defense against the industry changes. Can your business withstand an industry change? You need to stay current in the industry and my advice is to stay ahead of changes. You should always remember that your industry may change and you need to stay on top of it.

Have a defense against financial downturns. There will probably be a financial downturn at some point in your business ownership and you need to be able to withstand it. In a financial downturn, you'll need cash reserves. In addition, you should have lines of credit for emergencies, not to use for bills and payroll.

Have a defense against legal issues. Once you get hit with legal issues, you can feel helpless. A customer or vendor may sue. Whatever the cause of your legal issues, a strong legal agreement or contract can protect your business. You need to have professionals prepare these to protect yourself against legal issues.

Have a defense against staff turnover. You need to build depth within your staff. You need to have knowledgeable, cross-trained, overlapping people who can carry other responsibilities than their own for the short term. Also, you should have noncompete agreements for key people.

A DURABLE COMPANY WITH A GOOD DEFENSE SYSTEM ATTRACTS INVESTORS.

JANUARY 9
CRISIS MANAGEMENT

How do you handle a crisis?

Know when you're in one.

There's no time to think; sometimes you have to react. When you know you're in a fire, get out a hose. You don't wait to figure out how the fire started. You put out the fire first, then you can figure out how it started. Know when you're in a crisis, that's number one.

Know the potential damage and the casualties.

When you're in a crisis, you need to figure out what the end result could be: how bad could this get? You need to know your potential damage and casualties. You need to envision your worst-case scenario.

Consider your options.

Sometimes you don't have a lot of good ones, but you need to know what your options are. This is where you brainstorm with smart people. You collaborate with people who also have skin in the game, and you've got to do this fast.

Assess collateral damage.

What is the damage? OK, if we fire a person, this division might be crippled for a while. Or maybe it's a social media issue. How do we respond to this? Whatever the case may be, there's usually collateral damage. You have to ask yourself whether it's an acceptable level of collateral damage or whether it's too much.

Take action.

After you have put the fire out, considered all of your options, and evaluated the collateral damage, now you have to make a plan and take action. At some point, you have to move forward. You've got to solve the problem. Sometimes this is where people get paralyzed and just can't take any action. You must act to save your business.

Reflect later.

Don't reflect while you're in the middle of the crisis. In a crisis, you're trying to solve the problem as fast as you can with the least amount of damage, fallout, and cost. At some point, however, you need to reflect on the crisis and crisis management because you're going to learn from everything that happened.

KNOW WHEN YOU'RE IN CRISIS AND HOW TO HANDLE IT.

JANUARY 10
NEVER READY

"The way to get started is to quit talking and begin doing."
—Walt Disney

I was never completely ready to start any of my businesses. Not one of them. And none that I started went in the linear direction I thought it would go.

Gary Ryan Blair agrees about why you can't wait for things to be perfect: "You cannot afford to wait for perfect conditions ... pportunities are easily lost while waiting for perfect conditions."

Things often don't work out the way you want them to. If I had known all the obstacles I would encounter with the various businesses, I would never have started them.

As an entrepreneur, you're never going to be perfectly ready to start your business. You may never be perfectly ready to expand your business, and you may never be perfectly ready to franchise your business. There is no "perfect." You need to understand and accept this. You'll figure it out and adapt along the way.

So, never stall on starting any business because you feel like you're not ready. You'll never be ready. Just take the first step. Start your business. Follow all necessary procedures to ensure your business stays afloat and is profitable. Along the way, you'll adapt to the changes and challenges that will inevitably occur.

YOU'LL NEVER BE *100* PERCENT READY TO START A BUSINESS.

JANUARY 11
TRAINER

If you want to be a great entrepreneur, you need to be a trainer. You need to be able not only to train your existing employees but also to train new hires. I never want a new team member to leave my organization without having improved. The only way to have a great team is to maximize the potential of each player. Without training, that will never happen.

Undeniably, not everybody that you hire is going to be great the second you hire them. But you can make them so much better if you just spend a little time training them or investing in educational opportunities for them.

I have personal experience with going to large retail stores that have new hires who have no idea what they are doing. Trying to get questions answered is not only frustrating for the shopper but the poor employee as well, as they stare at you helplessly. They have no idea where everything is in the store and are not able to complete any one job with confidence.

I think this is the area where small-business owners really miss the mark. They don't invest enough money in training their staff when a time-management seminar, a communication seminar, or an accounting or office-management conference would really help their understanding. With so many webinars available today, there is no excuse not to advance the knowledge of your staff.

How good could your staff be if you were committed to investing in training? It is an investment, and the payoff is not always immediate, but there will be a dividend in time.

LEARN TO BE A TRAINER SO THAT
YOU CAN EQUIP YOUR TEAM.

JANUARY 12
IT'S NOT JUST ABOUT THE MONEY

Before you take the leap and start a business, ask yourself, "Why am I starting this business in the first place?" Does this reason excite you? This reason needs to be more than money, as this will probably be the last reward for your hard work. Yes, you want to start and own a profitable business, but you need to have reasons other than money to motivate you in challenging times.

There are many reasons why you might want to start a business. The most obvious one—according to nearly every survey—is the desire to make more money. That translates into improving your standard of living. The second most popular reason is greater flexibility and independence, meaning the opportunity to have more control over your future.

Gladys Edmunds of *USA Today* writes, "The primary purpose of having your own business is so that it can become the catalyst to affording you a life worth living."

However, there are usually deeper reasons for owning your own business. A passion to innovate. A need to challenge yourself to achieve things that others would find difficult—and may not dare attempt. A desire to put your unique stamp on the world. The determination to build a great team. Willingness to serve others.

In fact, to be totally motivated by the idea of making money rarely breeds success. If it did, a lot more start-ups would succeed. Think of the great entrepreneurs of recent times. After launching Apple, Steve Jobs had plenty of opportunities to cash out and live a life of ease. But he was constantly driven to make better products and dominate more of the technology market, leading him to work up until his death to build an even stronger company.

Ask yourself why you are going into business in the first place. Does the answer truly excite you? Remembering your deepest motivations is likely to sustain you in your business over the long haul, especially during difficult times, when you could otherwise be tempted to turn back.

OTHER THAN MONEY,
WHAT IS YOUR MOTIVATOR?

JANUARY 13
NICE GUY, NOT A LEADER

If you want to build a great company, you have to duplicate yourself. That's how you make the real money. So, though I love recruiting leaders, oftentimes, I need to develop recruits into leaders.

I was reading about McDonald's and their vision for their employees. It's really powerful the way they stress leadership. Considering their turnover, leadership is a daunting task. The company's website reads: "As the world changes and new business challenges arise, we need leaders who can inspire and guide McDonald's to new heights. Our future success requires leadership not just in management roles but at all levels of the organization. We expect every employee to live McDonald's values and demonstrate leadership no matter what your level or position."

McDonald's says the success of their company is in its leadership, and leadership needs to be in every employee. So, from the people who turn on the lights all the way to the top of their business, they need to have leadership.

The value of developing leadership within your company is critical. It starts with recognizing the value of leadership. Just this week, one of my partners went on vacation, and the company he oversees was a disaster. It was his first multi-week vacation, and there was a cash-flow nightmare. Nothing operated at full capacity because he did not have another leader in place. When I pressed him on this, he shared the name of his most talented and tenured worker to whom he gave the keys to the place. I replied, "Nice guy, but not a leader." I explained leaders don't just oversee or manage; they lead. They will confront problems and fix them as they happen. He then had his "aha" moment and said, "I need to develop some leaders."

THE SUCCESS OF A GREAT ORGANIZATION RELIES ON ITS ABILITY TO RAISE LEADERS.

JANUARY 14
TEN QUALITIES OF A GREAT SMALL BUSINESS

You have a vision, and you're working toward it.
If you're an entrepreneur and don't have a vision for your company, you're never going to get great staff. Nobody talented wants to work at a company that's not going anywhere.

- **You have accountability.**
  Are leadership and management being held accountable for the goals they have set? Are lagging team members held accountable for not contributing to the expected level?

- **You have a culture that attracts and keeps quality employees.**
  Your company will only be as good as the people that work with and for you.

- **You have opportunities for advancement.**
  You're not going to keep great players if there's nowhere for them to advance.

- **You're committed to customer service and growing your customer base.**
  Great companies are always marketing and branding. You don't want other people to take your existing customers, and you want to add new customers.

- **You have strong sales. You're a profitable company.**
  Are you making money? Because great companies are very profitable, this allows you to reinvest in your company and allows you to pay your people well.

- **You have a great reputation within the community or industry that you serve.**

- **You are always reinvesting in growth and expansion.**

- **You've got to grow.**
  If you're not growing, you're dying.

GREAT BUSINESSES HAVE THESE QUALITIES.

THE $100 START-UP

The "$100 start-up" is a fantasy. I say a real business is defined by having employees. Any business that involves only you is being a "solopreneur," a fancy term for "you do all the work." It goes against everything I believe in regarding business.

First, you are doing all the work, so your income is earned and not passive. Your earning is limited because it is in relation to your personal productivity. This is also how I feel about "side hustles," which have become very popular. Let me tell you, those are really just second jobs.

I am still trying to figure out how you get incorporated, buy a domain name, and launch a website for $100. Let's talk about what it really takes to start a business, and escape Fantasyland.

Start-up Cost Cheat Sheet:

One-time costs: One example is getting incorporated and obtaining the needed licensing to do business. Another is buying needed equipment, such as an oven or stoves for your restaurant. These costs can be large or small but are normally made once during the start-up phase.

Ongoing costs: These include rent, utilities, and insurance. These are the expenses that crush cash flow and must be met each month.

Essential costs: These are crucial for survival. Without these purchases, your company could not open its doors or grow to scale.

Variable costs: These are inventory or production costs that may vary based on the demand you have.

GO INTO YOUR START-UP WITH ENOUGH CASH TO HAVE A CHANCE TO SUCCEED.

TEN COMMANDMENTS OF BRANDING

1. **Find something unique to lay claim to.** Differentiate yourself from your competition.

2. **Make a bold promise.** Make sure that you can fulfill that promise, but be bold. Make an audacious promise, one that if you could deliver on it, customers would arrive in droves. Don't use a benign word like quality or integrity.

3. **Commit to your brand.** You are not branding this year and changing it next year. You may change your advertising because that is just a vehicle, but you must be committed to your brand.

4. **Make it believable.** Cheap and high quality don't exist together. If you are trying to build a brand, and you market yourself as being the least expensive and highest quality product, your credibility will suffer. Most people know that the two don't go together.

5. **Deliver.** You'd better be able to deliver on your promise. "Perfection," "always," and "lowest" are very hard things to deliver on.

6. **Make your results repeatable.** You can't deliver on your promise this week but not deliver on it next week. Repeatable means you have set up a system that can produce consistent results.

7. **Make your brand position measurable.** Very few companies can get away with words like innovation, integrity, and trustworthy. Have a brand that you can actually measure to determine whether you are delivering on the brand position.

8. **Make it teachable.** Can you train your staff to deliver this? Can you put it in your manuals? Is this something that you can build up through your staff?

9. **Make it memorable.** Craft a message that is simple and easy for a customer to remember.

10. **Make it marketable.** What advertising methods are you going to use to market this brand? How are you going to get customers to hear about and understand your brand?

HAVE YOU FOLLOWED THE TEN COMMANDMENTS OF BRANDING?

JANUARY 17
ADVERTISING

Nobody should sell you advertising. They should assist you to reach your ideal customer via radio, TV, digital marketing, direct mail, postcards, or whichever way you can best reach the most people most affordably. It's your job as the business owner to discern what's best for you.

First things first: you need to know who your ideal customer is. Ask yourself, "Do I know my ideal customer?" Well, you don't know if you've never tracked how people are currently finding out about you. The first thing you need to do is track, maybe over the next 30–60 days, who your customers are and where they are coming from. If you don't know who they are and where they're coming from, advertising is never going to work.

Pretend you're an FBI profiler. In your case, you're not dealing with a crime. You're dealing with who is purchasing from you, but you need to look at it forensically. You need to really study it. By doing so, you will discern who your ideal customer is, and understand which media will reach them.

So again, the first thing to find out is who your ideal customer is, and then find out the means to reach them.

Which method is best able to reach them? Is it radio? Is it digital marketing? If every method could reach 50,000 of my ideal customers, which one can reach them the least expensively? If it reaches my ideal customer, it's affordable.

GREAT COMPANIES ADVERTISE.

JANUARY 18
BUILDER OR SUSTAINER

Are you a builder or a sustainer? It's important to find out which you are. Who is a builder?

A builder in entrepreneurial terms is the person who starts the business, the catalyst. Who is a sustainer? That's the engineer who comes in and makes sure that the rocks don't fall on everybody.

For me, I'll blow the thing up, but I can't create. I don't want to be involved in all the other stuff. So, I brought on partners, and they helped me sustain my idea. Again, I know what my strengths are and what my weaknesses are. I know that I get excited about an idea for about eighteen months maximum. So, I'm going to get super excited in the first six months. I'm going to launch it in six months. I'm going to develop my partnerships in about six months, but after eighteen months, I'd better be getting paid really well to stay engaged.

That's been my game plan. I'm a builder. I know the value of sustainers, and they're typically different personalities. Sustainers are great managers, typically even-tempered, structured, and detailed.

I encourage you, if you're an entrepreneur, to hire or bring on your staff or into your partnership somebody who is the opposite of you.

You've got builders, you've got sustainers, and if you want a business to continue, you should be smart enough to hire sustainers.

KNOW WHERE YOU LIE IN THE BUSINESS:
ARE YOU A BUILDER OR A SUSTAINER?

JANUARY 19
INTRAPRENEURS

An *intrapreneur* is a person from within your company who isn't the owner but brings entrepreneurial ideas to you. They have an entrepreneurial mind, and sometimes they're the best entrepreneur that you can have because they have nothing to lose, so they'll just keep bringing you idea after idea. Sometimes an intrapreneur is a young staff member who doesn't know yet what is impossible, so they have an optimism that is irreplaceable.

Don't be the only person bringing ideas to your company. Encourage other people to share their profitable ideas with you. Then they can be an intrapreneur, and that'll make you a better entrepreneur. Having a few of these people on your team will challenge you. Remember it was not Steve Jobs who came up with the iPod or iPad; he was just the biggest fan. Both ideas came from someone who thought, *What if?*

I have learned you tend to get what you value, and if you do not value team members with an entrepreneurial spirit, you won't have any. At the very least, they won't speak up and share the seeds of a new profit stream, improvement, or innovation.

Fan the intrapreneur's flame and reward their efforts with bonuses and accolades, and they will rain down more ideas. It would be wise to identify those who you may want to partner formally with on something.

As the saying goes, two heads are better than one. Bring in intrapreneurs to your business, have weekly or monthly meetings with them where you just bounce off ideas, and, trust me, one of them will be a moneymaker.

SURROUND YOURSELF WITH INTRAPRENEURS;
THEY'LL GIVE YOU INVALUABLE FEEDBACK.

JANUARY 20
UNDERSTAND THE RISK

It is a common misconception that to start a business and succeed, you must take big risks.

The truth is that smart entrepreneurs take well-thought-out risks. Lawyer Steve Strauss warns against unnecessary risk: "Risk is part of the game. It is the juice. The problem is because entrepreneurs have that gambler's mentality, they can, at times, underestimate the risk involved. Or maybe they know the risk, but like it anyway." A well-thought-out risk means being prepared if things don't go your way.

It is a rare situation where you would "bet the ranch" on your business idea. The only time you can bend this rule is if you are in your twenties or thirties so that you will have time to recoup your losses if your business idea doesn't work out.

In his late fifties, my dad received a disability settlement and thought it would be a great idea to own a bar. Of course, it failed for all the reasons businesses fail. The worst part was that he was not at an age where he could ever earn his money back. To this day, he laments what this failure has cost him regarding his current standard of living. It was a risk he could ill afford to make at the time he did.

Be careful how much personal capital you put at risk. If your business fails, would you lose your home or your kid's college fund? If the answer is "yes," then, in my opinion, the potential for loss is too great to move forward. I would also strongly encourage you to communicate to those whose lives failure could affect that you have not "bet the ranch" and that you have carefully thought out the risks. I have been fortunate to have an amazing wife who has supported me on my business ventures, but I have also always communicated to her, in detail, what I was investing, and what the potential losses were prior to moving forward.

MOST ENTREPRENEURS DON'T BET THE RANCH.

JANUARY 21
CONDUCT BASIC MARKET RESEARCH

I often share that just because you love golf and could use a driving range to improve your game, that it doesn't mean a driving range is a good business idea. It shocks me how many businesses are started based purely on an individual's personal interests and not on good business sense.

In one shopping center where my office was located, there was a store selling model trains. A few doors down, there was another store selling NASCAR memorabilia. When you entered these stores and talked to the owners, you could tell that this was their passion.

I would always see the same people hanging out—but never spending money—in their stores. These business owners had a few friends who shared their passion. The problem was they thought there were enough people who shared their passion to sustain their companies. Neither of these would-be entrepreneurs is still in business.

Great businesses grow out of a need for their service or product. However, this need must be both substantial enough and consistent enough to sustain a business. How do you know if there's a viable market for your product?

The internet has made market research so simple. You can develop digital ads and surveys to gauge the interest in your ideas before dumping your money into something that does not have an eager market for what you are offering. I have made a fortune in service companies. Before I expand to a new area, I print and mail 5,000 postcards to people I believe are my ideal customers. I also purchase a phone number for that area so we can track calls. I spend a bit of money to test the market before I go all-in.

CONFIRM THROUGH MARKET RESEARCH
THAT YOU HAVE A VIABLE MARKET.

JANUARY 22
BUILDING SYSTEMS WITHIN YOUR BUSINESS

"In order for any business to succeed, it must first become a system so that the business functions exactly the same way every time, down to the last detail." —Rick Harshaw

When you can build a system that produces a desired outcome that is repeatable and can be done with average people, you have created the golden goose in business. I have also learned the opposite is true; when I launch a business and I can't figure out how to create systems, I have a one-off business. It will make money for a while, but its success is strapped to the talent I can hire. I prefer a business where I can put a new, average hire in place who can perform a critical task because we have systematized their job.

When you think of great companies like McDonald's, they can consistently produce thirty or forty menu items perfectly every time. They produce more food in their restaurants than anybody else in the world, and they do that because they have systems.

In one of the five books I encourage all would-be entrepreneurs to read, *E-Myth Revisited*, author Michael Gerber introduced the gospel of systems: "Organize around business functions, not people. Build systems within each business function. Let systems run the business and people run the systems. People come and go, but the systems remain constant."

What you want to do in your business is to look at how you do things. How do you greet customers? Is there a way that you greet customers that has a positive result? How could you streamline an office system, such as how you receive money or how you follow up with customer service?

These are the things within your business that need to be made into systems. Systems create repetition, and with repetition, you can achieve a single task over and over again to near perfection.

SYSTEMS HELP AVERAGE PEOPLE EXCEL IN YOUR BUSINESS.

JANUARY 23
ENTREPRENEURS THINK DIFFERENTLY

*E*ntrepreneurism is my word of the day, but the problem is, I cannot find a definition of it. When I look it up, it says it is another word for *entrepreneur*. I don't think that is true, because I want a word for a person who studies entrepreneurs. OK, maybe entrepreneurist is a word, but my computer spell check just highlighted this word informing me it is not a word. This is bothering me. Who studies entrepreneurs?

The groundbreaking book, *Effectuation: Elements of Entrepreneurial Expertise*, by Saras D. Sarasvathy, is the first and only book I have read that says entrepreneurs are unique in how they think and process information. This is the most exhaustive look into what and who an entrepreneur is. I will warn you, this is some tough reading, as the author provides countless studies written out in detail.

I have said all this to point out that entrepreneurs think differently from other people, and the book *Effectuation* lets me know I am not crazy or alone in how I think.

Remember from Algebra I, where A + B = C? Most people have to know what A and B are to know what C, the desired result, is. Entrepreneurs start with C, an idea for a successful business that provides freedom or money, and know *either* A or B. They rarely know both.

The fact is you cannot know or control all the factors needed to guarantee a successful business. Your original business and its plan, which is important, will evolve. As Scott Allison of *Forbes* put it, "You don't know what you don't know, and you don't know what the market wants until you build something and show it to them." Ten years from now, you will laugh at what you and this original business are doing. It will morph, and I am just letting you know in advance, that this is great, because it is what makes us unique.

DO YOU THINK DIFFERENTLY?

JANUARY 24
MAKING PROFITABILITY YOUR PASSION

It is great if you can do what you love to do and get paid for it. However, in many cases, your passion will not earn you a living. I wish someone would pay me to play golf and tennis, but I have yet to meet this person.

I establish businesses, in some cases, for no other reason than to make money. That is the motivation I need because having money allows me to do the things I am passionate about. I know early in this book, I said money should not be your first and only motivation to start a business.

What I am saying here is that your passion is not always profitable.

Years ago, I had trouble finding good contractors for a home improvement project. No one showed up on time, and the contract price kept changing. I saw, firsthand, that there was a need for this type of business. My thinking was that answering the phone with a friendly voice, providing a fair written estimate, showing up on time, and doing quality work would make a profitable business. It was not my passion, but that was beside the point.

Within two months, I launched Advantage Handyman Services. Now eight divisions, numerous sister companies, a name change, and millions of dollars later, it has paid for a lot of golf and tennis, among other new passions that I can now afford to have.

The illustration I share is that I love golf, but I have no interest in owning a driving range or golf course. Why? Because in most cases, they are very bad investments (money pits). However, being a successful entrepreneur has allowed me a membership at one of the finest country clubs in America. I can also afford to play any course in the world.

If you are passionate about something that also seems like good business sense, you are one of the lucky ones who can go into a business that you have a passion for. In *Creating a Business You'll Love*, Tim Berry, founder of Palo Alto Software and bplans.com, explains, "There is nothing as important as offering value ... The clichés say it's about doing what you love, being passionate, and sticking to it. I say yes, that is important, but you absolutely must temper that with making sure you're doing something that offers value to others. Maybe you love playing the guitar or painting with watercolors, but will people spend their money to hear you play?"

Of course, keep in mind that when you turn your passion into a business, it can turn fun into work. Sometimes it is best to pursue your passion purely as a passion and find some other way to pay for it.

A PROFITABLE BUSINESS WILL PAY FOR YOUR PASSIONS.

JANUARY 25
ATTITUDE

"A positive attitude causes a chain reaction of positive thoughts, events, and outcomes. It is a catalyst and it sparks extraordinary results." —Wade Boggs

Your attitude is the way you think or feel about someone or something. If you have a bad attitude, it can limit your personal success and will impact the culture of your company. Author John Maxwell has great insight when he imparts, "Your attitude is like the mind's paintbrush. It can paint everything in bright, vibrant colors, creating a masterpiece."

A winning attitude just gives off vibrancy. It's the energy that people can feel from you because of how you look at something. Attitude costs nothing but makes all the difference. It is one of the few things you have complete control over. You can either look at everything positively or negatively.

You need to ask, "What type of attitude do I display? Is it positive or negative? Do I have an optimistic outlook on things?" What type of attitude does your key staff have? Is a person's attitude something you consider in the interview and hiring process?

It is not hard to pick up on pessimism. A great attitude in your staff is like a turbo booster, as it just adds energy and speed to everything they do. The opposite is true as well, as Bikram Choudhury warns, "Negative attitude is nine times more powerful than positive attitude."

This is what I can tell you for sure: bad attitudes are like a cancer in the workplace. They just metastasize. I have let people go for no other reason than they had a bad attitude because I know the power of attitude, good or bad.

CHECK YOUR ATTITUDE TODAY—GOOD OR BAD?

JANUARY 26
THINK BIG

"You have to think anyway, so why not think big?"
—Donald Trump

I completely agree! Big thinking, also called "big picture thinking," means you take the frame off the picture and you expand the view. There are no limits to what you can see happening. I love what Arnold Schwarzenegger says, "I welcome and seek your ideas, but do not bring me small ideas; bring me big ideas to match our future."

Great entrepreneurs think big. There is no limit. They are always thinking, "If we had unlimited resources, what could we get done? Where could this project go? Where could this business go?"

Too many small-business owners open their businesses, and they are there for thirty years, and they only survive. Why is that? Because they never took the time to start thinking big. Remove the frame and start thinking big. Aristotle Onassis said, "To be successful, you must act big, think big, and talk big."

I'm reminded of George Mallory, who aspired to climb the world's tallest mountain, Mount Everest. When asked why he wanted to do it, his reply was simple yet profound: "Because it's there." Elaborating on his reasoning, Mallory said, "Everest is the highest mountain in the world, and no man has reached its summit. Its existence is a challenge. The answer is instinctive, a part, I suppose, of man's desire to conquer the universe." Now those are the thoughts of a man who knew how to think big!

ARE YOU A BIG THINKER?

JANUARY 27
ALWAYS HAVE A HOOK IN THE WATER

We run employment ads throughout the year, and I don't always list our company by name as sometimes I am just testing the employment waters. I like to see how fertile the hiring market is. Sometimes my own employees have replied, and I learn that these are people that we definitely don't have complete buy-in with. This prompts us either to consider replacing them or, if they are valuable, to sweeten their employment packages.

The main reason that my team and I try to interview someone every week for one of our companies is that we are always looking for talent. I run ads when I have no openings and I always do interviews optimistically, thinking I am going to find a potential superstar.

Sometimes I'll interview somebody from my competition, and I start finding out what's going on in their company. There is no downside of spending some time each week interviewing potential talent that you can add to the roster. I don't interview just to interview, as I make sure each candidate has the background that supports the position we are looking for. I can tell you without fail every few months I will be interviewing someone I thought would fill position A, and the longer I talk to them, I see so much potential in them for positions A, B, or C.

Always interviewing allows us to have a shortlist in place to fill key positions if someone valuable leaves. I don't wait until I need to hire. There are too many good reasons to have a hook in the water at all times. This single hiring secret has allowed me to build great depth in my staff and not to have to panic when someone leaves.

ALWAYS BE INTERVIEWING.

HAVE A PLAN FOR SUCCESS

People who have a plan for success should always be asking themselves, "What is it that I'm trying to accomplish?" If you can answer this question, it basically means you know what your goals are, you'll initiate steps necessary to attain those goals and ultimately succeed.

I define the goals that I want to achieve. If I don't ever hit any of those, I may close the business down. If after one year I didn't hit any of my measurables, it probably was a bad idea. So, in my business plan, I want to list my measurables. I want to find out what it is going to cost to start this business What is it going to cost to keep it up and running?

You need to plan for success. You need to have a business plan that considers operating costs and everything that you could possibly need to start the business, your to-do list, and deadlines. This is your battle plan, and it needs to be an active business plan. What do I mean by that? You can't be rigid with it because it's going to change. You must try to account for that, and you've got to be nimble enough to move.

You need to have an active, fluid business plan that gives your company a clear direction, shows your values, and reflects your mission statement. Why are you starting this business? What are you hoping to accomplish? What is your game plan? What resources are you going to need?

IS YOUR BUSINESS PLAN VIABLE AND ATTAINABLE? IS IT DESTINED FOR SUCCESS?

JANUARY 29
INVALUABLE

What qualities do you want in every employee? When interviewing or considering a business partner, what value could someone bring to the table? I have had the opportunity to talk with college students desiring to graduate, get an interview, and get offered their dream positions. I'd like to share how to win in the interview. Business owners, I would tell you to look at it in reverse. Job candidates need to display or offer one of these in a grand way, and you need to be able to identify these skills in your talent search process.

The Big Five:

1. **Solve Problems.** I want someone who does not make me aware of problems but solves them.

2. **Sell Products/ Services.** There is no one more valuable than the person who can sell what you offer.

3. **Lead People.** You will never grow your company without having leaders.

4. **Execute.** The ability to accomplish set objectives is what makes someone stand out.

5. **Have an irreplaceable skill or expertise.** There is no substitute for someone who is just great at what they do.

Your interview process needs to find ways to determine if a candidate possesses any of the above because a resume can only tell you if a person has the experience or training needed to do the job you are filling. It does not tell you if a person is the right person for the job. I believe you want not only someone qualified, but you also want someone irreplaceable.

LEARN TO IDENTIFY WHAT MAKES A TEAM
MEMBER INVALUABLE TO YOU.

JANUARY 30
PROTECT YOURSELF AND YOUR BUSINESS

When you start your business, do not take shortcuts that in the end will only make you and your business more exposed to potential expensive losses.

Five Shortcuts that Will Save You in the Long Run:

1. **Set up a corporation from day one.** This single decision will, in most cases, remove you from personal liability and litigation. With the countless online legal service companies or a simple visit to your state's corporation commission, this is a simple hurdle.

2. **Set up a partnership agreement.** At the very least, just write it yourself. Define everything upfront. Obtain the needed signatures and get it notarized. The worst part of ending a partnership is when it can't be dissolved amicably because responsibilities and consequences weren't clearly defined in the beginning.

3. **Have a noncompete agreement.** The last thing you want is for an ex-business partner or high-level employee who knows your formula for success to become your competition.

4. **Utilize an experienced accountant.** An accountant is a must on your team to keep you from tax problems and to help you understand your financial position. You should personally learn the key measurables in your balance sheet: profit and loss, debt, and cash flow are just a few.

5. **Use a payroll company.** This is one of my golden rules for a start-up, and this will not be the only time I mention it. It is too easy to pay bills with money that is not yours, not to mention the mad scramble at the end of the year to prepare needed tax documents.

BUILD A MOAT OF PROTECTIONS
AROUND YOUR BUSINESS.

JANUARY 31
ACCESSIBLE AND APPROACHABLE

I have seen too many business owners who make themselves nearly impossible to find, let alone available, to their staff for questions they as owners could resolve in a minute or less. Too often new business owners believe that since they are now the boss, they can hide from critical interactions and make themselves invisible. Their office is like a Sensitive Compartmented Information Facility (SCIF) on Capitol Hill. It is a highly protected area within the building with access that is by invitation only. What is said there does not leave the room.

As the leader of your company, you must be accessible, and employees must find you effortlessly, as finding you should not be a scavenger hunt. You must be approachable, so your employees are not afraid to bring you questions and problems when necessary.

In my office layout, I have removed any full walls of separation. I joke that my favorite intercom system is that I can yell from my office, and everyone who needs to hear it will. I don't have a door in my office, only a cased opening, because I want to be able to talk to anybody at any time I want. We have a conference room on a separate floor for interviews, arguments, and the like.

I have decided within the culture of our company that I wanted to be accessible and approachable. To be clear, this does not mean that I allow myself to be interrupted by anyone at any time, as leaders should naturally establish qualifiers for the intrusion. Is this important, and am I the only one who can provide this information, or solve this problem? If I can solve the problem ten times faster than anyone else, even if I am not the only one who can solve it, please bring it to me.

BE ACCESSIBLE AND
APPROACHABLE AS NEEDED.

FEBRUARY 1
BETTER THE DEVIL YOU KNOW

Regarding employees, I tell my staff all the time, "If we have someone who shows up to work every day, they're performing at a C level." But when they have a good attitude, that's a person that I would keep and wouldn't consider replacing right away. Too often we want to replace people and get new people we think will be better, but I always say, "Better the devil you know than the devil you don't."

I have hired too many people who have great resumes but ended up not being nearly as good as their resume said. What ended up happening is we lost someone who was average but available and replaced them with someone more expensive in most cases who ended up being a disappointment. Listen, I have no problem letting go of poor performing or unreliable team members, but not everybody on your team, if it's a good-sized team, will be superstars.

In short, don't rush to replace an employee who is not on par with your expectations. You may want to train them further. I also have learned to give value to the intangibles: has a good attitude, works well with others, and is liked by customers. You give me a combination of a few intangibles, and I will place that person where they can be a contributor to my company.

SOMEONE NEW IS NOT
ALWAYS SOMEONE BETTER.

FEBRUARY 2
WHEN YOU SHOULD START BRANDING

I believe you start branding before you ever open your company. Branding should be in your business plan.

You want to begin branding from day one. You have got to create this image or quality that you think would help your company be successful within its industry. To do this, you should answer this question in your business plan: If there was one thing that you could deliver to your customers that would make them choose you over your competition, what would it be? That is what you want to brand.

Maybe it is speed. Years ago, Domino's Pizza found that thirty-minute delivery was a unique position to brand. Papa John's didn't take that route. They went with, "Better ingredients, better pizza, Papa John's." Their brand promises that with better ingredients they will be able to deliver a better pizza pie. You should be branding from day one. Your brand is the DNA of your company.

How do you brand? Ask this question: What is the one thing, if we could deliver on it, that would draw customers in droves to our product or service? Once you find that, then you need to look for your wording, tagline, logo, or maybe just an image, to represent it.

You want something that effortlessly conveys what you are promising. Create an emotion around it, such as "fun" or "easy," if you can, when you are building your brand. Also, you want to create a promise that you can continually deliver on. In other words, you don't deliver the quality one week but not the next. You don't have low pricing for nine months out of the year, and then when there is a crunch financially, raise your prices. Your brand is something that you are repeatedly committed to delivering.

START BRANDING FROM DAY ONE.

FEBRUARY 3
BUSINESS AXIOMS—PART ONE

"**Better the devil you know than the devil you don't know.**" My staff will share with me somebody that they may be thinking of getting rid of, and I review a few things: Does this person show up every day? What do the customers think of this person? Don't necessarily get rid of this person because with a little bit of work, maybe you can make this person better.

I have only regretted the jobs or clients I have taken and never the jobs or clients I have not taken. Why? Because when you get a bad client, it is a nightmare. So, when I get that vibe, I have no problem turning it down, because I've never regretted a job from a client I've turned down.

We are a for-profit company. I'm constantly surprised by how many customers still want us to work for less than what I think is fair, or what we're worth. We are a for-profit company. We want to be a sustainable and durable company, and the only way to do that is to be profitable. We do not give away our time and talent for free.

When you pay peanuts, you get monkeys. If somebody's accepted a job for little pay, you haven't hired the right person. You never overpay talent, but whatever you pay, no matter how little it is, if they are terrible or can't perform the job, you overpaid them.

Starting a new business or a new division is like flying a kite. Your business starts as light and fragile as a kite. Your goal is to build it into a battleship so strong that the only thing that can sink it is an iceberg or an island.

WHICH ONE OF THE ABOVE
DO YOU NEED TO APPLY?

BUSINESS AXIOMS—PART TWO

Insanity is doing the same thing over and over, expecting a different result. You need to be more alert and aware, and you had better change something because if you don't, the results are not going to change.

My contracts don't promise happiness. My contracts don't promise happiness because there are some clients who you are just never going to make happy. We have deliverables there in the bullet points, but I can't guarantee that we're going to make you happy at every turn.

Coming in second stinks. Have you ever seen a person who was a runner up smiling as big as the person who won? No. Everything about winning is better, and it is no different in business. Be number one!

Cut your losses. There are some times that you must get out of a business, out of something you've started, out of a partnership. The problem is, people think if they keep the business going, somewhere down the line, they're not going to lose. Cut your losses and move on.

Cash is like oxygen. When you don't have oxygen, you're going to die. As a company, you need to be profitable. You need to store away cash always; put it in reserves.

Just add water. What does this mean? I will hear people share with me a business idea and act like it's going to be so turnkey and so simple, and I tell them, "You just think you're going to add water. It's never that way." You always have to add something to that mixture, you always have to add more content to make something just a little bit better. Very few things in business are so simple that you just add water.

LEARN FROM YOUR EXPERIENCES AND COME UP WITH YOUR OWN BUSINESS AXIOMS.

FEBRUARY 5
BUY YOUR COMPETITION

Why do you buy your competition?

- It will give you immediate growth, growth that you currently don't have.
- It could jump-start a division or an industry in a new area that you want to expand into.
- It eliminates a competitor.

When do you buy your competition? I try to do it when I know they're struggling. Sometimes you can just hear people bringing information to you. Sometimes you can interview people and it comes up.

Also, I only buy them if they have a customer base that fits our customer base, and I can get their phone numbers, emails, domain, and market share.

Sometimes you can buy warranties and existing problems. You have to be careful about what you're taking on. They may have a great domain that's good for you, or they just have a position or market share that you want, so I buy them when they're struggling, based on a few of those conditions.

Have they stopped advertising? Whenever I see somebody stop advertising, I know they're struggling because great companies advertise. If the owner comes across like they're looking to get out of it, I'm going to politely call them and very respectfully ask them what their transition plan is. Whatever the case may be, show class when you do this.

How much do you pay? There are a lot of ways to look at this. A lot of times I read articles, and it's ridiculous what they say to pay for a business, and I would never pay it. Never pay a dime more than you need to. Personally, with local businesses, I pay per customer. This is really easy. Look at their QuickBooks to determine how many customers they've served. The problem with most small businesses is that they have horrible records. You really need to find out what you're buying, and I have found that their customer base is the easiest way for me.

BUY YOUR COMPETITION:
IT'S AN EASY WAY TO GROW.

FEBRUARY 6
VALUE CREATION

Value creation is the primary aim of any business entity. Creating value for your customers means creating something that your customers want to buy.

When you create your first business plan, you do a value creation. Let's say a lightbulb. The value creation is that customers need lightbulbs. When you set up your business, this is the number-one part of your business plan. What value are you bringing to the marketplace? You need to bring something of value to customers.

You should go back and look at why you started your business. Is that need that you tried to solve or that value that you brought still a need? Some needs once existed that are no longer that important.

You have to continually ask yourself, "Is our core business changing? Is it still needed?" Well, if it's not, then you need to evolve.

You must continually ask yourself, "Who is our ideal customer? What is it they buy from us? What is it they would like to buy from us? Why do they buy from us? Can we possibly provide more value to this customer? Are we providing something they need, want, or desire?"

Apple only used to sell computers. They kept adding value, and now they're the most profitable, highest-valued company in the world. Amazon started with selling books, and they've now morphed into selling all things retail.

You need to keep building value within your business for your core customers, or you will be out of business.

VALUE CREATION IS THE GENESIS
OF YOUR VISION STATEMENT.

FEBRUARY 7
VETTING YOUR START-UP IDEA

If you're going to start businesses for a living, you're going to fail occasionally. Hopefully, if you follow my vetting process, you won't fail as often. When I have an idea for a business, I notice that there's a need for something, and I think it could be profitable. Then I need to vet this idea. I want to confirm for myself that this is a good idea and that there is data to prove it.

The Vetting Process:

- I want to know my competition and figure out where I'm going to rank. I want to make sure there's an opening in the marketplace.

- I want to find out what it's going to cost to engage in this business and that the cost is in line with my previous estimate.

- I want to make sure that there is research confirming that people are looking for the product or service that I'm offering.

- I want to have a test market and do test marketing and advertising to make sure that I can attract those buyers for the cost of acquisition that I expected.

- I want to make sure there is hiring ease. I want to make sure I can get people on my team as fast as I need to, and I want to make sure I'm paying enough to keep them.

- Finally, I want to review my exit strategy: how long would it take, what will the collateral damage be, and what will the cost be if I have to close this business up.

I encourage you to go through all these steps when you are vetting a business. They will dramatically change your approach and they will talk you out of starting quite a few of them.

VET YOUR IDEAS TO ELIMINATE BAD IDEAS.

SECRETS OF SELF-MADE MILLIONAIRES—PART I

Last I checked, pretty much 99 percent of millionaires are self-made millionaires. Why do I want to talk about being a self-made millionaire? Because that's what an entrepreneur is.

Dream big dreams.

Everybody wants to be an achiever, but achievement normally starts with a big dream. Then, of course, it's going to take hard work, but it starts with a big dream. You will only go as far as your biggest dream, and that dream should scare you.

Set goals.

Achievers set quantifiable goals. You know when you hit them. You have financial goals, you have career goals, you should have family goals, and health and fitness goals. Some people have community service goals or faith goals. Whatever the case may be, high achievers start with big dreams first, and then they set goals.

Take responsibility for your life.

You have to take responsibility for your own life. And whatever happens to you, get over it. You can't change it, and blaming somebody for it will only impede your success.

Your career passions must be aligned.

It's hard to be great at something you don't enjoy. I figured out how to start businesses that feed my career passions, my goal not to have to worry about money, and my goal to be able to provide well for my family. So, these goals aligned with my career in that if I own a business, I can provide very well. But you need to have some type of alignment. There needs to be synergy between your career and your passions, even if your career pays for your passions.

Be committed to being successful.

You're not going to be great at anything to which you're not committed. Commitment means you won't quit when it gets tough. Commitment means you'll go through a little bit of pain. Commitment means there'll be a sacrifice. If you're not committed to something, then you will easily quit.

WHICH ONE OF THE ABOVE IS A WEAKNESS?

FEBRUARY 9
SECRETS OF SELF-MADE MILLIONAIRES—PART II

Work harder and smarter than everyone else. You've got to be willing to work really hard and to work smarter than everyone else.

Be a lifelong learner.

You must grow your area of knowledge. You never stop learning, and you always have to be growing. Smart people are voracious readers, they go to seminars, they listen to podcasts, they get mentoring, and they get coaching. They're committed to growing their expertise and knowing more than anybody else in their industry.

Save money.

If you don't save money, you're always going to be reacting to being broke. Make a habit of saving money.

Be frugal.

You should always try to save money. That's what rich people do. They may spend more than you can imagine, but they're still frugal.

Know your business and stay in your strengths.

If you look at wealthy people, they've figured out what they're really good at. You rarely see them veering out of their chosen lanes, and when they do, they typically partner with somebody else.

YOU HAVE TO WORK HARD AND BE DISCIPLINED IN YOUR EFFORTS TO ACHIEVE SUCCESS.

VISIONARY

Great achievement happens first in the mind. If you can't see a successful venture before you start it, it probably won't happen. You need to see what a successful product would look like, your product, picturing it perfectly. You need to see a thriving business. You need to see what the ideal team would look like.

If you could hire the perfect team, what would it look like? You need to start spending some time really visualizing and just picturing what the perfect company looks like.

Start seeing things before they actually happen.

1. **See what a perfect company would look like.** If you could put everything together exactly the way you want it, what would your team look like? How would your distribution look? What would the profit margins look like? Who do you need to hire to have that team?

2. **Ask, "What could this idea be?"** See it in the future. OK, I have this idea, but where could I take it? What could this business look like?

3. **If I had the perfect team in place, who would it consist of?** What would it consist of? I have a CPA that works in my office, which is very rare for a small business, but that was one of the positions that I always wanted and pictured from the beginning.

4. **This employee, where can I launch them?** When I'm being a visionary, sometimes I realize that employees are not going to be with me forever. I picture them for a season with me, and I'll picture where I could see them going. Maybe it's within my organization, maybe it's moving on to a different company that I have, but again, I don't only focus on today.

5. **Speak as if it already is.** This is a habit that I have. I will joke about a car, walk out into my garage, and say to my son, "Gosh, such and such is going to look so good parked here," and the fact is, pretty much every car I've ever talked about has sat in my garage at some point.

GET IN THE HABIT OF SEEING
THINGS BEFORE THEY HAPPEN.

FEBRUARY 11
THE COST OF EXPANDING A BUSINESS

After you have determined your "why" and you are ready to expand your business, you need to know the costs involved to start the business.

It shocks me how many business owners expand and never calculate the true hard costs.

They sign a four-year lease, and then they are not making money after one year. They automatically assumed that they would at least be able to pay the lease. If you are not making money, you may need to close the business down. You may need to eat that lease for four years.

You have to look at what the hard costs are and how long your profitable company is going to absorb these. You may end up killing the golden goose, so be very careful to calculate costs and determine how they are going to be paid for in this new business. Make sure that the profitable entity that you have is absorbing those costs.

Again, you need to vet this idea as strongly as you would a start-up. After all, you do not want a profitable business to get crushed because you started another business and it completely depleted your resources and sucked the oxygen out of a profitable business.

Know your "why," and know where and how you are going to pay for all the costs associated with this enterprise. Make sure these costs are not coming from your existing profitable business.

KNOW THE COST OF EXPANDING YOUR BUSINESS PRIOR TO UNDERTAKING THAT TASK.

FEBRUARY 12
BRANDING HAS A PAYOFF

Early in his career, Warren Buffett purchased companies or made great investments in companies that had strong brands. Some of his holdings include Coca-Cola, Fruit of the Loom, GEICO Insurance, and Dairy Queen. What he learned was that, at the time, people did not put a dollar value on what these companies had created in their brand. In other words, when you think of Coca-Cola, you know what it is. When Buffet evaluated those companies, he noticed that they had put a dollar figure on assets and revenue but not on the branding component. He bought brands before people realized the value of brands.

A brand gives your company value. It allows advertising and marketing to have a singular focus. Once you have a brand that you are trying to promote, the advertising and marketing follow suit. It puts you on track and creates guardrails and prevents you from having a shotgun approach to advertising.

My advertising will always reinforce the brand I have chosen for a given company. I own many service companies, so my branding is very simple. I identify the one quality or promise which, if we could deliver it, would make customers chase us down to do business with us.

BRANDING BUILDS VALUE THAT IS NOT REFLECTED ON YOUR BALANCE SHEET.

FEBRUARY 13
WHEN TO EXPAND

Is it time to expand the business? That is the question that all business owners wrestle with. They want to know if it is the right time and if the business is well-positioned to expand.

The first thing you need to ascertain is why you want to expand your business in the first place. You cannot expand simply because you feel like it or you think it is something you need to do. Here are some reasons to expand your business:

You are testing your business model for franchising.

To franchise a business, it needs to work in more than one place.

You may have a lot of talent under your roof and you need to give them opportunities to grow.

Within your business, you may not have enough opportunities or positions to take advantage of the talent you currently have under your roof.

There is a profitable opportunity that is undeniable.

You have the feeling that you have hit gold in a certain area and you'd like to try something in a similar area with similar demographics. You want to test this profitability engine that you have or plant this money tree somewhere else and see if it will grow.

You have brand potential.

Let's say that you have launched a brand in a certain city where it has taken off. You found an area of differentiation or perhaps you found a tagline. Whatever it is, you found something within the brand that people gravitated toward very quickly. You have great brand potential and you feel that you could expand it to another location.

You have a lot of available assets.

Your assets may be vehicles, warehouses, land, staff, or other infrastructure not being used that you would like to share. You could add another location within a certain number of miles from your existing area and share a lot of the resources. Maybe you have untapped customers. For example, let's say you were a roofing contractor. Your business has expanded really well, and customers are constantly reaching out to you. Maybe you could add a siding or a window division. These naturally go together.

VET YOUR 'WHY' BEFORE
EXPANDING YOUR BUSINESS.

FEBRUARY 14
"YOU'RE FIRED"

It was not too long ago that Donald Trump made the phrase "You're fired!" famous with his hit reality show, *The Apprentice*. At the end of each show, he would eliminate a participant with this legendary line. As a business owner, letting people go comes with the territory. Let me share a few pieces of advice on when to say, "You're fired."

When they can no longer perform the job that they're being paid to do.

Typically, they lack the skill or discipline to get the job done. If you think someone is going to improve, they rarely do. That is my experience. Ninety days is plenty of time to determine this.

When they need to be reminded to do the job they're being paid to do.

They constantly need to be reminded of what they need to do. *If we need to babysit you, we don't want you.*

They're not reliable.

It drives me insane when I have a person who will miss work and then tell me they had a personal situation. They'll ask me, "Don't you have personal situations?"

I reply, "Yes, but they don't make me miss work." I can compartmentalize. If you're not reliable, then you are not one we want to rely on.

They compromise your brand.

They don't play by the rules that you've set. I had an employee who was upselling our clients, which is a no-no. We honor our original agreement and have ways of presenting options later.

They're culture killers.

They have no positivity about them at all. They're not loyal to your company. They never fit the team mold. They're typically openly critical about leadership as well as about their coworkers.

When they're being overpaid for what they can produce.

You hire a person and then you look back six to eight months later and their ability, their capacities, is about 80 percent of what you expected. Sometimes you need to reposition them. Sometimes you need to give them a pay cut. *Once I know that we're overpaying for you, we are going to modify your salary, modify your job description, or let you go.*

YOUR BUSINESS IS ONLY AS GOOD AS YOUR TEAM;
DON'T LET A TOXIC PERSON RUIN IT.

FEBRUARY 15
WHEN TO FIX AND NOT FIRE

You can't fire everybody; that's just not reality. So, often, I need to fix or improve someone, which I would always prefer.

When to fix:

Are they reliable and likable? I can work a lot with reliable and likable. I'm not saying I can keep them in the position they're currently in, but I'm going to try to find something for them if they're reliable and likable.

Can they improve? Can they get better? You've got to analyze if this person can improve.

Decide if they're worth the time to fix. One person I can think of was older and it would have taken too long to fix their performance. If I can fix a person in three to six months, that's not a deal-breaker. You have to analyze if they were properly trained in the beginning. Sometimes when somebody is not doing the job right, you have to analyze who trained them or who is supervising them. You should consider those factors to see if your employee needs to be retrained.

Are they misplaced based on their skill and experience? Knowing what you now know, ninety days after their hire, you review their progress and find they're just misplaced. Maybe they don't have the skill for their current position, and you need to reassign them. Is your employee the right fit for the job they were hired for?

When I start trying to fix someone, I give them a measurable goal that must be met in a given time period. By the end of the month, you need to be able to do this, or, within sixty days, you need to be producing a given amount. I'm going to put you on the next two jobs, and if I get any client complaints, that'll be your last job. I give them fixed measurables in a fixed time period. I create guardrails, clear instructions with more training if needed. I don't want them to keep failing.

PEOPLE ARE WORTH FIXING.

FEBRUARY 16
MESSAGING

When you advertise, you're trying to communicate a message to your ideal customer. Before setting up to advertise, it's imperative for you, as the business owner, to have determined who your ideal customer is and the most cost-effective way of reaching them.

Now, you need to communicate a message to this customer that will build confidence in your product or service and remove any skepticism they may have. That's why you see infomercials say, "We'll ship it back free, no-hassle, free return shipping." Why do they do that? They're trying to remove your skepticism. If you don't like it, we'll come to your house, wrap it up, pick it up, take it back, and refund it that day. That's basically what they're trying to do, build your confidence and remove your skepticism.

It's also worth noting that in advertising, messaging plays a significant role. Messaging is simply the promise that, if made, would cause your company to attract the most customers. If this message builds confidence and removes skepticism, it will attract customers. Assuming you're selling a product to your ideal customer, you need to discover two things: how your customers are currently finding out about you, and how you can reach them in the future.

Remember, a message is basically a promise that is going to remove skepticism and build confidence. This message is going to be used and advertised through various media that you've determined are the most cost-effective.

What promise can you think of, that if made to your customers, would cause them to have confidence in you, remove their skepticism, and make them buy more from you? It's important to understand the significance of advertising because if you don't make more sales, you'll be out of business.

WHAT IS YOUR ADVERTISING MESSAGE?

FEBRUARY 17
WHY PARTNER

I would like to share with you just a few heralded entrepreneurs who were big believers in partnering in business: Bill Gates, Steve Jobs, Walt Disney, Ray Kroc, Warren Buffett, and I can keep going. So, to review, Microsoft, Apple, Disney, McDonald's, and Berkshire Hathaway all owe their creation to the idea of a partnership.

So, when should you consider partnering?

When you lack expertise in a critical area.

You either don't have the expertise or specialty in an area of business. You just simply don't understand it. As an example, if you are getting into manufacturing, and you have no idea how to get something manufactured, you should partner with somebody who does.

You lack the time to do it.

I'm an entrepreneur. I'm always looking for new opportunities, but I'm not looking for opportunities that take my time. So I need partners to run the businesses I create.

You lack a critical recourse.

A critical resource is something without which there will not be a business (cash, technology, real estate, credit, etc.). Business is very much like a well-known algebra equation, $A + B = C$. You are A. You are missing B (need) and without it, you will never get C.

LOOK AT YOUR BUSINESS.
DO YOU NEED A PARTNER?

FEBRUARY 18
COURAGE

"Courage is being scared to death and saddling up anyway."
—*John Wayne*

When is the last time that you made a decision which, if it failed, would have a dire consequence? Courage is making tough choices. This may be risking money or your reputation on an idea. It is easy to make decisions that have minor consequences, but we need a big dose of courage when we go all-in. I like what Peter Drucker says to this: "Wherever you see a successful business, someone once made a courageous decision."

I am not a big fan of all-in bets, and I recommend you keep those to a minimum and preferably take them in your early twenties, but there will be times where a dose of courage will be needed. Is there a longtime employee who no longer carries their weight? It is easy to let them hang around; that requires no courage. Courage is having a difficult conversation and letting that person go and taking all the criticism that may come with it.

Courage is taking that loan to expand the company when your house is the collateral required to get it. I believe leaving college or your current job to chase an entrepreneurial dream takes courage. There is a reason why risk brings reward: because it requires you to gather up some courage. But the good news, I have discovered, is that most people lack this courage, and that is why they spend a lifetime wondering what could have been.

WHEN WAS THE LAST TIME
YOU DID SOMETHING COURAGEOUS?

FEBRUARY 19
LACK OF TALENT

Small businesses lack highly talented staff with the skills and expertise to alter the trajectory of a company. I find lack of talent is one of the most common areas of weakness within many small businesses.

Let me show one example of the effect of poor staffing. In almost every company, you need to have a proven and very driven salesperson or sales staff. You need to have somebody who can sell your product or service. It's amazing how many small businesses put this responsibility in the hands of a friend or family member who has no skill set for this and no experience. And even worse, they have no track record of sales success. If you cannot sell your product or service, guess what? You don't have a company or a business.

Let's start thinking about putting the best people on your team. You might say to me, "How can I even get these people?" It starts with first recognizing that you need a talent overhaul. It is always good to start with sales and move into sales those who can generate the most profit for your company. Next, after you recognize the key hires, you need to run ads in places that will give you qualified candidates. When you interview and identify someone with proven experience and a track record of success, pay the necessary salary that is required to bring them on board. Remember when you pay peanuts, you get monkeys.

HIRE EXPERIENCED, PROVEN
INDIVIDUALS IN KEY AREAS.

FEBRUARY 20
BEING A SELF-STARTER

Starting a business requires the ability to make something from nothing. This is more important than just having an idea. The ability to initiate something from nothing more than an idea into a functioning organization is what is required. Allow these words from noted motivational speaker and author Tony Robbins to shed light on initiative: "Success comes from taking initiative and following up, persisting... to produce a new momentum toward success in your life."

Did you ever have a lemonade stand as a kid? You decided you needed extra money, it was hot outside, and your mom had extra lemonade mix. So, a half hour later, up went your creative sign to attract those driving by as you enthusiastically served your product.

In short, you had all the needed components, so you took initiative and made something happen.

I have read more articles than I have fingers on the qualities needed to succeed as an entrepreneur. And without exception, being a self-starter was consistently in the top five of each list.

Did you organize fraternity parties in college? As an adult, maybe you started a neighborhood watch or a fantasy football league. It is this initiative, the energy to take the first step, and organizational skills, that are required to get something going.

The entrepreneur must be a doer. Think back on a time in your life when you were a doer, and ask yourself whether you can be that person right now. If so, you might be able to start a business.

I have met many people that have good business ideas but zero initiative. "The most common cause of start-up failure is the entrepreneur just gets tired, gives up, and shuts down the company," writes start-up mentor and blogger Martin Zwilling. "Many successful entrepreneurs, like Steve Jobs and Thomas Edison, kept slugging away on their vision, despite setbacks, until they found the success they knew was possible."

Starting a business requires personal dynamite. When you leave the area, everyone knows something happened.

BEING A SELF-STARTER IS NOT AN OPTION;
IT'S A REQUIREMENT.

FEBRUARY 21
YOUR SUCCESS INSTINCT

An instinct is a natural impulse. Do you have the success instinct? In other words, do you expect to succeed in the things you do, or do you constantly harbor fears and doubts?

I start every day saying the following phrase to myself: "I expect to be successful today." This may seem silly, but psychology has proven that what we expect tends to become reality. In a column for the *Huffington Post*, William Zinke, chairman of the Spotlight on Entrepreneurship Summit, listed a "positive attitude" as one of the top three characteristics of successful entrepreneurs.

You must have personal confidence that expects daily success. It is an inner wiring that naturally expects the best result in situations. This does not mean you are in Fantasyland, only that you genuinely believe most coin tosses will go your way.

If you are a pessimist and expect things not to go well, it is best not to start a business. I am being perfectly serious. In business, there are plenty of outside forces telling you that you are going to fail and that you should never have started a business. You don't need to lend your own voice to that chorus.

Pessimists tend to stop going the extra mile that it takes to be successful as an entrepreneur.

Optimists feel that their extra effort will be rewarded, and this becomes a self-fulfilling prophecy.

Start each day with a positive outlook, expecting the best outcome of each situation. This attitude is contagious and will permeate through to your employees. This creates an exciting work atmosphere.

I like what author Brian Tracy says: "Winners make a habit of manufacturing their own positive expectations in advance of the event."

BEGIN BY EXPECTING TO SUCCEED.

FEBRUARY 22
MORNING ROUTINE

Your morning routine is so critical. What you do in the morning sets the pace for the day.

I'm going to share with you just a little bit about some people that get up really early.

Your mind is critical to success.

When I wake up in the morning, I want to feed my mind first. So, the first thing I do is review my goals. I have a journal, and I write down my five big goals for that year —I do this nearly every single day. I want my brain to be very clear on what it is I'm trying to accomplish today. If I have one major overriding goal, which is typically a five-year goal, something I want to achieve, something really big, that's in there as well.

I start every morning off with, "I am a very successful entrepreneur, New York Times bestselling author, and a highly sought-after speaker, teacher, and coach." I do this every single morning because that's what I need to accomplish every day.

Reading.

I have a few minutes in the morning where I read. I will absolutely start every morning reading a couple of pages of something that I find important and encouraging. This is something that feeds my mind and is parallel to my values and encourages me.

I plan my day.

I blueprint it. If you don't plan your day, somebody will plan it for you. Let me show you a quick way that I plan my day. I want to know what my main event is that day. What is the one thing I have to be *on* for? Maybe it's a meeting. Maybe it's a presentation. I might need to meet with my accountant or lawyer, perhaps have a big interview or a confrontation. Whatever the case may be, I need to know at this time, I've got to be *on*.

Exercise.

It doesn't take long to exercise. You could do it in ten minutes. It allows you to think more clearly. You're healthier. I think image is important, and I know that if somebody came to my house to give me an estimate looking sloppy and undisciplined, if that person was the one doing the work on my house, I probably wouldn't hire them. You're the most important person in your business. Let's just start there. It's not your customer. It's you, because if we take you out of the equation, there will be no business.

HAVE A MORNING ROUTINE THAT BENEFITS YOU.

FEBRUARY 23
5 WAYS TO BUILD A BUSINESS THAT CAN SURVIVE ANYTHING

As an entrepreneur who has started more than 20 companies and has survived 9/11, the economic collapse of 2008 and the coronavirus, I have learned there are in fact ways to create a durable company that can withstand once-in-a-lifetime events.

1. **Survival Is Not Guaranteed:** Too many business owners assume they will be in business a year from now. Let's be clear, we now know from the 2008 market collapse to the virus we now face NO company is guaranteed to be alive a year from now.

2. **Play War Games:** You need to always ask what would it take to put us out of business? How Blockbuster Video did not notice the power of online content and streaming, not to mention those red boxes in front of grocery stores, is a mystery to me. You need to do a war assessment: where are we vulnerable for attack?

3. **Never Have All Your Eggs In One Basket:** What crushes many businesses is they have all their revenue coming from minimal sources and when an industry change or something you have not foreseen coming wipes out your enterprise. You must think of multiple sources of revenue based on expanding product lines and services.

4. **Get Credit When You Don't Need It:** What I learned during the economic collapse of 2008 is when you need money nobody will give it to you, as lenders don't like to put money in companies trying to survive. They much prefer companies thriving. Get credit when you don't need it is my advice.

5. **Guard Cash Like A Toddler At A Playground:** We have all heard the wise saying "it is not what you make, it is what you save." This is true as well in business. I don't care what your revenue is. It is what you systematically save, putting in reserves that matters.

SURVIVAL IS GUARANTEED TO NO ONE. (ONLY 12% OF FORTUNE 500 COMPANIES FROM 1960 STILL EXIST!)

FEBRUARY 24
IT TAKES A TEAM

"A vision becomes a nightmare when the leader has a big dream and a bad team." —John Maxwell

If you plan to build a profitable, growing company, then you will need the ability to attract and retain talent. Attracting a great team will be critical if you have any intention of succeeding as an entrepreneur. How can you have multiple locations if you can't build a team? How can you build a $10 million company if you can't build a team?

You can't do everything yourself, and you *shouldn't* do everything yourself. Your ability to identify, attract, retain, and motivate talent will be what makes the difference regarding how large and profitable you can make your business.

Your team is not only your employees; it is your partners, vendors, contractors, banking relationships, and the professionals (lawyer, accountant, consultants) you have assembled. These all become the pillars of a strong company.

Assembling a team starts with identifying all your staffing needs. Who do you need to open your doors? What expertise do you lack? What positions do you need filled that could help your business grow the most? What level of expertise, if you could bring on staff, would take your company to a higher level?

Your capacity to put together a winning team will be the difference between success and failure, possibly more than any one thing you can do.

YOUR GOAL IS TO BUILD A SUCCESSFUL TEAM.

FEBRUARY 25
KEEP YOUR BUSINESS MODEL SIMPLE

Is your business idea simple? Your first business should be simple, if possible. Sometimes we over-complicate our business models. In the planning stage, a business model describes how your company creates, delivers, and captures value. It is designed to change rapidly to reflect what you find outside the building in talking to customers. Entrepreneurs get into trouble because they overreach, overcommit, and overborrow.

Start simple and stay simple. Know what your customers want and figure out the most efficient way to provide it. Then, make sure they keep coming back.

I recently ate at Waffle House. It's a good example of a company that has made the most of simplicity. Its menu is focused primarily on a single meal (breakfast). Moreover, the menu reads like variations on a central theme. It's easy for a short-order cook to prepare. It's also easy to serve.

Customers eat in a compact, diner-style environment. Because a small wait crew can serve it efficiently, wage costs are kept down. The truth is that you don't have to find and cultivate exceptional employees to manage a Waffle House. Plentiful, "average" employees will do just fine.

By the way, this golden rule of simplicity isn't just a by-product of the mass consumer industry. Even industries that offer niche products have applied this rule successfully.

The fragrance company that produces "Clean" started with the premise that many consumers are attracted to a "fresh out of the shower" scent. It built a product line accordingly and is thriving at a time when more sophisticated perfume companies aren't.

To sum up: Start with a simple idea, and keep the execution simple, too. The simpler the operation, the lower your operating costs will be, and the higher your expected profits will be.

SIMPLE CAN BE REPEATED WHICH
IS THE GOLDEN RULE IN BUSINESS.

FEBRUARY 26
COMMUNICATION

Your ability to communicate effectively an idea, a vision, sell your company, or sell a product or service is one of the most valuable skills you can have as an entrepreneur. You are going to interview people, and you're going to have to sell that person on your vision. You might have to offer them less money than they're being offered elsewhere, so you're going to have to communicate something that makes them want to work for *you*, something that makes them want to be a part of the culture that you're building.

I have often asked my partners why they joined forces with me on a start-up, often quitting their jobs or businesses, in order to collaborate on my vision. Though the wording varies, the point is always the same: "You were so excited about it, and you talked as if you knew it was going to happen, so I wanted to be a part of it."

Communicating by sharing your story or your vision in a way that excites people is a gift, and it's something that you can learn and improve on. You can take speech classes, read books, and take seminars and workshops to become proficient in this area.

Work on looking people in the eye and talking with enthusiasm. Your ability to communicate a big audacious vision that excites your team is a game-changer. I encourage you to constantly grow your communications skill set.

COMMUNICATION IS A SKILL YOU SHOULD SEEK TO IMPROVE.

FEBRUARY 27
OBSESSED

"Be obsessed, or be average."
—*Grant Cardone*

All great entrepreneurs are obsessed with their start-up ideas. When I have an idea that I believe has the potential to be very profitable and to make a mark in the marketplace, I am consumed by it. I wake up and go to bed thinking about how this business will look and function when I get it going. I daydream about the potential it has. Billionaire entrepreneur Mark Cuban warns, "Don't start a company unless it's an obsession and something you love."

When's the last time you were obsessed with a business idea? Something that might improve or add profit to your organization? Do you still love your business, or do you dread it? When's the last time you had an idea that just absolutely consumed you?

A weakness you need to avoid is what I call "temporary obsession." This is where you move from one consuming idea to the next, never following through on any. Ideas with no execution are just wasted thoughts.

I encourage you to be totally obsessed with something involving your business. Let this become a singular focus. That's how you become a great entrepreneur. Your team will catch hold of your excitement.

WHEN WAS THE LAST TIME
YOU WERE OBSESSED WITH AN IDEA?

MARKETING ISN'T OPTIONAL

"Marketing is no longer about the stuff that you make, but about the stories you tell." – Seth Godin

You can't just be a word-of-mouth company. It's not enough to grow. At best, it's enough to survive. The most formidable businesses in the world aggressively market their products or services. They're always trying to attract new customers. At the very least, their marketing effort reminds their existing customers why they love and use their company.

You should always try to attract new customers. So, when you're starting a business, you need to understand who your ideal customer is and how you are going to attract them. In which advertising vehicles are they most likely to hear and see your message? Maybe that's radio, TV, digital marketing; there are countless ways you can do that. It could be billboards, direct mail, but whichever you choose, you've got to have cost-effective vehicles that will reach your ideal customer with a message that will prompt them to buy.

If your goal is to build a great company, marketing is not optional. If you don't know how to do it, hire someone who is a proven pro. You can listen to a podcast, read books, or take workshops on marketing.

WHAT IS MY STRATEGY TO ATTRACT NEW CUSTOMERS?

MARCH 1
DON'T BE A LONE RANGER

"One is too small a number to achieve greatness. No accomplishment of real value has ever been achieved by a human being working alone."
—John Maxwell

Over the years, I have found four reasons why companies stay understaffed with low-level talent:

They're just cheap: The first and foremost reason owners do not have high-caliber staff on their roster is they are cheap and know talented people cost more.

They think they can do it on their own: The second reason is that they don't think they need anyone. Are you really that talented an individual that you can do everything better than anyone else? Every growing company needs someone on the team. You cannot be skilled in every facet needed to grow.

They don't want to be challenged: Third, they don't want to be challenged by anyone. We've all met this owner. They're stubborn and they think they know everything. I would encourage you to bring people in that will challenge you and improve your ideas.

They're afraid of competition: Fourth, they're afraid that if they impart their knowledge to someone, that this person will leave and start their own company. The fact is, that could happen. However, if you're not that talented yourself, don't worry about it. They're not going to be that much of a threat. And if they really are talented, then they are going to help your company grow. And if you're smart and you take care of them through compensation or ownership opportunities, they're going to stay.

RECOGNIZE AND VALUE TALENTED,
VALUABLE TEAM MEMBERS.

MARCH 2
BE ABLE TO ADAPT

I encourage you to heed the advice of Richard Branson: "Every success story is a tale of constant adaptation, revision, and change." You need to be able to adapt your company. By adapt, I mean change positively to align with the current business trends, industry changes, and the ever-demanding needs of your customers.

Is the marketplace moving? Is your industry changing? You can't always be the same old.

You need to adapt. That's why I've encouraged you to be a learner within your industry. Are you adapting to current technology or are you possibly even ahead of your industry? You need to constantly look to where you need to change. What are your customers requesting that you're presently not providing? You need to adapt. What are your competitors offering that you are not?

I can share that I have never—not once—had a company that has not had a major incident that I never planned for in my business plan by year three. Somewhere early on, we had to adapt to something I never accounted for, good or bad. Not all adaptation is survival. Sometimes an opportunity requires the same.

You need to morph, that means change into something you currently are not, for the very reason of survival. Warren Buffet always has a folksy style of communicating this point: "Should you find yourself in a chronically leaking boat, energy devoted to changing vessels is likely to be more productive than energy devoted to patching leaks."

YOUR COMPANY'S ABILITY TO ADAPT
WILL DETERMINE ITS SURVIVAL.

MARCH 3
COLLABORATIVE THINKING

"Many ideas grow better when transplanted into another mind than in the one where they sprang up." —Oliver Wendell Holmes

Collaborative thinking is a method of brainstorming with other people. This is where you allow others to improve upon as well as to be critical of your idea. You allow others to take your idea further than you originally conceived it.

Collaborative thinking is how I allow others to improve, to add to, or to criticize and challenge my ideas. You need to have ideas that are shared with other people. That's why I love partnerships because I get excited about my ideas for a few days, then I run it by my partners, and they say, "Did you consider this? How are you going to hire that type of person? What about that competition over there?" And they start bringing me all these things to consider. I don't give up on my idea, but I do go back to my critical thinking. I go back and adjust my strategy to include the considerations that I had missed before.

As an entrepreneur, you will always work with a team if you are smart. Not every idea or solution to a problem will at first be great, so you'll need to collaborate with other employees to come up with the best ideas and solutions to problems.

I am an idea machine and come up with what I believe is a great idea nearly every week at a minimum. However, when I bring these ideas to my team, quite often they share with me something I had not thought of that makes this idea less great. Other times they take a good idea and take it further than I could take it on my own. Either way, I cannot lose. They help eliminate bad ideas, saving me money, or improve an idea or confirm my original plan is a winner.

Learn to incorporate collaborative thinking in your organization. Two heads are better than one, and having a multitude of experienced teammates to bounce ideas off of results in smart profitable decisions.

ARE YOU A COLLABORATIVE THINKER?

MARCH 4

STAY IN YOUR LANE

"My success, part of it certainly, is that I have focused in on a few things." —Bill Gates

In business, you're going to find an industry that you understand better than others. You're going to find areas where you've made money effortlessly. There gets to be a point where you really do have a lane, and you need to learn to stay in it.

I know somebody who lost a tremendous amount of money trying to get into an industry that they had no knowledge of or experience in. You can get cocky as an entrepreneur and you start to think that you can succeed at all things business-related. I'm warning you, "Pride goeth before a fall."

If you look at Shark Tank, each business owner has an area of comfort: Mark Cuban, technology; Kevin O'Leary, licensing; Lori Greiner, retail products; and Daymond John, branding and clothing. Each one of them has an area they feel most comfortable with.

You're going to find that most entrepreneurs have a lane. This may be an industry or a certain type of deal or partnership that they have had success in. As an entrepreneur, always be opportunistic, but know the lane that you're best in and stay in it.

KNOW YOUR LANE, AND STAY IN IT.

MARCH 5
CHALLENGE YOURSELF AS AN ENTREPRENEUR

"A challenge only becomes an obstacle when you bow to it."
—Ray Davis

Every year, I challenge myself to start a new 20 percent profit stream in one of my companies. Throughout the first six months of the year, I vet my ideas, and then I start narrowing them down. I work on the business plan the last three months of the year and begin to implement my plan in order to launch it early in the new year.

I have done this for the past twelve years. I define success as being able to create 20 percent of new revenue. It is the standard I have set for myself. Is it ambitious? Absolutely, but it keeps me sharp and challenges my team.

I force myself to be an entrepreneur. I am always honing my entrepreneurial skills and reading books on how to be an entrepreneur. Every week, I read a book on how to start and grow a business or what it takes to be a successful business owner.

SET A GOAL EVERY YEAR FOR AMBITIOUS GROWTH.

MARCH 6
CLARITY THINKING

"It's a lack of clarity that creates chaos and frustration."
—Steve Maraboli

Clarity thinking is how you analyze your priorities. What do you need to focus on completing? What initiative will have the greatest payoff? What division within your company is no longer carrying its weight? As the owner, what should you be spending your time doing?

I had to do this recently with one of my businesses and I thought, "Why are we offering the service anymore?" I realized that it wasn't as profitable as I thought, and it was taking more of my staff than I realized and had become a major distraction for me.

A simple way to begin clarity thinking is to ask yourself, "Why?"

- **Why are we doing what we are doing?**
- **Why are we doing something the way we are?**
- **Why am I spending my time on project A?**
- **Why should we continue to do something the way we are?**

    Let us take this exercise further:

What is critical for our company's survival? What one thing, if achieved, would have the greatest payoff? Just begin to put every initiative under a microscope and question how important it is.

HAVE CLARITY ABOUT WHY YOU ARE DOING WHAT YOU ARE DOING.

MARCH 7
CLIENT CONCENTRATION

Client concentration measures how much any one client is responsible for your company's revenue or total clients in general. A simple way to determine if your client concentration is heavily dependent on one client is to ask yourself, "Is there one client who, if we lost them, could put us out of business or cripple our business?"

I have a friend who does contracts with a large general contractor on massive construction projects. It becomes very easy to have one job where only that one client makes up 50 percent of your total revenue for the year. Well, my friend got crushed because he had a client that was not so quick to pay. So, each week his ability to meet payroll was dependent on a timely payment from *one* client.

Never have one client or one job make up more than 15 percent of your revenue. It really should be 10 percent, but I'm going to say 15 percent for some wiggle room because you're getting off the ground. If you do have more than 15 percent of your revenue concentrated in one client or job, you have a company that's nearly impossible to sell.

If you have a client generating 50 percent of your revenue, trust me, you're taking every phone call night or day. You become hostage to this one client. You become dependent on every check that is owed. It is just a terrible position to be in.

If you have a client like this, look at it like a separate business that can go out of business every six months. Do not dare consider it part of your existing business. Be grateful that you have it, but don't count on it. Prioritize bringing on new clients. Replace them as fast as you can.

NEVER HAVE A SINGLE CLIENT MAKE UP MORE THAN 15% OF YOUR REVENUE.

MARCH 8
CLIENT DISPUTES

"Your most unhappy customers are your greatest source of learning."
—Bill Gates

How do you know you have a dispute? Typically, you have a dispute when a customer starts expressing dissatisfaction with your services or products to the point where there will be financial loss or noticeable costs involved to resolve it. Anything that is minor and costs you little is just customer service.

As a business owner or a high-level leader, you should be able to tell when you're in a fire with a customer. I cannot tell you how often I have to alert my staff to a potential dispute that I see coming because the customer service is not being handled fast enough.

How to Avoid Disputes:

1. **Your contracts need to be written simply,** in such a way that a twelve-year-old could serve as the mediator.

2. **Contracts need to benefit both parties,** but they should always benefit you more. You're the one who drew up the contract; if it doesn't benefit you, shame on you. Get a new attorney.

3. **Don't let any client rewrite or make any major additions or subtractions from your contract.** It puts them in the power position, and I have found that you're just bringing on a litigious client.

4. **Don't take the job or client when you sense that the client will be extremely hard to satisfy.** You don't have to take every job because some jobs you're going to lose money on. Some jobs or clients simply are not worth the money.

5. **Set up some ground rules of engagement** before starting with this client, prior to engaging in a contract. Some examples I have used in the past: We agree to communicate openly, respectfully, and during business hours. I also make it clear that I do not want lengthy late-night emails; just call me the next day.

Don't go into a dispute trying to defend yourself. Your primary goal is to understand what your client is asking for and how quickly and inexpensively you can solve it. My goal when resolving a dispute is twofold: 1) satisfy the client with the least amount of cost and exposure to litigation; 2) maintain the client if possible. There are times at the end of disputes where it is best for both parties not to work together in the future.

HAVE A CLEAR PROCEDURE TO RESOLVE DISPUTES.

MARCH 9
STREAMLINING

How do you make everything more efficient in your life and especially in your business? You need to systematize and streamline your operations. Just because you have been doing things a certain way for a lengthy period does not mean that that way is the most effective and efficient way to do it now.

Always think about streamlining your business. This means removing all resistance to a task getting done. Remove layers of decision-makers. The faster you can do things, the more likely it is that you will become more profitable, as you'll increase the number of goods and services you provide to your customers.

As an entrepreneur, ask yourself, "Can I make things simpler? Can I consolidate one or two procedures in my company to improve efficiency?" If you can, you can hire employees without much experience, as most activities will be repetitive and wouldn't need a high-level skill set to perform.

Is there new software or machinery that can speed things up or make tasks less demanding on your staff? If so, you need to make this investment.

Always consider how you can streamline your business. Make this a regular part of your business evaluation process.

STREAMLINE THINGS IN YOUR BUSINESS
TO MAKE THEM MORE EFFICIENT.

MARCH 10
KNOW YOUR NUMBERS

I get a report each day at the close of business that lays out all my companies and all the numbers that are essential for me to know what is going on in my businesses: what came in that day, how many customers contacted us, and from what means of advertising. I can be anywhere in the world and have a dashboard of all the key measurables I need to see in order to be alert to a potential problem. I tell business owners, just as a fantasy football fan knows the stats of all their players, you need to have all the stats of your company at your fingertips.

If you think you're going to meet with your accountant every three months, and you're going to get a great update on your company, no, that's not how you do it. You've got to know your numbers:

- What is your profit margin on your products?
- What product is the one that is selling the most?
- What services are most in demand?
- What services are you offering that you're not making any money on?
- What are your daily operating costs? Have they gone up since last year?
- What is your profit margin on every employee?
- What are your expenses just to open the doors?

Every owner will have different numbers that are critical to them, but receiving a daily report will keep you in the know.

There's one reason why 99 percent of businesses go out of business. They run out of money. Why do they run out of money? It's because they don't know their numbers. Create a dashboard system. If you don't know these numbers, you can never make any adjustments.

THERE IS NEVER AN EXCUSE FOR NOT KNOWING YOUR COMPANY'S VITAL NUMBERS.

MARCH 11
SEEING THE UNSEEN

"You can make something big when young that will carry you through life. Look at all the big startups like Microsoft, Apple, Google, Facebook, Twitter, etc. They were all started by very young people who stumbled on something of unseen value. You'll know it when you hit a home run."
—Steve Wozniak

Seeing the unseen is basically faith, a confidence that something you are hoping for will become reality. Every visionary, which I believe an entrepreneur is, can see potential in ideas and outcomes that are beyond explainable.

It was Bill Gates who saw a computer in every home. It was Henry Ford who envisioned everyone having a car in America. That's what entrepreneurs do. They have this great vision of something that nobody else can see. They absolutely believe it's going to happen, and they work relentlessly to bring this vision to reality.

You need to have this great belief that this idea you have can happen if you put the energy and effort into it. If you want to be a successful entrepreneur, begin to see the unseen. I always have a goal so big that when it is achieved, it will be unexplainable. I will start my story with, "You are not going to believe what happened."

AN ENTREPRENEUR SEES THINGS BEFORE THEY HAPPEN.

MARCH 12
SMART

My daughter is a schoolteacher, and she is very sensitive to the word *stupid*. But as I have told her, "You can't hide stupid." In business, you know when someone does not have the common sense or the smarts to get the assignment done. That may not be politically correct, but it is reality. I am aware we all have areas of knowledge, but I need your knowledge to align with my business if you work for me.

There's no substitute for a smart employee. When you have smart employees, they can do so much more for you. I have also learned that you can't hide stupid. What do I mean? The less "bright" a team member is, the less capacity they have. They just have a much lower ceiling to what they can do for you. This is not an IQ test for intelligence. They just pick up on things fast with very little explanation. On the other hand, to this "not so bright" group, you have to explain things over and over, and they still seem like they are lost.

I have been fortunate over the years to have hired countless "smart" team members, most without a college degree, who have been a tremendous asset because they picked up on things fast, allowing them to carry many responsibilities.

People often ask me, "How can you tell when someone is smart or not so smart?"

My simple answer is, "They will learn fast." One way to find out is to ask them about previous jobs and see if they have been stretched before.

I have had countless college graduates who have worked for me, but I would tell you the two smartest employees I ever had were not college graduates. One was a waitress who eventually was running a restaurant, and to the day she left, I could not find anything she could not learn to do. The second was a bricklayer. Yes, I said bricklayer, and her capacity to learn was amazing. I could tell when I interviewed both that they had something special, an energy, a desire to learn that was easy to pick up on.

THE SMARTER THE EMPLOYEE, THE GREATER THE CAPACITY.

MARCH 13
LOVE A CHALLENGE

If you look at the great entrepreneurs, you will learn how competitive they are. They love a challenge. They love knowing that they could get something done that no one else could. You look at Amazon; they absolutely believed that they could ship a product, nearly any product you could ever want, and have it to you within twenty-four hours. Walmart believed you could have a superstore in smaller towns that its competition never wanted to serve.

A challenge will stretch you as well as your team. If you look at the great companies, you will see that they all overcame challenges that would have brought lesser leaders to quit. Each enterprise faced a challenge, whether it was getting products to market faster than a potential rival or adapting along the way.

If you want to be a successful entrepreneur, you need to love the challenge. You always need to be finding a challenge that stretches your organization. What begins to happen is with every small victory, your team gets a new level of confidence, which will lead to game-changing accomplishments.

If you don't have a challenge right now within your business, you're not growing. You're becoming stagnant. Stretch yourself and your team by setting a few challenges before them.

GREAT ENTREPRENEURS LOVE A CHALLENGE.

MARCH 14
INTUITION

"Don't let the noise of others' opinions drown out your own inner voice. And most important, have the courage to follow your heart and intuition." —Steve Jobs

Intuition is kind of a sixth sense. You get a "gut feeling" that your idea is going to be a success. You sense a problem before everyone else does. There is an opportunity you believe is available before anyone else seized it. Entrepreneurs know what I am talking about.

I can't tell you how many times I've shared an idea with a potential investor, a potential partner, and they just couldn't see it. I, however, could not understand why they didn't see what I saw.

What I saw in my mind and felt in my gut was just inside me. It was just a feeling, a confidence, that it was a great idea. I couldn't explain everything about it. I couldn't add up all the numbers. I just had a gut feeling that it was going to succeed.

There are other times where you get a sense that something is not right. I have had this happen more times than I have fingers, where I just knew the numbers did not add up. So, I asked my accountants to dive further and, sure enough, we found problems. There are other times when I heard a partner discussing an issue with a client, and I interrupted and said, "You are getting ready to have a major problem with this client." They think they have it under control, and I say, "Trust me; you do not."

Great entrepreneurs have great intuition. They have tremendous confidence, a gut feeling that their idea is going to succeed. They are very alert to a gut feeling that tells them they are on the right path. They equally sense problems before anyone else does.

LISTEN TO AND TRUST YOUR INTUITION.

MOTIVATED

"Be motivated by the fear of being average." —Pinterest

A re you still motivated to succeed by growing your company? Are you just getting by, glad to be paying the bills and still in business? Is your only goal survival? You need to find motivation, a desire that wakes you up early because you want to pursue it.

Often, the last time we were excited and motivated was when we had that initial start-up idea. Sadly, you have not had a great idea since your genesis moment. You need to find something that excites you and that gets you out of bed in the morning. You need to be motivated to take your business on to a new level.

You need to have that motivation because that passes itself on to your staff. The culture in your business will reflect you. If you're just walking around the office with no level of excitement, your team will have the same level of enthusiasm. I like what Coach Lou Holts says: "Motivation is simple. You eliminate those who are not motivated."

Be motivated about something. Have something within your business that excites you, that your staff can tell that you're consumed by, and they want to be a part of it. Leaders set the course and the temperature of the enthusiasm within the organization.

ALWAYS WAKE UP WITH SOMETHING
YOU ARE EXCITED TO ACHIEVE.

MARCH 16
FACILITATOR

Great business owners are facilitators in that they are always looking for ways to make work easier for their team. Think about a point guard in basketball who constantly distributes the ball to the players who can score.

You need to be a facilitator. You need to give your staff the resources they need to succeed. You need to know the positions that allow your players to be most valuable to you. It is possible you have staff that are in limited roles within your organization and you need to provide more opportunities for advancement.

As hard as it may be, sometimes you need to help a person advance outside of your company because they have outgrown you and your company. Your company may have a ceiling for them regarding opportunities because of its size or structure. There are times when you have someone exceptional for only a season.

Speak to your staff, and find out what they need. Maybe your staff needs more training. Maybe they just need more staff because they are under siege with too much work. Begin facilitating. Begin giving your staff the resources needed to succeed.

BE A FACILITATOR.

MARCH 17
COMPANY NAME

I am constantly shocked by how many bad names I see for new start-up businesses. They are either too cute or too clever. And I have no doubt the person who came up with the name had great intentions, but the name is not clear enough. Only online businesses can get away with names none of us know the meaning of because they need an odd or distinct URL that people can remember. Examples are Google, Bing, etc. But an everyday storefront or service business would be wise to have a name that quickly identifies what it provides.

Recently a new retail storefront in a quite pricey shopping center opened with the name "Fruit Fixed." I would later learn it is a cell phone repair company. After a few minutes of racking my brain, it hit me that they repair Apple phones or devices. When I first saw the sign and saw the word fruit, I thought for sure it was a smoothie company.

I recently received a local magazine with a cell phone repair company named "CPR Cell Phone Repair." When I hear that name, I know exactly what it is that they do.

You need to have a name that doesn't take somebody all day to figure out what it is you do. It makes marketing so much harder. You've got to introduce your name, explain what you actually sell or offer, and then promote the business. That's way too complicated and costs too much money.

Make your name simple. Make it reflect exactly what you are offering in the marketplace.

TAKE TIME, RESEARCH, AND GET
A RELEVANT BUSINESS NAME.

MARCH 18
MARATHONER

You need to be a marathoner if you want to be an entrepreneur because it's a long-distance race. My son runs cross country for his school, and he also runs track during another season. I have learned the races are quite different. In track, many races range from a quick sprint of one hundred yards to the longest race of four times around the track: sixteen hundred yards. The longest race takes about four minutes. However, a marathon (26 miles) takes two-and-a-half hours or more. The older I get, the more I accept luck seems to come after years of hard work. And there are no "get-rich-quick" businesses.

If you're a sprinter, you are probably not prepared for an endurance race. A marathoner is prepared to run for hours in the elements on different terrains. To succeed as an entrepreneur, you need to be able to survive the long haul and all the different obstacles that you are going to face. Be prepared for disappointment, as it will come from either a team member, bank, or a failed idea. All these things are the life of an entrepreneur; they're marathoners. They know that they're in it for the long haul and are built for everything that might get thrown at them.

I encourage you today to know that if you're an entrepreneur, you're a marathoner; you're in it for the long haul. Don't get discouraged by the little bumps along the way.

BE A MARATHONER; ENTREPRENEURSHIP IS A LONG AND DIFFICULT RACE.

MARCH 19
OVERCOMING FEAR

"Don't let your fear of what could happen make nothing happen."
—Louise Armstrong

If you're going to be an entrepreneur, and you're afraid of going broke, of failure, or rejection; if you're afraid people won't like you and won't want to work with you, then you are never going to succeed.

I love what Henry Ford shared: "One of the greatest discoveries a man makes, one of his great surprises, is to find he can do what he was afraid he couldn't do." You've got to overcome fear. You've got to find out what is holding you back and just move forward.

One secret that I have learned when I was moving into risky water is to write down all the bad things that could actually happen. I also write down all the good things that can also happen. If I can deal with the worst thing on the list because the payoff is worth overcoming my fear, then I move ahead. Fear is the standard hurdle of all success journeys, and I am amazed by how many spend their average lives staring at this obstacle.

In my twenties, I feared nothing, and as I got older, some things were not worth the risk to me. The payoff was not worth it, but in most cases, the things I feared could be overcome with greater planning. And then when you get into your fifties, there are things that you absolutely can't take a chance with. You will find the balance that fits you and your circumstances. But just realize that to have a degree of fear is normal, and, in many cases, you can overcome it.

IT'S VERY HARD TO BECOME SUCCESSFUL IF FEAR PARALYZES YOU.

MARCH 20
MINIMALIST

To be a successful entrepreneur, you should start being a minimalist. It means you don't start a business with everything. A minimalist starts the business with just enough to get it going, but not much more than that. The illustration I share with people is this: when you are starting a business, you begin with a pup tent. Do you remember those? They are the smallest and cheapest tent you can survive in. At best, a pup tent might keep you dry during a mild rainstorm but nothing more.

Why do I encourage you to be a minimalist? Because you're going to waste so much money on bad ideas and things that aren't that important, and we need you to save money for the evolving and adapting phase that comes *after* you get the business off the ground. Start with a pup tent not a dream house.

Think of being a minimalist: what's the least amount it would take to start this business? What's the least amount of office space you need? What's the least amount of warehouse space? Whatever it is, start with the least amount. Spend enough to get a pulse (up and barely breathing) and not a dime more.

THINK PUP TENT, NOT DREAM HOME.

MARCH 21
RAINMAKER

A rainmaker is that one person who can bring in the big client, the one person you trust to close the biggest deal, the one person who you know is constantly working toward bringing in big revenue. In the launch phase of a business, this is the most important person on your team, and more than likely, it is going to be you or your partner. It's hard to ask an employee to slay the giant for you. If you are fortunate enough to have an employee with this skill set, *never* lose them.

I can give you a profile of what this person tends to look like. They have a confidence that cannot be shaken. It is borderline arrogance, and they do believe that they can walk on water when needed. They want the ball on the one-yard line. That is just a glimpse of their makeup.

When you look back at some of the great start-ups like Microsoft and Apple, Bill Gates and Steve Jobs were rainmakers. They created and closed the historical deals that made their companies household names. There needs to be somebody within the group who has no problem asking for the big checks and asking for the big client to sign on the dotted line.

ALWAYS HAVE A RAINMAKER ON YOUR TEAM.

MARCH 22
MANAGER

As much as you need a rainmaker, you also need a manager. Somebody within your group needs to be able to run the operations. Everybody wants to be an entrepreneur, but there must be somebody overseeing operations. There needs to be somebody who is constantly making sure that the organization is delivering on the promises made to their customers.

As the owner, there will be critical periods where you, and only you, will need to be the manager. You'll need to start this project. You will need to push it along, and you need to be able to set the objectives. But for a company to grow, you need to hand these responsibilities off as soon as possible so you can focus on the future of the company. If you are an entrepreneur, you will get bored with these day-to-day duties anyway. Most entrepreneurs have limited attention spans and are quickly attracted to the new shiny object.

I know that I need a detailed person next to me because that is not my strength. I am like a bulldozer in that I can break up ground that looks impenetrable, but I want someone else to manage the building I just constructed so I can start another project.

Here are some hints as to what a good manager looks like: they are averse to risk and can find five reasons why you should not do the expansion you are thinking of doing. That is good because they will find genuine concerns that you need to consider. They protect you from you. Value them, and balance their caution with your optimism. A great example of this balance was Walt Disney and his brother Roy. It was widely known that Roy kept Walt from running the company into bankruptcy.

THERE'S NO SUBSTITUTE FOR
HAVING A GREAT MANAGER.

MARCH 23
DEPENDABLE

Bob Jones, Sr. advised, "The greatest ability is dependability." A person who is dependable is simply someone who can be relied on and trusted. They will do what you are expecting them to do. Dependability is absolutely a quality anyone who works for me has to have. If I cannot trust you to show up and do what you are required to do, then whatever skill or talent you have is irrelevant.

You personally, as the owner and leader, need to set the standard if you want your staff to be dependable. If you're not credible in this area, you're not going to keep high-level staff members. That means you don't have to be reminded to get something done. My personal standard: I will do what you are asking me to do faster than requested and better than expected. I have heard it said that being dependable is doing what needs to be done before doing what you want to do.

Good luck running a great company when nobody in the business can be trusted to get something done. So how do you get team members to be dependable? For one, you demand it in the first interview. You tell them it is a nonnegotiable quality within your organization. I ask them to give me examples of how they have shown dependability in their past employment experience.

Warn them that when it is determined that someone lacks this quality, they will be dismissed with little hesitation.

BE DEPENDABLE TO YOUR STAFF
AND DEMAND IT BACK FROM THEM.

POTENTIAL

"Potential is a priceless treasure like gold. All of us have gold hidden within, but we have to dig to get it out." —Joyce Meyer

Potential is the capacity to become something in the future. Someone has the ability or capacity to do something they may not even realize that they can do. Potential is a latent skill or quality that is yet to be developed. It is inside of them, and you can help discover and develop it.

Great leaders see potential in people well before they see it in themselves. Why? Because we are always looking for it. We expect people to have the skills and talents that they have yet to recognize in themselves. You need to create an environment and provide opportunities for talent to reveal itself.

Let me give you a piece of advice that will save you thousands and millions if you use it throughout your life as an entrepreneur. It is too expensive to hire people who come to you ready-made. Always be looking for potential in new team members. Begin to be alert to potential in the interview process. Create a culture where potential is given the opportunity to bloom. Share this priority with everyone who hires and manages new talent within your company.

I have found that about 60 percent of our employees come to us slightly better than average.

They have potential skills and valuable traits within them that we need to pull out of them. I have found very few things as rewarding as discovering the potential in someone and developing it so that they are better than when they arrived. Henry Ford said, "There is no man living who isn't capable of doing more than he thinks he can do."

***ALWAYS BE LOOKING FOR AND
DEVELOPING POTENTIAL.***

MARCH 25
COMPETITIVE ADVANTAGE

"An organization's ability to learn, and translate that learning into action rapidly, is the ultimate competitive advantage."
—Jack Welch, legendary CEO of General Electric

You don't ever want to fight fair in business. I am not encouraging you to do anything unethical. In business, you always want to create an advantage from the beginning, then you want to continue that advantage, and if possible, expand your advantages.

Amazon exemplifies growing your competitive advantage. They begin with one great competitive advantage: offering the most exhaustive online store on the planet. They did not just settle for this one advantage. They added providing the fastest shipping possible. To make the customer experience effortless, they created the simplest ordering and return process available. They did not stop there, as you can actually call them on the phone and receive what I have found to be spectacular customer support. This is what I call building one competitive advantage after another, which creates a moat of security around your business.

Look at Blockbuster Video, the former largest video store. Somebody didn't notice those little red boxes going up everywhere. Somebody didn't notice Netflix streaming movies online. They lost their competitive advantage.

Can you do something faster than your competition? Do you have better pricing than your competition? Do you have better innovation?

You've got to find something that allows you to do something better, faster, with more creativity, and be more exhaustive in your service or product offering. Do you offer something unique that gives you an advantage over your competition? You need to create this from day one.

BUILD ONE COMPETITIVE ADVANTAGE AFTER ANOTHER.

MARCH 26
SCARED MONEY

"Scared money doesn't make no money."
—Rapper Young Jeezy

I'm borrowing Jeezy's elemental truism about scared money's inability to make money so that I can make a point today. This is an absolute truth that every entrepreneur should know. When you're going with an initiative, and you're scared to death that you're going to fail, and you're scared to death of the risk, you're never going to make any money. People can tell when you're scared.

Facebook founder Mark Zuckerberg warns, "The biggest risk is not taking any risk." I try to stack the deck in my favor on any project I am involved in, keeping the risk to a minimum, but I have never seen a sure thing in business.

So again, don't just throw money around, but when you have made a calculated risk, it's time to put aside doubt. You need to put on your game face, as your team will lose confidence if you start showing signs of questioning your decision. Yes, there are times when you fake it until you make it.

SCARED MONEY DOESN'T MAKE ANY MONEY.

CRISIS THINKING

"In a crisis, don't hide behind anything or anybody. They're going to find you anyway."
—*Legendary Coach Bear Bryant*

There are times in business when you have a crisis, and this means there's going to be a heavy consequence if you don't resolve the crisis. This is much different from problem-solving because of the time factor to solve the problem, as well as potential consequences, which are never good if not dealt with. In crisis thinking, you need to be able to make the correct decision *fast*. You need to be able to identify the threat and to identify the collateral damage.

My strategy when facing a crisis is to bring in intelligent people whose expertise and experience I trust. This is when having an experienced staff is so advantageous. I have always tried to build a cabinet, much like the president has, of advisors that I can call in when I need critical advice. Hollywood, in countless movies, has shown a president, facing a grave threat, with his closest advisors in the Situation Room, where they go through every option available with the possible collateral damage.

Crisis thinking is a skill you will need to learn if you intend to lead a growing organization. Lee Iacocca advises that "trouble shared is trouble halved."

This is sound advice from someone who navigated Chrysler Motor Corporation out of a massive crisis that would dictate the fate of the company. Your leadership will be forged in times of crisis. At no other time will you earn or lose your team's confidence in your leadership more than in these challenging times.

ARE YOU PARALYZED WHEN FACING A PROBLEM?

MARCH 28
ENERGY

"Without passion, you don't have energy. Without energy, you have nothing." —Warren Buffett

Billionaire investor Warren Buffett has often shared that energy is one of the three qualities he looks for most in people who come to work for him. I would encourage you to do the same. There is just something different about a person who has that extra bounce in their step. They tend to be tireless with an endless reservoir of enthusiasm for what they are doing. It is like getting two people for the price of one.

You'd be surprised at the energy level of different people, especially as you grow older. I know as I've gotten older that I don't have the energy I had when I was twenty. I like to think I am a great deal smarter than I used to be, but energy does at times decline with age. One strategy I use to harness the energy of someone younger is to look for interns from colleges. They are like the Energizer Bunny. You need to give a great deal of direction, but they will run in any direction you ask without stopping.

You need to look at the job description that you have and where you need energy. You need to hire somebody who has that, as they're tireless. I would encourage you to really look at your staff, look at your needs, and find out who you have who can go further than anybody else. Look at the people that barely get to the goal line.

GET A TIRELESS TEAM THAT
NEVER RUNS OUT OF ENERGY.

MARCH 29
LIKE FLYING A KITE

When you launch a start-up business, it's like flying a kite. Anything can bring it crashing to the ground. Your goal is to turn it into a canoe eventually, then into a battleship. The battleship is a well-fortified company, and if it doesn't hit the corporate equivalent of an iceberg or an island, it can withstand nearly any challenge.

The advantage of a kite is it's nimble. You can bring it down from the sky, make a couple of adjustments, and send it back up again. With a mere tug of the string, you can maneuver it as you wish. This allows you to make quick adjustments to fit your market or competition.

Maybe the branding position you picked is not applicable. Maybe you need to veer off in another profit direction because what you thought was profitable isn't as profitable as you hoped. Take advantage of the fact that you have a nimble little kite out there, and you can just pull it quickly in any direction.

In time, you will build this company into an unsinkable vessel by cementing your brand into the minds of customers. You will manage profit, building reserves that can withstand a down economy. If you are wise, you will build depth in your staff. All these will transition your kite into a canoe, then a barge, then a battleship.

TAKE ADVANTAGE OF YOUR NIMBLENESS.

MARCH 30
POSITIONING

"Positioning the brand and regaining trust are all the smart things for us to do, and those are the litmus tests for any decision we make."
—*John McKinley*

Do you even have a brand with your company? A brand is your unique position within the marketplace. It's the one quality that people think of when they think of your company. For safety, you may think of Volvo cars. When you think of BMW, it's the driving experience. If someone asked you quickly to name the best watch, most people would probably say Rolex. It has been the standard of all luxury timepieces for decades. They have relentlessly built a brand of excellence showing their watches on the wrists of the most famous people in the world.

You need to think of positioning your company. Where would you best fit within your marketplace? Do you serve high-end customers? You may not be able to position your company as the least expensive within your industry, so you may want to position it toward quality or toward great customer service.

Walmart, for example, has chosen two positioning points for their brand and reflected these in their advertising and their stores: lower prices and large selection. They are not targeting high-income customers. They will attract anyone wishing to save money followed by a secondary position of a large selection. One stop and you can get everything you need for the week or month. This large selection naturally brings in the third position without even trying: convenience.

DECIDE WHICH POSITION YOU WANT YOUR COMPANY TO TAKE.

MARCH 31
YOU DON'T NEED A DEGREE

It is no surprise to learn that doctors earn the highest income in America. From surgeons to dentists and orthodontists, the average income for these professionals ranges from $160,000 to $260,000 per year. However, consider all that is required to get into one of these occupations: the smarts, the long years of schooling, and the large student loans. I am happy to report that you can make the same income, or more, as a savvy businessperson.

That's right. I started one of my second businesses with less than a $1,000 initial investment. I made as much money as a surgeon typically does. In more recent years, I have earned far more.

On this year's *Forbes* 400 list of the wealthiest Americans, 70 percent are entrepreneurs who had no quality in common other than having a powerful business idea and the initiative to pursue it. Anyone—absolutely anyone—can be wealthy as a successful business owner if they have the basic aptitude and are willing to become the master of their own habits.

Another fascinating thing: no billionaires on the Forbes list who did not graduate from college ever went back to get their degree. Bill Gates, Steve Jobs, Mark Zuckerberg, Michael Dell, and the list keeps going. They learned how to lead billion-dollar companies without a business degree.

Perhaps you've clicked past job listings that required advanced degrees you don't have. That career ceiling typically disappears for successful entrepreneurs. College graduates experienced the largest slump in new business creation for 2011. Unlike a Human Resources Department, most of your customers aren't worried about what pieces of paper are hanging on the business owner's wall.

AMBITION, EFFORT, RISK, AND SOME SPECIALIZED SKILLS ARE WHAT YOU REALLY NEED.

APRIL 1
CULTURE

"A company's culture is the foundation for future innovation. An entrepreneur's job is to build the foundation."
—Brian Chesky, cofounder and CEO of Airbnb

What is culture? Essentially, corporate culture is the accepted norms, values, and behavior that is acceptable within a company.

Within *your* current company, how do you do things? For instance, how important is the customer? In my businesses, we are extremely customer-centric with the caveat that we do believe that customers can be wrong. We have a cultural belief of, "We want to do whatever we can to help you as well as provide extraordinary service."

Team is important in our company culture. No lone rangers. If someone needs help, there is always someone willing to lend a hand.

Clean language is important. I don't curse, so I don't want to hear my staff curse. I don't mind an occasional slip, but I don't accept profanity as the common language used. I also don't think customers want to hear profanity, so it is not acceptable in our company culture.

Clearly, these three cultural standards we have set will eliminate people, and we are good with that. But the ones who are on board fit and stay forever because they like and endorse the culture.

CREATE A CULTURE THAT FITS YOUR VALUES AND BE RESPECTED BY YOUR CUSTOMERS.

DAILY DISCIPLINES

Discipline is normally understood as a punishment for not following a given rule. Discipline is used to correct unwanted behavior. However, the Olympic athlete loves discipline because this is an often-difficult routine or regimen they have set for themselves to improve in their area of competition. If you are an entrepreneur, you should have a few daily disciplines that you routinely do.

The first daily discipline you should have is identifying what your main event is. What's the one thing that will have the highest payoff today? What's the one thing that will have the greatest consequence? This will allow you to prioritize your day around first accomplishing that most important thing. Too many people accomplish a broad to-do list but never accomplish the "main thing."

What did you learn today? I spend some time every day reading or listening to a podcast and in many cases both. You can listen to a podcast on your way to work. There are so many ways you can learn today. A discipline you should incorporate is learning something every day.

I spend time thinking, not every day, but at least multiple times per week because I want our companies to be innovative. I want to improve on things that we are currently doing as well as to think about things we may want to stop doing.

I lift weights and exercise every day. It gives me energy. It's a daily discipline. I have a variety of daily disciplines.

In your mind, what do you say to yourself? Do you constantly focus on the negative? Begin a routine of looking at things from a positive paradigm.

Daily disciplines will be what make you successful. The greatest athletes and the greatest musicians in the world have incredible discipline because they do something every day to improve their craft.

WHAT DAILY ROUTINES WOULD DRAMATICALLY IMPROVE YOU?

APRIL 3

DEFINE A WIN

"You play to win the game."
—*Coach Herman Edwards*

In my company, we want to constantly schedule a win, and we game plan for one every week.

You must learn to define a win for your employees and your partners. What do I mean by that? Because some of my partners initially didn't know what a win looked like, I would sit down and tell them, "This is what a win looks like. This number, right here, is how many customers need to contact us every week. This is what our advertising needs to bring in each week. This is the amount of income that needs to come in. This is where we need to keep our labor costs, or whatever the case may be." I defined for them a win. So, on Friday, they know whether we won or lost.

How can they game plan a win if they don't even know what a win looks like? The problem in business is, it's too abstract, it's too ambiguous. My goal in business is to be highly profitable, so I set ambitious weekly goals for my companies that, if hit, will naturally produce a successful company.

If you aim for nothing, you will hit it every time. I want to set clear objectives, and I choose to set most of them for each week. I structure these into weekly wins. My thought has always been that if we win the week, over and over, we will win the quarter and the year.

DEFINE A WIN EVERY WEEK.

APRIL 4

FOCUS ON DURABLE GOOD AND SERVICES

You may remember the "dot com" bubble that crashed in the late 1990s. Companies that had no profits were valued at hundreds of millions and even billions of dollars. Investors learned a very expensive lesson. Warren Buffet, who is going on ninety and has spent time as the richest man in the world on and off over the last three decades, has so many good insights on business. I talk about having a competitive advantage, but he emphasizes that unbeatable force when he says, "Any business that enjoys a durable competitive advantage is likely to have a long history of profitability."

A company needs a product or service that is profitable but also durable. Durability is another one of the famed investor Warren Buffet's favorite qualities when investing in a company. So, as you would guess, he was not interested in investing in the internet companies of the "dot com" era. He was criticized, but he had the last laugh. Do not get caught up in what is popular today.

There is always that rare company that initiates a new product or service, but it's an outlier.

Don't overthink business. In its simplest form, you need a product or service people want, with a price they are willing to pay, that allows you to make the net profit you need to meet your financial goals.

To be successful, this product or service needs to be in demand for a long period of time. Think about what is durable and how to make it better and more efficiently than anyone else. Resist the siren song of "hot properties" and "quick kills." Master the fundamentals of start-up success. You can always venture out later with a solid track record and business foundation.

WHAT COULD MAKE YOUR COMPANY MORE DURABLE?

APRIL 5
LEARN TO DELEGATE

If you can't delegate, how can you grow your business? If the business is so dependent on you to do everything, then it will always stay small. You are not going to bring on any leaders and highly talented people if you cannot give them challenging jobs to do.

You need to learn to delegate. You need to learn to be above your business and not get caught in the minutiae of what it takes to run a business. Often a failure to delegate is the result of an inflated sense of self-worth. "The company needs me there eighty hours a week." That is a rare situation. If I am working eighty hours a week, I'd better be running eight businesses at a minimum. If I am working eighty hours a week running a small business, that means I am doing the jobs that quite often can be done by others.

We need to learn how to delegate. High achievers delegate items that are not imperative to the success of their project. They know what is important and which tasks only they can do. The rest they delegate. They have a team of people.

Quick Tips on How to Delegate:

- Look to delegate. Your goal is to get as many responsibilities into the hands of others as possible.

- Assign these tasks to capable people who have a track record of handling them.

- Give every assignment a deadline.

- Follow up to make sure the task is completed.

BECOME ADDICTED TO DELEGATING.

APRIL 6
CUSTOMER SERVICE

Customer service is not a department; it's a culture. This is not an assignment for any one person or department, this is something everyone participates in. Leadership will tout it as a core value, and if so, it needs to be rewarded by those who perform exceptionally at it. At the very least, there needs to be a system in place so that every customer receives a level of acceptable (I would argue exceptional) service.

3 Tips for Better Customer Service:

1.   Create a culture where serving the customer is paramount.

Your staff needs to know that what we're trying to accomplish here is to meet the requests of our customers based on our guidelines, our commitment to our contract, and our mission statement. Whatever you have posted or promised, your staff needs to know about, and they need to know that they are encouraged to always provide that level of customer service. From day one, create a culture where serving the customer is paramount.

2.   Train your staff to genuinely listen to and handle a complaint.

The best advice I can ever give you is that when a customer is sharing a complaint, you shut your mouth. Shut your mouth, nod to them to continue talking, and encourage them to get it all out, but do not interrupt, interpret, or defend the company, yourself, or your employees. Your only goal is to listen and understand exactly where the problem lies. You can't solve a problem if you don't know what it is. When you train your staff, equip them to resolve the problem. Train them to listen and equip them with the training to solve these problems.

3.   Have customer service guidelines with goals.

You want to set a time frame for how quickly customer problems will be solved. They should not linger for thirty days. All customer service problems should be resolved within forty-eight hours, and if they can't be, then they go to Level Two. You need to have a time frame with a deadline defining how quickly you are going to resolve a customer issue. Next, you need to determine what the outcome is that defines success. You need to define success for every customer service experience.

GREAT CUSTOMER SERVICE IS NOT OPTIONAL.

APRIL 7
ABUNDANCE MENTALITY

There are a couple of ways you can look at things. You could have a poverty mentality, and that just means we're broke, have always been broke, and will always be broke. We don't even look at nice things because we know we can never afford them.

You can have a survival mentality in that you are hoping for and are satisfied with just enough to get by. But I want to encourage you to have an abundance mentality. This is where you expect more than enough. I expect my companies to be very profitable. Anything less is a disappointment. I have learned that you tend to get just what you expect and no more.

It doesn't mean that you are in a fantasy world and make purchases you cannot afford.

However, you don't want to get trapped in a negative mindset regarding money. Some people can never see themselves wealthy and able to give generously. I grew up "not so rich" but always had my sights set on the best. "Why not me?" was my attitude. Was every rich person I ever met smarter than me? No! Were they harder workers than me? No. I knew I could achieve whatever I set my mind to, and from early on, I chose an abundance mentality.

The choice is yours, but I cannot think of one good reason not to have an abundance mentality.

MAKE THE CHOICE TO HAVE AN
ABUNDANCE MENTALITY.

APRIL 8

ONE THING

"Be like a postage stamp. Stick to one thing until you get there."
– Josh Billings

What is the one thing you need to get done today? Start your day with just that one thing and then build your to-do list from that. What is the one thing that is going to have the highest payoff? What is the one thing you need to get done every week? Set your week up the same way, identifying your top objective. We all have a lot we can do, but successful people identify the main things that only they can do and focus on that.

This also works well when leading your staff. Give each of them, or give to the entire company, one single objective to shoot for. Sometimes it will be the need to increase profit. We need to increase the speed of production. Maybe it's customer service, maybe it's acquisitions. Whatever the case may be, trim things down to just the one main thing—for the day, for the week, for the year, for your company.

This creates a singular focus. Do you remember the magnifying glass experiment? Hold a magnifying glass in one position facing a newspaper, allowing continued heat from the sun to pass through it. Soon it generates enough heat on the newspaper to create a flame. That is the same focus you need to have on key objectives.

WHAT IS THE ONE THING?

APRIL 9

START A BUSINESS—OR PURCHASE ONE

Do you want to be a business owner, or do you want to be an entrepreneur? Here's the difference: A business owner is someone who owns a business, while an entrepreneur is someone who starts a business.

The key word is *start*. I love the excitement of starting a business. I have started several over the years. However, I've found that purchasing an existing business is often the fastest way to reach my desired goal.

There are quite a few advantages to buying an existing business. You have the opportunity to look at existing financial records and customer lists. You may be able to speak with the staff. You may already be familiar with the company. This removes many of the risks of starting a business.

Often existing businesses are making money but could make a lot more with a few tweaks, such as more advertising and new enthusiasm. Also, you may be able to purchase a business for equal or less than what it takes to start a business.

Additionally, the owner may be willing to do some owner financing, which reduces your initial costs. Usually, the asking price is in relation to how much the owner has personally made or the gross receipts. Since most small businesses are S Corporations or LLCs, this figure is on their personal tax returns.

BUYING A BUSINESS CAN ELIMINATE A GREAT DEAL OF INITIAL RISK.

APRIL 10
PROBLEM-SOLVING

"If I had an hour to solve a problem, I'd spend 55 minutes thinking about the problem and 5 minutes thinking about the solution."
—Albert Einstein

Problem-solving is why the owners and leaders get paid the big money. Do you become paralyzed when presented with a challenging problem? What do you do when you have a major problem? I'm going to give you a little piece of advice. When I have a problem, I sit down, take out a piece of paper, and write the problem on it, and then I brainstorm all the ways I can solve it. I bring in some other smart people, and we start brainstorming together.

You'd be shocked how many great ideas you will get solving problems, and once you begin solving problems, they just seem smaller and smaller when they present themselves in the future. Problem-solving is a skill that you can improve at, and all leaders need to have this skill. I have a section in the back of my journal where I keep problems that I faced and then overcame. This list has allowed me to face hurdles now with great confidence that they, too, will be overcome.

BE A PROBLEM SOLVER.

APRIL 11
PARTING WAYS WITH A CUSTOMER

This is the age of "The customer is always right," and I believe social media with its online posts and reviews has really emboldened customers. I also believe that just as a customer can choose not to use your company any longer, you can choose not to serve a client any longer. Obviously, this needs to predicate on this client being a losing proposition for your company.

The first reason is you can't make them happy. Simply put, what they want, you can't deliver. No matter what you do, they're just never happy. I have shared with clients that our contracts don't promise happiness anywhere in them. We do however have an agreed upon scope of work that we are happy to fulfill for them. Sometimes they are just never happy with what you do or provide. This wears on your staff, and the client's money is not worth it. Move on.

Secondly, they want more than what is agreed upon in the contract. You've met them, and they always want more. This type of customer also wants to renegotiate the contract at the end to improve the price. In short, they want more than what they agreed to.

Thirdly, customers who don't pay as described in the terms of the agreement. I don't like customers who you must chase down to get paid. If the payment process is difficult, we don't want to bother with you.

Finally, if I find that you talked to any of my staff rudely, I will absolutely get rid of you.

So again, I don't necessarily believe that the customer is always right. I believe 99 percent of the time, there's great merit in it. I believe that you can always learn something from the customer. There are times, however, when you do have to dismiss a customer and just part ways.

THE CUSTOMER ISN'T ALWAYS RIGHT.

APRIL 12
EMPLOYEE INTANGIBLES

I look at two things in a resume:

1. Do you have experience in the job that we're hiring for?

2. What is your employment history, and how long did you stay in places you have worked? Everything else is an intangible to me, and I've had great success with this outlook.

What are the intangibles?
What made this person so good?

- **Likability and great social skills.** When I met somebody and I liked them in under a minute, that's the first qualifier.

- **Great energy.** You can sense it when you see it even in the interview. They have a bounce in their step. They are excited when they talk.

- **A reason to come to work.** I want someone who cannot afford not to work. They have a family to feed.

- **Good communication skills.** They can effortlessly talk and communicate a thought or idea.

- **Smart.** It is one of my favorites because you cannot do much with stupid.

Every industry and company will have qualities that it values. What is important to me does not have to be what you look for in a new hire. You do need to identify a few intangibles that others who have been great for your company have had.

WHAT QUALITIES DO YOU LIKE IN YOUR EMPLOYEES?

APRIL 13
AN ENTREPRENEURIAL MINDSET

"I think anything is possible if you have the mindset and the will and desire to do it and put the time in."
- Roger Clemens

I have met countless business owners over the years as they started one business and held on for dear life, hoping it would survive and pay their bills. An entrepreneur is always looking for new opportunities to grow and expand their empire. They have an aggressive, offensive mindset in business. They are never content with just one small win in their portfolio. It has been said, "The best defense is a good offense."

Let's check your entrepreneurial mindset:

1. **Do you constantly see opportunities to grow and expand your current business?**

2. **Do you consider franchising your business?**

3. **When was the last time you started a business, invested in one, or created a new profit stream?**

4. **Do you crave the thrill of building something from scratch?**

5. **Do you give business ideas away?** I have given away business ideas that I did not have the time to act on. We don't hoard ideas because we know that ideas constantly come to us.

IT IS THE MINDSET THAT CHANGES EVERYTHING.

APRIL 14
ENTREPRENEURIAL COMPANY

Entrepreneurial companies are always strategizing about ways they can grow in size, market share, and revenue. As such, entrepreneurial companies purchase other companies, they partner when it is beneficial, and when necessary, they consume the competition. It's an aggressive mindset, but if you're going to be an entrepreneur, you need to have an aggressive mindset. The illustration I use is "Pac-Man." Do you remember the video game? Pac-Man eats everything in sight.

I'm a small-business owner, I still buy local competition. Why? I want their customers. I want to expand my demographics. I want market share. And sometimes I just want to remove competition.

So, why do small businesses need to acquire other companies?

- **It allows you to expand your offering**. Say you had a restaurant, and there was another restaurant that you could buy in a different part of town. You know how to run restaurants, you had overlapping staff, and you had incredible management already in place. This would be a win for you.

- **You may want to bring in a great partner.** I would never partner or buy a company unless one of two things happens. Either I can eliminate their ownership and their influence, or I want their influence. If I'm buying them, the reason might be that I don't think the company is being run very well, so I want to buy it and clean house. Or the opposite: I think they have great staff, so I want that team on my team.

- **Maybe you have the infrastructure to absorb this company and be able to put it on hyperspeed.** That's one of the reasons why I acquire companies. I know that we have a strong infrastructure: office staff, a huge client base—we know how to market to that client base—and, we have great talent. So, I feel like I can absorb a certain company in a certain industry and know that I can put it on turbo the second we acquire it.

THINK GROWTH MINDED, AND BECOME AN
ENTREPRENEURIAL COMPANY.

APRIL 15

EXECUTION

"Success doesn't necessarily come from breakthrough innovation but from flawless execution."
—Naveen Jain

Execution is accomplishing what you have set out to accomplish. I meet people all the time who share great ideas with me, but they don't ever get anything done. Successful entrepreneurs get things done: they execute!

You need to understand that execution does not have to be perfect. I think this is what keeps people from executing or following through on ideas. You need to take action steps, but understand that typically they never start perfectly, and they will evolve countless times in ways you never imagined.

How do you execute?

1. **Know what tasks and initiatives have the highest payoff.** First, identify the things that must get done and get working on them. Then identify what will have the greatest payoff. Be very intentional with your time and energy, focusing on the most important things to do.

2. **Keep strategies simple and adaptive.** Situations are going to change, and because I understand that, I don't need a perfect strategy to start a business. I understand that the strategy is going to change, so I try to keep it simple so I can keep adapting it.

3. **Recruit others to help you execute.** It's hard to do anything by yourself. You recruit others to help you execute.

4. **Stay focused.** You can't jump all over the place. Too many entrepreneurs do that. They claim to have lots of great ideas, but in reality, a lot of great ideas are no good ideas. One idea that is executed is the best strategy.

5. **Relentlessly persist.** Relentlessly pursue completing tasks and the initiatives that have the highest payoff.

SUCCESSFUL ENTREPRENEURS EXECUTE.

APRIL 16
EXIT STRATEGY

I am a big optimist, but in every business plan I have for a new start-up or an expansion plan I have for an existing company, I also create an exit strategy. You need to calculate, in terms of time and money as well as staff, how long it would take to shut the business down and what, if any, collateral damage would result.

I remember an interview with General Norman Schwarzkopf, who led the first successful war against Iraq, the one where we were smart enough to get in and get out quickly. After bombing everything in sight, we did not bring our soldiers into Baghdad, the capital city. When asked about this choice, the General said, "It is easy to start a war, but how do you end it?" The point was, we were not completely sure how we would get out once we started that fight, so the prudent thing to do was not to get into it. This is the mentality of a smart entrepreneurial general.

Every business I start, fully expecting it to succeed—as I'm 99.9 percent plowing ahead—always has, tucked away in a file, an exit strategy. I would advise you to do the same. Some simple things to consider are initially to keep commitments as short as possible even if you can save money. Think pup tent, not dream house. If needed, you want to be able to bring this whole thing down in days, not years. Here are some simple strategies to consider:

- Short leases on property (store, office warehouses, etc.).
- Month-to-month advertising agreements.
- Enough insurance to be prudent, but not anything extra.
- Used vehicles, not new.

HAVE AN EXIT STRATEGY READY NO MATTER HOW OPTIMISTIC YOU ARE.

APRIL 17
THE ENTREPRENEUR'S MUST-READS

1. ***Think and Grow Rich* by Napoleon Hill**
   The author interviewed five hundred of the most successful people of his time. They were introduced to him by Andrew Carnegie, the wealthiest person at that time. He distills thirteen key principles of success into the overriding principle: successful people think differently.

2. ***Rich Dad Poor Dad* by Robert Kiyosaki & Sharon Lechter**
   I don't necessarily endorse his methods toward the end of the book regarding real estate, because I believe the 2008 market broke down some of those pillars and made some of this not as accurate, but the book does a great job establishing the mindset that an entrepreneur has as well as the limitations of the everyday employee mindset. The authors share the power of passive and multiple streams of income.

3. ***E-Myth* by Michael E. Gerber**
   This is a fantastic book because he establishes the fact that most entrepreneurs are really technicians, in that they work in their business. He endorses working on your business, growing it and improving it, not in your business.

4. ***Speed of Trust* by Stephen Covey**
   He talks about integrity and competence; this is what creates trust. Likability has to parallel integrity. People need to trust you, and the only way they can trust you is by believing that you have character and you have competence. He illustrates this by looking at Warren Buffett, who does deals within a day or two, compared to companies that normally take a year to eighteen months. He attributes this to Warren Buffett's integrity.

5. ***Good to Great, How the Mighty Fall, and Great by Choice* by Jim Collins**
   He gets three books in there because he's going to take you through a decade, and he will introduce you to some great companies. Then, because of the recession, some of these don't survive, and he shares why they failed. He then shares with you how some companies are great by choice, in that they're durable companies. He shows what they did to become durable, and he shares the flaws of the companies that have fallen.

MY FIRST FIVE BOOKS EVERY ENTREPRENEUR SHOULD READ.

APRIL 18
ALIGNMENT

"Authenticity is the alignment of head, mouth, heart, and feet -
thinking, saying, feeling, and doing the same thing - consistently. This
builds trust, and followers love leaders they can trust."
– Lance Secretan

You want to have your goals in alignment with your values. It is great to be financially successful, but it is not great if you have not paid your taxes to do that, or if you're finagling things financially.

Do you treat your staff with respect no matter what their position is? There is never an excuse to treat people disrespectfully. Your position does not give you the right to talk down to or speak rudely to anyone.

Are you honest with your customers? Are your contracts ambiguous at best, leaving a way you can get away with not delivering on an assumed promise? I have learned over twenty years that when you don't lie or mislead, you can defend yourself and your company effortlessly when needed.

There is no customer of any business I have ever had whom I would avoid if I saw them at a restaurant. I went into business with the understanding that as a parent in a smaller town, I would see people that our companies served, and I never wanted to be embarrassed.

It is great to be ambitious, but it's not great to be ambitious and lose your family.

Get your goals in line with your values. I'm just encouraging you today to have better alignment in your life. Get everything totally squared up, and I think you'll be a lot happier.

YOUR GOALS NEED TO ALIGN WITH YOUR VALUES.

APRIL 19
MOTIVATE AND INSPIRE OTHERS

"When you are living the best version of yourself, you inspire others to live the best versions of themselves."
—Steve Maraboli

Have you ever seen a football team that flounders for years, until they hire a new coach and he turns the team completely around? He can motivate, get the team to do what his predecessors could not get them to do. A great coach brings out talent and energy that others cannot harness.

If you want to be a successful business owner, you need to learn how to motivate your staff, to get them excited about what excites you. Allow them to catch your vision for being dominant in your industry: to grow in size and influence.

The ability to motivate is a learned skill and very few skills will pay as big a dividend. I have always been able to motivate people to "rush hell with a squirt gun." My enthusiasm for anything just becomes contagious. People around me know my excitement is genuine, and they also feel my confidence that we can achieve big things. This is critical: you cannot fake your enthusiasm, and you will only earn their confidence if you deliver on small initiatives along the way.

Motivation also allows you to get more out of your team than you or even they think is possible at key times throughout the year. You cannot push them every day or you will burn them out, and they will just get tired of you. You need to balance motivation, approval of a job well done, and a rest period. I have found the balance of the three in that order, used a few times per year, has allowed our companies to achieve grand results.

Read some books on great coaches and generals, and you will see some key behaviors and skills they all share that allowed them to bring out the best in others.

LEARN TO MOTIVATE AND INSPIRE OTHERS.

APRIL 20

BUILD A BRAND

"A brand is a voice and a product is a souvenir."
–Lisa Gansky

Don't just be a small business. Be a business with a recognized brand (image, reputation). Branding made simple: Find something that is unique to what your company can deliver and that your ideal customer values, and lay claim to it with advertising efforts. It is a promise to your customers about something they can expect from your product or service. It should be in all your messaging. You beat this drum for years so that your customers associate your company with this quality. That's the idea.

Brand Examples

- **Volvo:** Safety

- **Rolex:** Perpetual Excellence

- **BMW:** Ultimate Driving Machine

- **Papa John's:** Better Ingredients, Better Pizza

What is the position that you're trying to establish in the marketplace for your company?

What differentiates your business from your competitors? What is that one quality, that one unique position that if you could deliver on it every single day, would make customers swarm to your company?

Lay claim to this position, and own it. Create a tagline that reinforces it. Have all your messaging echo it. Do not change it every year.

BUILD A BRAND FOR YOUR COMPANY.

APRIL 21
FAILURE

"Failure is the scar tissue left behind on your journey to success."
—Sean Castrina

If you fear failure, you'll never take risks, and if you don't take risks, you're never going to be a successful entrepreneur. Failure is the growing pain of success. You cannot have one without the other.

You need to view failure differently. Failure is only a temporary setback. It does not define you; it shares a single event. Often, it's only a launching point, and it teaches us lessons that in most cases could not be learned any other way.

There are countless things that I've learned in one failure that allowed me to do something so much better in another venture. The bigger the failure, the greater the lesson that failure inscribes, as nothing else has a louder voice of instruction than an expensive and painful failure.

Failure is only a temporary setback, and if you use it right, if you mine for gold, it could actually launch you further than an initial success.

For successful people, failure is a learning lesson. They move on; they don't dwell on it. When you talk to them five years later, they don't bring it up.

Every great lesson you'll ever learn will be expensive. I've also learned that very rarely are inexpensive lessons valuable. It's the big failures that teach you the most.

LEARN FROM FAILURE.

APRIL 22

FIVE PLAYERS YOU NEED ON YOUR TEAM

You're only going to go as far as the team you have around you. By this I mean that if you have a great team, they'll get you anywhere you want to go. On the other hand, if you don't have the right team, I don't care what your goal or vision is, it's never going to happen. So, who are the types of players you want on your team?

Pack mules

These people have a great capacity to take on extra work for the short term. They have a servant's attitude. They are typically in your administrative staff.

Utility players

You've got to have people on your team that will do anything. I'm not saying they do anything great. What I say is, they're C players from a talent standpoint, but they're A players from an attitude standpoint, and they'll do anything you ask.

Bulls

These aren't your social butterflies. These people don't play well with others. They've got sharp elbows in the sandbox, but they clear ground. If you have a major initiative, you send them in first. They have the capacity of a pack mule, but they have extraordinary talent that you just have to have. They are more like mercenaries.

MVPs

These are people that can balance both; they're like bulls in that they can get a lot done, but they have great social etiquette. They can basically oversee an area of your business and could even become a partner in a business. They have talent, great capacity, great intelligence, and great business IQ. Simply put, they could replace you in many areas of your business. These are the people you do not want to lose to a competitor.

The opposite of you

You need Ying and Yang. I'm a crazy optimist, so I need somebody who can reveal to me what I may have missed. Someone with more of a pessimistic critique. If you're not a numbers or detail person, you had better have someone who is.

A BUSINESS IS ONLY AS GOOD AS ITS TEAM.

APRIL 23
WHY BE AN ENTREPRENEUR

I want to remind you why you have chosen entrepreneurship, the most exciting career with the highest income. If for any reason you are still on the fence, I hope that after reading this, you will come join us.

Let's start with what do all NFL owners have in common, other than that they are all billionaires? They are all business owners or the heirs of an entrepreneur. What do Forbes 400 Wealthiest Americans all have in common? They either started a very successful company, or they are the heirs of someone who did. I have yet to find a practicing attorney or doctor on that list. The few doctors that litter the list actually made their fortunes starting a company in their industry of training.

Entrepreneurship—unlike becoming a lawyer, doctor, engineer, or teacher—requires no college degree. The highest-paid profession in the world rewards only initiative and great ideas. It does not qualify you based on your income or your credit score. If you can act on a profitable idea, entrepreneurship will reward you.

What I happen to like most is, unlike successful doctors and lawyers who have to work 70–80 hours a week, the more successful the entrepreneur, the less they actually work. Let me redefine work: having to go somewhere, do something, at a given time, without being able to say no to it.

Entrepreneurs can do what they want (because if they are smart, they delegate their areas of weakness) when they want (they are the boss). That might explain why I rarely hear of a billionaire business owner retiring. People retire because they are tired of being told to do something or they are tired of doing something they no longer want to do.

Finally, the most philanthropic people on the planet are far and away entrepreneurs. According to Forbes, the top five all founded companies that provided the wealth they were able to generously give from.

KNOW WHY YOU CHOSE TO BE AN ENTREPRENEUR.

APRIL 24
FOCUSED THINKING

"When every physical and mental resource is focused, one's power to solve a problem multiplies tremendously."
—*Norman Vincent Peale*

Focused thinking is what I believe allows a good idea to become a great idea. Sometimes you've got to drill down on one idea with the goal of taking it further than originally planned. I may start with a simple question like, "Can I improve it (the original idea)?"

This is where I put something under a microscope. If you're trying to solve a problem or you need a solution, focused thinking is the way to go. This is where you remove distractions. I put the problem or whatever I'm thinking about on the top of my legal pad and then I just drill down on it. I discipline myself to only think about this one thing.

Ralph Waldo Emerson said, "Concentration (focus) is the secret of strength ... in all human affairs." When someone puts their total focus on any one thing for a sustained period of time, improvement must happen.

Steve Jobs said, "This has been one of my mantras: focus and simplicity. Simple can be harder than complex. You have to work hard to get your ideas clean and simple, but it's worth it in the end because once you get there, you can move mountains."

So, focused thinking and problem-solving are solution-oriented, an improvement on an existing thought or idea. They may even bring forth that one great idea that changes the world. If you want to be a successful entrepreneur, you need to know how to get your thinking more focused.

TAKE YOUR THINKING TO THE NEXT LEVEL: GIVE IT A SINGULAR TARGET.

FORTIFYING YOUR BUSINESS

"A man in debt is so far a slave." —Ralph Waldo Emerson

When we talk about fortifying your business, that translates to how you avoid going out of business. How do you build a moat around your business? There are six ways of fortifying your business:

1. **Build cash reserves.** Until I had cash reserves in the bank, I never had peace of mind. My business pulled me around; I did not dictate my business. So, the first thing you do to fortify your business is to build cash reserves. You do this by establishing a fixed percentage of all income or profit that you will put in reserve. Cash reserves are the oxygen of your business.

2. **Establish lines of credit.** Banks don't loan money to companies in need. If they sense you are in trouble, they are not going to give you any money. So, you need to establish lines of credit before you need them. And you only use lines of credit in an emergency.

3. **Create new profit streams.** You've always got to create more income streams. You've got to keep discovering new ways to generate more money, more sales, and more profit.

4. **Cost sharing.** Do you have anything within your business that you can share the cost of with another company? (e.g., office staff, accounting services, extra desk space or specific machinery you could rent out). You have got to get creative and share your costs. Lease out some equipment, your office staff, and unused portions of your warehouse.

5. **Lower operating costs.** Lowering your operating costs enables you to have more cash reserves. You do this by looking at your operating costs quarterly, or at least every year, to see where you can cut back.

6. **Build depth in your staff.** Your employees should be versatile and able to handle multiple positions so that if you lose somebody, your business doesn't drop off. You shouldn't lose an income stream just because you lost a key person.

A VARIETY OF ECONOMIC OR COMPETITIVE RISKS MAY ONE DAY THREATEN YOUR BUSINESS.

APRIL 26
DEBT SNOWBALL

I'm not a big fan of debt. I have found that creating a debt snowball is the simplest and most effective way to eliminate its stronghold.

What bill are you going to pay off this year? I would recommend listing all your debts with their payoff or monthly payment. Start with the one with the lowest payoff, and set your sights on eliminating it as fast as possible. Then take that amount and roll it over to pay another debt. I've been doing this for years. Whenever I pay off a company vehicle, I take that payment and move it toward another vehicle or debt.

Sometimes I'll renegotiate a contract with a vendor, saving me money. I'll take that extra money and apply it to a debt. I'm always rolling a debt snowball. I constantly tell my CPA that the snowball is getting bigger and bigger. In business, sometimes debt is a necessary evil. It just happens, so you need to have a systematic strategy to eliminate it.

Consider a debt snowball. Pay one debt off, take that amount, apply it to another debt and just keep doing this. You'll be shocked at how sometimes you have $1,000, $2,000, or $10,000 a month rolling out debt every month. Soon you will be debt-free and can take this saved money and create a cash reserve.

CREATE A DEBT SNOWBALL.

APRIL 27
ARCHITECT

Consider being more like an architect if you want to grow your business, add new divisions, or expand to new locations. I have built houses from the ground up and can tell you that the first step is to determine what you want the final product to look like. This will, in turn, be determined by your needs and wants. If you want a first-floor master suite, that will dictate much of how the house will need to be laid out for it. This is not something you could add in the middle of the project.

Entrepreneurs have countless ideas, which is good, but the ability to draw up a blueprint to achieve the desired outcome is critical to the success of the project as well as to gain the confidence of your team. This blueprint will account for everything that will be needed to accomplish this initiative: time frame, manpower, resources, cost, design, etc.

I prefer the blueprint analogy over a business plan, as a blueprint shows visually the final product. I think this makes you focus on the final outcome and work backward with a plan to make it happen. I also like that an architect does nothing without a blueprint as it is the Holy Grail of the job. Too often a business plan is written and thrown in a drawer.

You need to think more like an architect and have a blueprint for any large project or initiative you are setting out to accomplish. Also, just like an architect has an easel that the blueprint is placed on so that it is always in front of them, follow your blueprint with the same diligence.

CREATE A BLUEPRINT, AND FOLLOW IT.

APRIL 28
ORGANIZED AND CLUTTER-FREE

We all have seen that person with a messy desk who swears to us they know where everything is. I don't believe it. I would encourage you to be organized because if you're organized, your staff will be organized. When I hire a lead secretary or a key person within the office, I look at how they organize and leave their space when they leave the first day.

Clutter is just distracting. I think every piece of paper and mail should go through a simple filing process:

- Do I need to take action on it? Then get it done.
- Do I need to delegate it? Then hand it off.
- Do I need to discard it? Then throw it away.
- Do I need it later? File it where I can find it.

I try to take twenty minutes at the end of every week, set a stopwatch, and go through all my mail and papers. I try to organize everything into tasks, basically listing what needs to get done next week. I delegate when possible and file and discard when applicable.

I encourage you to consider being more organized. It will save you a great deal of time, and it clears your mind of unnecessary distractions. Your staff just might follow your lead and become more organized as well.

SET THE EXAMPLE: BE MORE ORGANIZED AND CLUTTER-FREE.

BURNING DESIRE

"There is one quality which one must possess to win, and that is definiteness of purpose, the knowledge of what one wants, and a burning desire to possess it."
—*Napoleon Hill*

Every great achievement starts with a burning desire. What is your desire today? Do you have a burning passion to achieve something within your business? If you want to be a successful entrepreneur, you've got to have an obsessive want. Do you have a consuming idea you wish to act on?

My family would tell you that when I have an idea or project, the company I wish to start consumes my attention. I do not get distracted, but I'm like a dog with a bone. I don't let go. A burning desire—I love that description—takes a simple desire to a whole different level. Napoleon Hill's *Think and Grow Rich*, which I believe to be the standard for all nonfiction books, puts a burning desire as the number one thing you must have to be successful in your sought-after outcome.

Desire is what gives you motivation. It is the fuel that takes you up over the hurdles that will present themselves. This obsession gives you the energy to relentlessly pursue this achievement.

WHAT IS YOUR CURRENT BURNING DESIRE?

THREE PARTNERSHIP LESSONS

"A single arrow is easily broken." – Japanese proverb

You get these three lessons for nearly nothing, as they cost me a small fortune to learn:

Partnerships are not always 50–50.

This is where people make mistakes. I always try to get a majority by convincing the others that I'm bringing the most to the table. I'm willing to do 50–50 profit sharing, but what I want to avoid is bottlenecking every major decision. I'm entrepreneurial by nature, so I'm going to have aggressive ideas. I'm going to be very innovative, and I'm bringing you on because your strength is what I don't have time to do—manage the business.

You need to clearly define responsibilities.

You are responsible for A, B, C, D, E, and F, or whatever it is. That is what clearly defining responsibilities means. If you fail to perform those, you will lose your ownership.

Have a partnership agreement.

Have a legal agreement drawn up by a lawyer. I would never go into a partnership without a partnership agreement. Include responsibilities, and how to end the partnership with a predetermined buyout figure. At the very least have a written agreement notarized and signed by the partners.

PARTNERSHIPS ARE GREAT WITH A FEW SIMPLE RULES.

MAY 1
PREPARATION

"If you fail to prepare, you're preparing to fail."
—Benjamin Franklin

I try to stack the deck in my favor, preparing for everything I possibly can. I have a plan A, B, C, and so forth. I prepare for every high-level conversation, negotiation, or confrontation I may have. I don't want to get caught unprepared to answer or defend something. It is often referred to as due diligence. The Roman philosopher Seneca said, "Luck is what happens when preparation meets opportunity." Simply put, the more prepared you are, the better positioned you will be to take advantage of the opportunities that will come your way. The results will be a success, which others may call luck.

I like what Robert Schuller said about preparation: "Spectacular achievement is always preceded by unspectacular preparation." Preparation is never spectacular. Before I start a business, well before the business plan, I spend time in preparation to determine if this is even a good idea. I may need to study the area, market income, hiring ease, competition, cost of advertising, etc.

ALWAYS BE PREPARED FOR AN OPPORTUNITY.

MAY 2
MONETIZE

The goal of every entrepreneur is to monetize their ideas. This is when you actually earn money from them. Your ideas begin to earn revenue for you. Probably more than any single word, *monetize* defines what we are trying to do; we take our ideas and we turn them into profit. If you have an idea, but you can't turn it into profit, you just have an idea.

If you have watched *Shark Tank*, this is the one thing they focus on first: how much money is this invention, new business, or product making. Then they want to know the costs and how much profit margin is there. Then they spend time getting a feel for the person making the pitch. But first and foremost, they want to know if this is a moneymaker. I have had ideas that I thought could not fail, yet they did not make me a dime. I have also had ideas that I thought were average, but the need or demand was so overwhelming, more than I initially thought, that they became very profitable ventures.

My newest venture is a platform-building company for authors. Our tagline is "Monetizing your words, image, and influence." Set a new standard for your ideas. These brain creations should generate profit.

MONETIZE YOUR IDEAS.

EXCEEDING CUSTOMERS' EXPECTATIONS

"Exceed your customer's expectations. If you do, they'll come back over and over. Give them what they want—and a little more."
—Sam Walton, Walmart and Sam's Club Founder

Why do we want to exceed expectations? Well, because anybody can be average. Think about it, if you set your goal today, within your company, to exceed your customer's expectations, this is what may happen:

They purchase from or use your company again and again.

They share their experience.

They become an evangelist, promoting your services or products to friends, family, and neighbors.

This is where they actually sell your product or services for you so then you get a call, lead, or customer that is buying from you.

They defend your company when someone shares a criticism.

Always set a goal to exceed the customer's expectations. It's hard enough, sometimes, to make everybody happy, but if you set a goal to exceed their expectations, at worst, you're going to meet the expectations of even your most difficult customer. The mission statement of one of my companies has "exceeding our customers' expectations" in it.

EXCEED YOUR CUSTOMERS EXPECTATIONS.

VISUALIZE

"Having a mental snapshot of where you are, where you are going, and what you are moving toward is incredibly powerful."
—Sara Blakely

Hall of Fame golfer Jack Nicklaus once said he had never hit a golf shot that he had not seen first before he hit it, in that he saw the ball's flight, he saw it hit the green, and he saw how it would roll toward the hole. He wanted to have a vivid picture in his mind of what the perfect shot would look like before he swung the club.

In business, you need to see your business exactly how it will look and function five years in the future before you even create it. Visualization is so important. As an athlete, I was a wrestler. I never pictured myself losing. I was disappointed because sometimes it happened, but when I visualized it, I always wrestled the perfect match.

You need to visualize the perfect business today. This will allow you to set intermediate goals to make this vision a reality. This snapshot needs to be embedded in your mind so you can be an evangelist, sharing it to all who will listen. Bo Bennet brings this point home with "Visualization is daydreaming with a purpose."

CREATE A VIVID PICTURE OF WHAT YOUR BUSINESS WILL LOOK LIKE FIVE YEARS FROM NOW.

MAY 5
STOP SELLING CRAP

*F*orbes magazine had a story it shared courtesy of Nike CEO Mark Parker. He said shortly after becoming CEO, he talked to Apple Founder and CEO Steve Jobs on the phone.

"Do you have any advice?" Parker asked Jobs.

"Well, just one thing," said Jobs. "Nike makes some of the best products in the world. Products that you lust after. But you also make a lot of crap. Just get rid of the crappy stuff, and focus on the good stuff."

Parker said that Jobs paused, and Parker filled the quiet with a chuckle. But Jobs didn't laugh. He was serious. "He was absolutely right," said Parker.

I believe all business owners need to ask themselves, "What are we selling that we know is crap?" I have had to ask myself this a few times over the years. One of my companies, a high-end home improvement company with countless divisions that can provide nearly anything you could ever want to be done to your home, decided to offer driveway sealing.

The more I learned about the process, the more I did not like the offering. Basically, it's spray painting the asphalt. I came to believe that customers were expecting a new driveway look no matter what we told them, but in the end, every crack and imperfection was still there, only painted black. We were selling crap, and I closed it up as fast as I could.

I wish I could tell you this was my only experience selling crap, but over twenty-five years in business, I look back and can see some offerings that did not reinforce brand position, which in every company I have is excellence at the core.

IF YOU ARE SELLING CRAP, STOP.

MAY 6
CHANGE

"Your success in life isn't based on your ability to simply change. It is based on your ability to change faster than your competition, customers, and business."
—Mark Sanborn

Ask yourself these questions:

· What one change to your business would have the greatest payoff?

· What one change could bring more profit?

· What one change could save the most money?

· What changes do you need to make to keep up or lead your industry?

· What changes need to be made to improve the culture of your company?

· What one staff change could make the difference?

· What one change could you make to allow you to lead better?

It was Albert Einstein who said, "The definition of insanity is doing the same thing over and over again and expecting different results." Too many small-business owners get caught in this trap because change requires admitting that what you are currently doing is not good enough.

Change is something we don't want to do, but if we want to be successful as entrepreneurs, we have to constantly adjust our business to meet the needs of our customers and to adapt to our competition. If you want to grow as a leader, you need to make changes as well.

ALWAYS LOOK FOR AREAS YOU NEED TO CHANGE.

MAY 7
CONSISTENCY

"Success isn't always about greatness. It's about consistency."
—Dwayne 'The Rock' Johnson

What can you deliver on regularly, without fail? What do your customers consistently expect from your company? Are you able to consistently deliver on what you are promising? You can see the pattern here. Your ability to consistently deliver what you promise, and what is expected by your customers, is critical.

When you are starting a business, the tendency is to make promises that you cannot sustain long term. One of the biggest questions I consider when vetting a potential new business or division of an existing company is, "Can we sustain what we are offering?" If you have a new location an hour away, or multiple locations, will managing be a challenge? Can you adequately staff that area? Often, the answer is yes, but you need to be prepared to do what it takes to provide consistency and to be up to the challenge.

Do you have systems in place to deliver this consistency? Systems are the best way I have found to create consistency in anything. Whether you like them or not, a Domino's pepperoni pizza tastes the same no matter where you get it from. This is because they have a system in place. If you want to be a great company, you need to be able to consistently deliver on what was promised and expected.

*BE ABLE TO CONSISTENTLY DELIVER ON WHAT
YOUR CUSTOMERS EXPECT.*

MAY 8
BUYING THE COMPANY YOU WORK FOR

The traditional method of being an entrepreneur is to have an original idea that you turn into a business. As I have noted, you might also buy an existing business or purchase a franchise.

There is still another way. You can try to buy into—or buy out—the company you presently work for. I have personally allowed people to buy into my businesses. I have also seen friends buy the companies they work for. Allow me to explain.

I have a friend who worked for a small steel erection company whose owner was nearing retirement age. The owner had no transition plan to secure his company's future. My friend offered the owner a "buyout" plan. Not having any capital of his own, he offered to take profits from the company to purchase the business over time.

Here is an example of how this "buyout" may actually work. Say the current owner is presently making $100K per year. The buyer offers to pay the owner $50K for ten years and $25K for another five years. The total payout is $625K. All the money comes from the annual profits of the company. You might be surprised at how many older founders would take an annuity like this.

For the owner, this amounts to a fifteen-year retirement plan. For the "buyer," it's an opportunity to acquire a company without any start-up capital. The buyer continues to draw his regular salary, plus all-new profits above expenses from the new innovations and energy they bring. The owner turns the company over to someone who knows all the ins and outs and can keep it running profitably. It's a win-win deal.

Caution: Under no circumstance should this be a "handshake" agreement. Have an attorney draw up the papers.

THERE ARE MANY WAYS TO OWN A BUSINESS.

MAY 9

DESTINATION DRIVEN

"When you establish a destination by defining what you want, and then take physical action by making choices that move you toward that destination, the possibility for success is limitless, and arrival at that destination is inevitable."
—Steve Maraboli

Are you familiar with *reverse engineering?* This is when you work backward from a finished product to figure out how it was built. This is why when one of our military planes goes down, we hope it is completely destroyed so that an adversary cannot reverse engineer the technology.

I encourage you to set a big goal (destination) and then reverse engineer it by listing all the necessary steps or achievements that will be required to make it happen. A simple example would be a goal to have a secondary location for your business. Working backward, what would it take?

- Capital

- Find a location

- Management and staff

- Marketing plan

- Etc.

You need to have a destination that you're shooting for. What is it? Maybe it's to have your company on the New York Stock Exchange. That single destination is going to make you do a lot of things differently. You are obviously going to need to bring in some investors and you're going to have to grow that company. You're going to have to keep track of all the numbers. Nobody is going to invest in a company where you haven't kept track of everything. This is just a snapshot of how you would do things differently. Author Stephen Covey would say this is "beginning with the end in mind."

WHAT IS YOUR DESTINATION AND WHAT DOES IT TAKE TO MAKE IT HAPPEN?

MAY 10
DON'T QUIT YOUR DAY JOB

I want everyone to live a purposeful and passion-driven life, and I understand how owning your own business can bring this into reality. However, I do not believe quitting your day job is always the best route to accomplish this. Determine exactly what you need to be involved with to make this new business a success.

Let me drill down on this: What specific tasks and responsibilities have you determined that you will be in charge of? I have started businesses where my key responsibilities were hiring, marketing, and setting the direction of the company. I was able to perform these functions before 8 a.m. and after 4 p.m., which allowed me to keep the very high-paying job I held at the time. By keeping my day job and the guaranteed income, my stress level was much lower than if I had jumped into my new business full-time.

You can also begin part-time at your new start-up. Set measurable income goals for the company, and when you reach those goals, is the time you make the transition to full-time. This method has always motivated me since I had to grow the company to a certain level before joining its payroll. If you can maintain your current employment while starting this company, I think you should do it. Avoiding an initial cash drain on the company is always a good idea.

LAST I CHECKED, THERE ARE
168 HOURS IN A WEEK.

MAY 11
PEOPLE VS. TALENT

I am a huge football fan. My team, the dreaded Washington Redskins, has no quarterback, and the result is a losing team. The quarterback is the centerpiece of the football team, as this person has the ball more than any other player. With this said, if your team cannot identify a quarterback in the draft, they have failed in the single most important task they have. And sadly, my team is the worst at this.

Now, let me share with you the New England Patriots, a team I admire. They have three quarterbacks they have drafted who all start for an NFL team. Not only do they start, but between the three, their records so far this season are nineteen wins with one loss. When other teams cannot figure out how to find a quarterback, how do they draft three elite players for this position?

My neighbor, who has been a college coach for some of the most-recognized college programs, answered this for me in a quick text. I shared with him my discovery that Coach Bill Belichick of the New England Patriots had drafted basically 10 percent of all the starting quarterbacks in the league right now.

My text asked, "How does he do this?"

To which my neighbor quickly replied, "Bill (like they are friends) drafts *people,* not talent."

His point, which he would later share in person, is that to be a great quarterback requires many intangibles, and a high-quality person has a great deal of these. They are smart, want to learn, and can handle criticism and pressure. He said they can all throw the ball. It is these qualities that Coach Belichick knows will make them great.

DRAFT PEOPLE, NOT JUST TALENT.

MAY 12
GREAT TIMES TO START A BUSINESS

Before you get downsized: Sometimes you can see the writing on the wall, sadly. I see it a lot around the ages of 50 through 60. You're the highest-paid person in your position. They start hiring people in their thirties that they know they can get for a fraction of what they're paying you. Before you get downsized is an opportunity to start a business. If you have a great skill, a unique talent that you can monetize into maybe a consulting business, this is a great time to step away.

Two to three years before your kids are going to college: They start their freshman year of high school, and you've got no money put aside. The kids are putting together all these exciting plans, and you and your spouse wonder how to pay for them. Again, before they go to college, consider starting a business. By the time they get there, you should easily be making a few thousand dollars a month, which will make a major dent in their college tuition.

In retirement: By age 60, you should be pretty good at something. Why should you stop getting paid for it? Warren Buffett is eighty-nine and sharp as a tack. You don't ever see these successful people saying they're done. It's when you've stopped something that you lose that step. I'm not a big fan of retirement, so why not start a business in your retirement?

When you're in college: We know the great Facebook story, and we know of Bill Gates, and we know of Steve Jobs; this is just a good time. You're so creative at this point, you don't have any financial worries, and you could sleep on the floor in a friend's apartment. This is the time you're least stressed financially, so it is a great time to run with an idea.

IS IT A GOOD TIME FOR YOU TO START A BUSINESS?

MAY 13
SELF-CONFIDENCE

"Always have self-confidence because that can take you a long way."
—Baker Mayfield, NFL Quarterback

In my experience, when your staff or your clients determine that you lack self-confidence, it can be like sharks when there is blood in the water. You become hunted. I have heard it said, "Show me a man with no confidence, and I will show you a loser every time."

There is a fine line between confidence and arrogance, so let me quickly define self-confidence in business. This is purely my definition. Self-confidence is when you believe in yourself even when no one around you sees or believes in your vision. However, they believe in your self-confidence enough to support you. This is something you will need to earn, but you cannot start fast enough to grow this quality. How do you grow self-confidence?

- Know your area of giftedness. You can't bring everything to the table.

- You're growing an area of strength that brings value to the organization. Know that you have a strength that has monetary value and that the company needs you to bring it.

- You remember past achievements.

- You associate with people who believe in you and verbalize it to you.

- Associate with those who also have high self-confidence. Birds of a feather flock together.

- Try a little self-talk. Tell yourself every day, "I'm fantastic. I've got a great vision. It's going to happen." You may not think this works, but athletes use it all the time.

GROW YOUR SELF-CONFIDENCE.

MAY 14
GUT INSTINCT

"In the same way that I tend to make up my mind about people within thirty seconds of meeting them, I also make up my mind about whether a business proposal excites me within about thirty seconds of looking at it. I rely far more on gut instinct than researching huge amounts of statistics."
—Richard Branson, Billionaire Entrepreneur

Gut instinct is simple. When something feels right, you know it. When something doesn't feel right, you know it. It is like a radar detector. When you are getting ready to make a costly decision, it sends your gut an alert, and, equally, when you are getting close to your desired target, it just lets you know from the inside out.

Great entrepreneurs trust their gut instinct and give it equal weight with facts. Notice I said *equal*, not *overriding*. I do think when facts are overwhelming, you must heed their directive.

When I hear an idea, I get that feeling about whether it's right or wrong. I definitely have a gut instinct about people. Gut instinct makes me look further and do a little bit of research. But if you are an entrepreneur, you just have that feeling when things are right and when they're wrong.

You need to cultivate a gut instinct for things. You'll get it over time, but remember that the great entrepreneurs trust their gut instinct.

WHAT DOES YOUR GUT FEELING TELL YOU? LEARN TO GROW AND TRUST IT.

HANDLING CRITICISM

"The final proof of greatness lies in being able to endure criticism without resentment."
—Elbert Hubbard

If you want to be successful in anything, prepare to be criticized. I recently saw an old clip of Tiger Woods being interviewed when he first turned pro. The interviewer, a Hall of Fame golfer, was criticizing Woods because Woods said he expected to win every tournament he played. The HOF golfer looked at him incredulously, and with much sarcasm, in the most condescending voice, muttered, "You are gonna learn." Then, with a big sarcastic smile, he repeated with emphasis, "Oh, you are gonna learn."

Well, for the first ten years of his career, Tiger Woods won over 40 percent of every tournament he played in—an unthinkable record. He handled the criticism by just winning. And that is all he has done since. He replied so calmly to his peer interviewing him, "I would not play if I did not expect to win every time I tee it up."

You're going to get criticized by your staff, customers, partners, friends, and even family when your dream is crazy big. You will also be criticized when you deserve it, and you need to be able to handle it. I am not a fan of criticism, but when it comes from anyone who loves or cares about you, it normally has a morsel of truth in it, so heed it.

As long as you're doing anything that amounts to anything, there'll be criticism. You need to be able to handle criticism. Don't let everything offend or affect you; toughen up. As my wife tells me, "Suck it up, buttercup."

LEARN TO HANDLE CRITICISM; IT WILL ALWAYS COME ONE WAY OR ANOTHER.

MAY 16
YOUR WORD IS TRUTH

Do you want to be a successful business owner? Do you want to have staff clamoring to work for you? Do you want customers who want to do business with you? Make sure your word is truthful and can be counted on. It is said that investor Warren Buffett can do a billion-dollar deal in a couple of days, which would normally take other people months because his counterparts know that everything he speaks is truthful. He has a sixty-year track record of delivering exactly what he promised.

When you say something to your staff, when you make a promise, do you follow through on it? Do you make grand claims to your customers and not deliver on them? Your word is the most important thing you have in business. If your customers and team members can't trust what comes out of your mouth, you are destined for failure.

I have learned to make fewer promises, and when I do make them, I send them in a text or email confirming my commitment. This confirmation holds me accountable to deliver on what I have agreed to. What I have learned is that when people can count on your word, deals get done faster because they are confident that everything you have assured them of is accurate. Clients and peers will tell others of your integrity and equally, of your lack thereof.

How to improve on this: think before you make a promise—*Can I deliver on this?* Keep a record of commitments you have made, so you can check them off when completed.

CAN PEOPLE TRUST YOUR WORD?

CREATE A RECIPE FOR SUCCESS

A recipe is a set of instructions that will yield a given result if followed. When you do A, the result will be B. Some CEOs and coaches have a recipe for improving any team or company they lead. They have a few axioms that they hold to because they have seen the results in previous situations.

Legendary college football coach Lou Holtz has taken six different teams to bowl games. Each one of the programs he took over had been dreadful losers prior to his arrival. What does he have that others lacked? Clearly, he has a recipe that works. When colleges hire him, they have confidence, based on his record of achievement, that his formula will turn things around.

How do you create a recipe? First, start paying attention to things that work *repeatedly*.

Examples:

- What qualities commonly make for successful hires?

- What advertising brings the most responses?

- When is the best time to do certain advertising?

- Has a partnership worked well in the past?

- Are there certain demographics, areas, and markets that have been easier to attract?

- Do you have systems that have allowed you to successfully deliver according to expectations?

- Is there a sales script that has been overwhelmingly positive?

- Do you have a script that allows for customer disputes to be handled effectively?

Entrepreneurs have a recipe for success that they use over and over. I have learned that success always leaves clues.

DO YOU HAVE A RECIPE FOR SUCCESS?

MAY 18

POWER OF A MISSION

Do you have a mission that your team and company are working toward? I just recently sponsored a mission trip to Cuba. The objective was to share the Gospel with children through a camp setting. I encourage businesses to set out on a mission to accomplish something big that involves a group to achieve the objective. Achieving a mission creates a bond among your staff and confidence that more can be attained.

I attended Liberty University and, as crazy as it sounds, during a teardown of an old building, they threw away a sign from 1971 on the mission of the then-Lynchburg Baptist College. I have this sign as a reminder of why you want a mission and the power it has.

You can set out to be voted the best in your area in your given industry if, like our area, your various newspapers and magazines have an annual "Best Of." This is a worthy accomplishment, and we have achieved it in every local publication in our area. My team sets this as an annual mission to accomplish. We are always on a mission every year to increase revenue by 20 percent. At one of my companies' annual Christmas parties, I loved sharing that we had achieved this level of growth for eleven straight years.

When I owned a direct mail magazine, I had a mission: I wanted my publications to go to more homes than the Sunday *Washington Post*, which we achieved. A great mission requires the participation of many, not just one, to achieve it. That is what I believe makes it special. Example: Seal Team Six's mission to take out Osama Bin Laden. I doubt any participant on that mission will ever forget their place in history. Another example would be our great astronauts who first walked on the moon.

I have found the secret to accomplishing the mission is to clearly define it and share the reason why it is a critical mission. This may be the payoff that would follow the successful mission or the publicity that would result from success, but there needs to be a reason that motivates people.

GET YOUR TEAM FOCUSED ON A MISSION.

BE A DISRUPTOR

"Disruptors are innovators, but not all innovators are disruptors."
—Forbes

Harvard Business School professor and disruption guru Clayton Christensen says, "A disruption displaces an existing market, industry, or technology and produces something new and more efficient and worthwhile. It is at once destructive and creative."

I must confess I think disruptors are the entrepreneurs that I stand in awe of because they take something further than I could imagine. To disrupt a marketplace, you must see something needed or different so much in advance of everyone else. It is as if they had a sneak peek at the future.

The payoff for being a disruptor is a billion dollars or more. What do I mean? It seems to me that when I see a business that was the one who broke the previous mold, the payoff was equal to the risk. Some examples of these businesses are Uber, Airbnb, UFC, Tesla, Ruyan (E-cigarette), Draft Kings, and Walmart. These innovators and risk-takers all are billion-dollar disruptors. The ideas these companies were based on would in time disrupt existing industries as well as create new industries. They would displace all competition.

Heather Simmons said, "Those who disrupt their industries change consumer behavior, alter economics, and transform lives." I hope that someone reading this book will be inspired by today's reading and that it would light a fire that would inspire a "Disruptor."

DON'T JUST BE AN ENTREPRENEUR, BE A DISRUPTOR!

MAY 20
SPEED, PRICE, AND QUALITY

As a company, you need to find one of these three that you're going to drill down on and dominate within your marketplace. You're either going to choose speed, price, or quality. Warning: it is hard to have all three.

Domino's and Amazon have mastered speed. Domino's was the first pizza chain to lay claim to fast delivery with its iconic "30 Minutes or Less Delivery Guarantee." Amazon has now taken that mantle when it comes to online retail outlets.

Walmart has laid claim to low pricing in the brick-and-mortar retail category. Not to be outdone, Dollar General has carved itself out a nice and lucrative niche in the discount pricing category. Remember, only one company in your marketplace can be the cheapest.

Rolex, Mercedes, BMW, and Louis Vuitton have equally laid claim to the quality division in their industries. If you choose quality, it may take time to earn this recognition in the marketplace. With creative marketing, this recognition may come faster. Boll and Branch bedding came out of the gate with "Our products are slept on by three US presidents."

Quality, speed, and price; they're the three pillars in the marketplace that you need to hang your hat on, but you can normally only hang your hat on one. So, decide what your business is going lay claim to: speed, price, or quality.

IN WHICH ONE OF THE THREE DO YOU
ASPIRE TO LEAD?

MAY 21
MAKING BIG GOALS HAPPEN

Decide on goals (measurable and motivating). You must start by setting measurable and motivating goals. You should be able to know when you achieve it (lose 10 lbs., earn $100K) and it should be motivating. If it doesn't motivate you, you're never going to stick with it.

Set a deadline.

If you don't set a deadline for your goal, it just becomes a lifelong wish. There is no urgency. If you set a deadline, you can create mile markers (see below).

Create a plan.

You must create a plan. You're not going to achieve a goal if there is no list of things that need to get done to bring this goal into reality. If your goal is to start a business, there would be a fairly large list of things needed to get it off the ground.

Set mile markers.

You need to know what needs to be done first. If you are setting up a business, getting a business license takes precedence over hiring. Hiring is extremely important, but you can't open the business without a license. If you want to run a marathon, you first need to be able to run a mile.

Add a new habit.

What one habit could you add to your routine that would bring your goal to pass? Writing for thirty minutes each day is a step toward bringing a dream of publishing a book to reality.

Take advice or mentoring from someone who has achieved your goal.

That's how you achieve a goal. Find somebody who has already done it. If you want to write a book, find an author. See what they did.

Take action daily.

You need to take action toward the goal daily. What I have learned is that when you take 365 action steps, something big is going to get accomplished.

Review your progress.

Have you accomplished what you set out to accomplish in the last ninety days? Are you on target for that deadline date?

A GOAL WITHOUT A PLAN IS WISHFUL THINKING.

MAY 22

HOW TO BUILD A WINNING TEAM

"I've learned that the only way to build a company with great success and scale is to build a great team."
—Dave Kerpen

How do you build a winning team in business? First, decide what the key positions are and if they are currently adequately filled. You need to create a measurable for each position in your business and set the bar for each team member who plays this position. Second, you need to know what an all-star looks like.

Begin by analyzing all the key positions within your organization. Look at who you have in each critical position, and give them a letter grade. Could you replace their production easily? When they are on vacation, can you see a decrease in production? Do they play a role that no one else in the company can substitute for during their time off? Would it bother you if they worked for your competition? The answers to these questions will tell you if you have the right player.

Then, think about what talent looks like. I have a rule when I interview someone, whether or not we need to hire a person right now. If I think they're that talented, I will hire them on the spot and figure out where I'm going to put them later. Have you ever had an interview for one position, and this person comes in and while they're not a perfect fit for that position, you know you're staring at raw talent? I'll walk out of the room, look at my staff, and say to them, "We've got to get this person on staff. I'm not really sure where we'll put them, but we don't want to lose this person." You need to start knowing what talent looks like. You can tell that they have energy and quick and solid answers to problems. They start asking questions about how they can grow the position even in the interview. So, you need to know what this talent looks like.

GRADE YOUR TEAM AND SEARCH FOR TALENT.

ARNIE'S ARMY

According to *Forbes*, Arnold Palmer is third on their list of highest career-endorsement earnings with $1.35 billion. What is shocking: Arnold Palmer has not played on the PGA Tour in over fifty years! (I am not counting the Senior Tour, which when he participated was a limited field involving very little money). In 2019, he still made the Top 10 List of Most Endorsed Athletes, even though he passed away in 2016 shortly after turning eighty-seven.

Palmer ranked seventh last year for his aspirational score in Repucom's Celebrity DBI, which measures the degree to which people feel that a celebrity has a life to which they aspire. Palmer was tied with hoops icon Stephen Curry out of 3,652 celebrities in Repucom's database, one spot behind the world's fourth-richest man, Warren Buffett.

Arnold Palmer can thank Arnie's Army for creating what would become an iconic following. This loyal band of followers adored him. Before there were books like *Raving Fans* and *SuperFans,* Arnold Palmer figured it out. He had Arnie's Army, the genesis of what we now call a *following.* It was this following that garnered endorsements from the most coveted blue-chip companies. Companies such as Mastercard, John Deere, and Pennzoil, just to name a few, sought his image to tie to their brand.

Consider following Palmer's lead by creating your own army of loyal followers who are "Raving Fans" of your business. They'll tell everyone how great your company is. Some tips for creating SuperFans:

- Give them a reason to be your fan. (Give an outstanding job performance.)
- Communicate with them. (Engage your customers.)
- Be likable. (Be the company they will admire.)
- Be different.
- Let them know how much you appreciate their patronage.

FOLLOW ARNOLD PALMER'S EXAMPLE AND CREATE AN ARMY OF FANS.

MAY 24
HOW TO CREATE COMPANY CORE VALUES

If you're not communicating your personal core values, which should lead the way to your company's core values, your employees are likely not to display them. Your core company values should be displayed in a statement for all to see in a prominent location within your company. It is hard to go wrong with a large professionally-made sign in a strategic location. Maybe your statement is on a slip of paper in every paycheck, or the signature portion of all of your companies' in-house emails.

Here is how to create core values:

1. They should be personal principles that guide our behavior.

2. They should guide how we act with others and guide our business.

3. They should be the standards or rules of conduct we use to conduct business.

4. They reflect how we treat our customers and partners.

5. They should not be strategies or tactics.

WHAT ARE YOUR COMPANY'S CORE VALUES? DO THEY REFLECT YOUR PERSONAL CORE VALUES?

MY ONE BIG SECRET TO EFFECTIVE DELEGATING

"Be able to delegate, because there are some things that you just can't do by yourself."
– Meghan Markle

You need to delegate if you want to be successful because it's not possible to do everything yourself. But how do you delegate? The formula that I use when I'm trying to get someone to help me with a big task or project is the 20–70–10 method.

I put 20 percent of my time on the front end: defining the project, explaining the outcome that I want, and giving them whichever tools I think can help them achieve that outcome. This may be information, contact people, etc. Then I take the time to tell them what a win looks like, defining exactly what the goal is for the project.

Seventy percent is heavy lifting. They do that. However, if there's something I can do in one phone call or something that I have access to or can solve quickly, they know to give it to me. I do not mind that.

Finally, and this is critical, I come back in on the last 10 percent to pull it all together or to coach them to the finish line. If they handle all that themselves (in time they will), great, but in the meantime, plan to reconnect at the end of the project.

THE MORE TALENTED THE STAFF, THE GREATER THE RESPONSIBILITIES YOU CAN DELEGATE.

MAY 26
PROTOCOL FOR TERMINATING EMPLOYMENT

Years ago, when I had to let an employee go, I had a very wise business partner share some advice with me. He said, "Sean, if you keep firing people the way you are, we are going to have to fistfight someone every Friday around here." He had a great way with people even when he had to let them go. By the end of the conversation, they were apologizing to him for being a bad hire!

This is what I learned:

Always do it in private.

Let me say that I fire people in private 95 percent of the time unless I know that I have a loudmouthed, obnoxious person, and then I bring in a second person so they can't twist what I said.

Don't be arrogant.

Give them respect and take a hit. They're going to criticize you. Let them get it out in under a minute. Don't defend yourself. There's nothing you can say. Just be direct, don't overexplain it, and don't defend your decision. My objective is to get them in and out as fast as possible.

Don't terminate when you're angry.

You will never go wrong sleeping on your decision for twenty-four hours.

Don't punish yourself.

Sadly, I have been dumb enough to get frustrated and angry with someone mid-job and have let them go, resulting in needing to bring someone else on in midstream. This is always a catastrophe. My advice is that if it is at all possible, ride them out to the end, even if you need to send someone to help them.

Make sure you can replace them.

I have made this mistake before as well: letting someone go, assuming they would be easy to replace, only to find out just how valuable they were. My advice is to run employment ads for their replacement in advance of letting them go. Be confident you have an adequate replacement. I hire a person and give them a trial before letting the person they are replacing go. Advice: don't tell them whom they are replacing.

MOST IMPORTANT LESSON: DON'T DEFEND YOUR DECISION.

FINDING A LEADER IN THE MIDST OF MANY

When you are interviewing somebody, can you determine if a person is a leader? Can you see a potential leader who just needs to be mentored a little? The number-one thing I am always looking for is leaders because I know that without leaders, I can't duplicate myself. I can hire all the managers I want, but they cannot take over a complete company and lead and grow it. Managers oversee the directives that leaders set. Leaders have an "X Factor" you cannot go without. How do I identify a leader in just a simple employment interview?

I ask them, "Have you ever overseen anybody? Give me some details." I want to know if they have ever had subordinates. Have they ever been completely responsible for other people and their performance?

Do they have a military background? When someone has a military background, they tend to understand the value and role of leadership.

I'll ask them, "Were you ever responsible for the complete results of a project? What were the details and results?"

I also look for the intangibles that leaders tend to have: confidence, great communication skills, and energy. They generally have a track record of achievement. If they cannot lead themselves, they will never lead others. I ask myself, "Would I want this person's qualities in others on my team?" Leaders set the example.

You will see leadership potential, but they may need some work. There is often an area that we need to develop. If they were perfect, I wouldn't have the opportunity to hire them. Think about that. If the perfect leader was in front of me, why aren't they working somewhere else?

THERE IS NO SUBSTITUTE FOR A LEADER.

BUILT TO SELL

At some point in the life of a company we have started, we're all looking to sell our business. This allows us to be compensated for our years of time, risk, and energy. Even if you hand it over to a family member, it still needs pillars that make it durable. Some generational businesses are like hand grenades being thrown in the lap of an unsuspecting heir.

How do you build a company that is built to sell?

Validate that it's a profitable company.

Nobody is going to buy your company if none of the numbers can be validated. If you don't have legitimate tax returns, validation is difficult. I want to see profit and loss statements that can be validated with a supporting tax return. I want bank statements.

Does the small-business owner document their own income?

If you can't put it on a tax return, you're not going to sell it. If you can't validate what your revenue is, nobody's going to buy your company.

Do you have a complete customer database?

If you don't have very good records on recognized software programs of customer information (names, buying history, email addresses, phone numbers, etc.), you cannot support your claims to have a strong customer base.

Is the business in a fertile market?

Are you in a dying industry? For example, if you own a retail shoe store right now, I probably wouldn't be really excited to buy your business.

Do you have systems that allow for a seamless transition?

People want to buy systems. They want to know that they can seamlessly transition into your business or merge it with theirs.

Reputation

You want to build a good name, a good reputation, a good brand.

How good is your staff?

How much talent do you have on your team? Will they support the new buyer?

BUILD YOUR BUSINESS TO SELL.

MAY 29
IT TAKES MORE THAN A VISION

I love a vision statement, but it takes more than a vision statement to be successful. A vision is a highly optimistic picture you see of your business in the future. It may be a bold initiative you have. After creating this vision, you have to cast your vision. You've got to be able to communicate your vision to your followers. If your followers don't buy into your vision, then it is no more than your private daydream.

Next, you need to make it a shared vision. Make other people feel like they're a part of it, so they have a buy-in. You can modify your original vision with input as you bring on valuable team members. After you've cast this vision, it becomes a shared vision, and that creates the culture within the company that everybody's excited about.

Finally, you execute the vision. Executing the vision means you have a detailed strategy to achieve the vision. This plan must have deadlines, accountability, a team in place, and expertise to make it happen. It's great to have a vision, but if people don't believe you can execute this vision, you have only a speech.

GOOD BUSINESS LEADERS CREATE A SHARED VISION.

MAY 30
TWO EARS FOR A REASON

"Seek first to understand, then to be understood"
—Stephen Covey

Author Stephen Covey, in his international bestseller, *The Seven Habits of Highly Effective People*, which I believe is one of the ten best self-help books ever written, extols the value of listening. I am a very good speaker, which I always thought was a strength, but the older I get, the more I realize that the value is in the ability to listen. I call it active listening. I liken it to how a child listens to a bedtime story. They look like they are going to jump with excitement on your next word. Sadly, most adults tend to listen only to identify a break so we can jump in and clutter the conversation with our thoughts and opinions and an even better story.

I would encourage you to work more on your listening and focus a little less on your speaking. It takes discipline to be attentive to what someone is saying. To listen to their tone, to gather how emotionally vested they are in what they are sharing. Do you want to put a deal together? Keep your mouth quiet. Sometimes you need to hear what the opposition really wants. If you're the one doing all the talking, you'll never know.

One of my biggest mistakes when I first started dealing with client or customer complaints was in trying to defend myself, or the company, aggressively. This is a huge mistake and the wrong approach, 100 percent of the time. My approach now is to shut up. It is not always easy, and at times, the client is spouting nonsense that I could effortlessly refute, but I let them finish. I nod in agreement on some comments, which tends to make them lower the intensity. When they have finished, I try to address what they see as the problem. If you don't listen, you will never know what it is. Defending yourself just elevates their frustration.

BECOME AN ACTIVE LISTENER.

MAY 31
IT'S NOT ALL ABOUT THE MONEY

When you are starting a business, your motivation can't be *all* about the money because that's probably the last thing you're going to see. However, I think that if you don't generate some income in the first sixty days, it's the wrong business 90 percent of the time. There are always outlier businesses that take greater time to generate income, but most everyday start-ups should generate some income early on.

Even when I started my own business, it wasn't about the money. I was excited about building a team. I was excited about the challenge of it, and yes, I thought I'd make money, but I wasn't thinking I was going to be a millionaire in the first year or two.

So, when you start a business, please note that the money *will* come if you build a great business, but that can't be your sole motivator. Based on my experience, I think you're going to face poverty first because initially, you are going to be the one making all the sacrifices.

I can't tell you how many times my secretary said to me, "Are you on the payroll this week?" and I said, "No." I even brought in a partner early on, forfeiting a paycheck, because that person had the expertise we desperately needed.

I don't think there is anything wrong with having material wants and great ambitions to motivate you. I currently have a large framed picture of a private jet membership I want, and it is my motivator for a new start-up I have. However, I have countless other reasons to keep me highly interested until I get this big payoff.

WHAT OTHER THAN MONEY MOTIVATES YOU TO START A BUSINESS?

JUNE 1
AIR TRAFFIC CONTROLLER

I would like you to view your role as owner in your company akin to an air traffic controller. An air traffic controller has a vital role to play when you travel. It is the air traffic controller who keeps track of all the planes in their air space. Keeping each aircraft at a safe distance from one another, as well as giving the order for who can land, requires a unique set of skills. They are choreographing a Broadway play in the sky.

This illustration of organized chaos represents your company. Everyone in your orbit has what they believe is the best goal, decision, and outcome for their team or the organization. It is your job as the leader to prioritize the planes (goal, initiative, job). They may all have value, but they cannot all be priority one. You bring down each plane in the order that is your priority. Only you can do that.

In a company's infancy and most situations, the owner sets the initiatives and defines the priorities for the company. If you don't take on the role of "air traffic controller," you are going to have some big-time crashes. They can be avoided when you are the leader that is required for a great organization.

BE THE AIR TRAFFIC CONTROLLER.

JUNE 2
DESIRE ZONE

Michael Hyatt in his book *Free to Focus* shares four zones in which people spend their time (Drudgery Zone, Disinterest Zone, Distraction Zone, and Desire Zone). He has a great view of how we spend (waste) time in areas we should not be spending time in.

I have often preached about how far too many business owners—and for that matter, people—who flounder in mediocrity don't know how to effectively use their time and energy. They either get trapped into feeling like they need to do everything themselves or get ensnared by urgency. This is where whoever is "yelling the loudest" takes precedence over whatever should be getting accomplished. This type of owner runs from one fire to the next. Finally, people don't actually recognize their strengths and spend time in areas they are not gifted in, which always leads to poor results.

Hyatt lays these out in his Four Zone Theory, which I think is well organized and offers clarity as to how you should seek to spend your time. I put my take on his zones below.

- **Drudgery Zone:** You simply hate doing these things.
- **Disinterest Zone:** You can, in that you have the skills to do this, but you don't enjoy it.
- **Distraction Zone:** You have a passion for this, but you stink at it.
- **Desire Zone:** You not only are passionate, but you excel at this.

I have heard this (Desire Zone) called your Core Competency, which is where your passion meets your proficiency. As a business owner, you want to spend 80 percent of your time in this zone because it should bear the most profitable fruit for you. For me, this is creating the next big thing to go after, marketing, and sales. When I am in any of these three areas, it is effortless, like breathing, as I love all three of these. Now if you put me in meetings all day, resolving conflicts, or any level of busywork, I am miserable. If I could stay in my "Desire Zone," I would never want to retire.

WHAT DO YOU LOVE TO DO? WHAT DOES EVERYBODY TELL YOU IS YOUR STRENGTH?

WHAT IF?

*"There is no passion to be found playing small—in settling for a life
that is less than the one you are capable of living."*
—*Nelson Mandela*

If you had all the money you could ever need or want, what would you do? The answer to this question may reveal your true passion in life. When you remove survival from the equation, it tends to reveal what actually makes you tick.

What if nobody would ever see it, and you would never get credit for it? What would you be doing? So, no pat on the back, recognition, or reward for doing it. This will uncover your true motivation.

What if you only had six months to live? How would you spend it? This will surely disclose whom you love and what matters to you.

What would a life well lived look like to you? Too often we get caught up in just trying to survive. Sometimes our lives become mundane, with nothing but routines, and nothing in our schedules excites us. The older I get, the more intentional I get about life and my correlating schedule with its accompanying to-do list. I want to make an impact. My passion is equipping entrepreneurs for success. My purpose, which is a combination of my passion and my belief that God put me here for a reason, is to equip, encourage, and evangelize entrepreneurs throughout the world through my books, curriculum, and events.

I just wanted to encourage you today to ask a few "What ifs?," knowing that the answer to these questions may prompt some intentional living.

DOES YOUR LIFE HAVE INTENTIONALITY?

ADDITION THROUGH SUBTRACTION

The last time a Washington, DC baseball team won the World Series was in 1924. It has taken this storied MLB franchise ninety-five years to get back into the World Series and win it. They did it in epic fashion, winning four road games, which has never been done in any professional sports championship. What I think makes this historical sports accomplishment even more fascinating is that the team lost what many would have said a year ago was their most "talented" player to another team. I put the word *talented* in quotes because talent alone does not guarantee a championship player.

I am speaking of the Washington Nationals' young phenomenon Bryce Harper, who was lost in free agency to the Philadelphia Phillies. On paper, the Nationals lost their most productive hitter, who was also an outfielder with a cannon for an arm. The team soon experienced the phenomenon of "addition through subtraction." It is often what you get rid of that improves the organization.

Washington got rid of a "culture killer." Harper was a young, brash, selfish player who was not a team guy. He brought with his "talent" an equally negative force of energy. Washington had a new look this year and a new attitude in the clubhouse. What allowed them to survive countless elimination games and win a World Series Championship was having a great team of talented players where the whole (entire team) was greater than the players' individual contributions.

You may want to look at your team differently today. Whom can we subtract so that we can grow and get better?

WHOM DO YOU NEED TO SUBTRACT?

JUNE 5
COMPELLING CHARACTER

What if you could have a superpower? What if you could attract people to your ideas and vision? What if others wanted to include you in their projects and plans? I am going to share with you a simple way to stand out in the crowd of choice potential hires, consumers, and associates. I want to teach you how to be a *compelling character*. This means you evoke interest, and you become irresistible to those who come into your orbit. Remember, "ordinary" and "average" will not attract people to you.

While watching *Millionaire Listing New York* with my son, I saw the power of becoming a compelling character. He loves the show, as it profiles an eclectic group of real estate agents in the Big Apple striving to close the biggest deals. One new character was trying to gain the listing of a property worth $13 million, well above anything he had ever listed before. When presented with the question from the sellers, "Have you ever listed or even sold a property in this price range," he froze, and you could feel him melting under the weight of this potential disqualifier.

He then pivoted to depicting himself as a compelling character, sharing his personal story of losing 200 pounds in the last two years and how hard a challenge that was. He said he would bring that same commitment and dedication to this endeavor. The sellers, who two minutes earlier had said, "We will think about it, as we have many potential brokers to consider," became engrossed in his story. He changed their paradigm through the power of a story that made him a compelling character—someone they now wanted to succeed.

HOW CAN YOU BECOME A COMPELLING CHARACTER?

BIG HAIRY AUDACIOUS GOAL ("BHAG")

Do you have a goal that is so audacious that it inspires others to want to be a part of what is to come? This is what great entrepreneurs have. This is what great companies have. It sets good businesses apart from great businesses. In his book, *Good to Great*, Jim Collins introduced us to the term *Big Hairy Audacious Goal*, which he coined *"BHAG."* He explained that this is a strategic business statement similar to a vision statement that is created to focus an organization on a single medium- to long-term organization-wide goal that is audacious, likely to be externally questionable but internally regarded as not impossible.

I think President John F. Kennedy set the standard for a BHAG when he shared with our country that he intended to put a man on the moon by the end of the decade. What made this unlike most politicians' words of inspiration (or bull, however you look at it) was that President Kennedy gave a deadline. He gave NASA the resources and support to make it happen. NASA set goals and achieved incremental victories in space before the big landing.

The Bill and Melinda Gates Foundation has an audacious vision to enhance healthcare and education and reduce extreme poverty around the world, but it plays itself out in bold strategic initiatives where it provides grants to address these concerns. The foundation has an endowment exceeding $50 billion to address this vision. Because the vision for the foundation is not only audacious but extremely strategic, it must be led by someone with tremendous credibility. Bill and Melinda Gates had donated more than $35 billion themselves as well as founding one of the most valuable companies in the world—Microsoft. The Gates Foundation is the standard of all philanthropic foundations. Notice the three qualifiers I have shared: an audacious goal, a strategic plan to accomplish it, and the leadership of someone who inspires credibility.

DO YOU HAVE A "BHAG"?

LAW OF TALENT

The law of talent knows that any company is only as good as those who toil inside. Simply put, you're only as good as the people who work for you.

If you want to be a great company, you've got to have great people working for you. The biggest problem with small businesses is a lack of talent. They play defense only, filling holes (positions) as needed. The owner never has a strategic staffing plan. Oftentimes, they fall into the trap of surrounding themselves with relatives, people that don't push the owner to be better. As the Good Book advises, "iron sharpens iron." You need to have a staff that challenges you as well as provides the skill, expertise, energy, management, and leadership to achieve growth that no one person can achieve alone.

If you want to be a great company, recruit great talent, and don't forget the law of talent. You're only as good as those who toil inside the walls of your business.

HAVE YOU BEEN PLAYING DEFENSE? CONSIDER A STRATEGIC PLAN FOR HIRING.

JUNE 8
THE LAW OF DEVELOPMENT

The law of development understands that great organizations develop their staff, improving their talent and assessing their capabilities, as well as providing opportunities that will challenge and expand their value to the organization. I don't ever want someone to come work for my company and leave without growing in their given trade or area of responsibility. In the very first interview with someone, I assess the talent and qualities they can immediately bring to the organization, but I am also a "talent scout," always looking for potential areas that I can help them grow and develop. My in-house term that I share with my partners is that we need to "expand their capacity." "They come to us being able to do A, and we need them to be able to do A, B, and C."

You want to create a great company? You need to develop your employees. This needs to become a core initiative. When they start with your company, they must begin to improve and expand. You will accomplish this by providing training and educational opportunities, as well as assignments that stretch them. Think of it like a "training camp," where you have a system in place for improving your employees, to get them ready for the season ahead.

HOW CAN YOU SYSTEMATICALLY GROW
NEW HIRES?

JUNE 9
THE LAW OF GREATNESS

"I am the greatest!"
—Muhammad Ali

The law of greatness says that customers and employees want to be associated with great companies. I have personally experienced this countless times. Once I am confronted with quality and service at an extraordinary level, I cannot go back. I am in their tribe forever.

I remember the first time I went shopping at a Nordstrom store. I vividly remember having to go up an escalator to the men's clothing department, where someone dressed in a tuxedo was playing the piano just to set the mood for what would turn into my clothes-shopping addiction.

What would cement my loyalty would be their exceptional service. I would become a "raving fan" when I returned a pair of pants that I purchased but never really liked. I stared at them in my closet for two or three years before returning them.

I had heard a story of an elderly woman who once returned tires to Nordstrom's—yes, automobile tires—and not to embarrass her (they do not sell tires), they politely took them back with the same enthusiasm they did with my trousers. I had experienced "the law of greatness," and I am a customer for life.

Their employees evolve into "Nordis" with a cult-like loyalty, heralding every positive thing they can share to whoever will listen. I know this because I was at a wedding, seated next to a proud "Nordi" who could not tell enough stories of his experience working for greatness. Had I not already experienced Nordstrom, I would have sought them out, having to see what would make a new, base-level employee so excited to gather more followers.

Once you experience the law of greatness, you become a proud member of the following, touting stories that attract all who will listen.

GREATNESS ATTRACTS CUSTOMERS AND TALENT.

JUNE 10
THE LAW OF EXECUTION

"Execution is the ability to mesh strategy with reality, align people with goals, and achieve the promised results."
—Larry Bossidy

Great companies execute industry-changing initiatives that move the marketplace. The ability to execute routine tasks as well as large-scale initiatives grows out of their leaders' track record that earns the respect and buy-in from team members. It starts with executing the obvious and routine, such as following through on base-level commitments you make at a staff meeting. It grows into a year-long initiative to add a new division that you successfully deliver on. One victory after another builds a leader's reputation for being able to execute plans. This creates a management team that expects to be held accountable for outcomes. Finally, you have grown a corporate culture where the successful execution of initiatives is the measuring stick.

The bottom line is this: if you can't execute daily routines, weekly routines, and large-scale initiatives, you will never be a leader able to build a great company. It takes consistent victories over the small (routine) to lead to the great victories that change everything.

Author and business expert Larry Bossidy, who provided our opening quote, lends more insight in his book titled *Execution*. He sees execution as the missing link between aspirations and results. We have all listened to—or worse yet worked for—people who share grand ideas with no plan that would bring about their desired outcome. Leaders know that an ambitious idea must be equally yoked to a commitment by all involved to execute the given plan in a timely manner.

IT IS ONLY EFFECTIVE EXECUTION THAT
BRINGS RESULTS.

THE LAW OF GROWTH

"Growth comes out of a healthy competitive atmosphere."
—Edward Felten

The law of growth says that if you're not growing, you're dying. I think it is important to define healthy growth within an organization. A company must continue to grow in market share, industry dominance, profit, or company value. There must be a growth mentality within the culture of leadership. Great companies that no longer are with us all shared a similar life cycle. They reached a point of dominance, which led to complacency or false confidence, which in time resulted in extinction.

We can all remember how Blockbuster Video once dominated the market, but it never took those Redbox vending machines outside the grocery stores very seriously. Blockbuster never picked up on the way Netflix mailed movies directly to people's homes and later made the seamless transition to streaming over the internet, bringing movies directly into our homes without us having to go anywhere.

The list of extinct or dying retail giants is endless—Sears, JCPenney, and Toys R Us—just to jar your consciousness. A strategic growth move would be to purchase an online winner to learn from their model as Walmart has done with its seemingly under the radar purchase of Bonobos. This purchase, although only $300 million, allowed the retail giant to get a successful blueprint for how to market and sell to a niche market online.

I would argue that when your business can no longer grow, it should be like a "smoke alarm" sound going off in your executive meeting. It is possible with certain industries that growth is no longer possible, like in the coal industry. However, alert and growth-minded entrepreneurial companies stave off extinction by always investing in complementary industries or find completely new opportunities.

Jamie Dimon, president and CEO of JP Morgan Chase, gives time-tested advice: "Companies that grow for the sake of growth or that expand into areas outside their core business strategy often stumble. On the other hand, companies that build scale for the benefit of their customers and shareholders more often succeed over time."

LACK OF GROWTH IS YOUR WARNING LIGHT.

JUNE 12
THE LAW OF BRANDING

"If your business is not a brand, you are a commodity."
—Donald Trump

The law of branding will make us lay claim to an admirable quality, a compelling promise to our customers, and an even bolder position in regard to our competition. I encourage new start-ups to begin with their brand in mind. Work back from the most attractive brand in your marketplace. If you could deliver on one promise that would make customers rush to do business with you over all your competition, what would that promise be? What is a quality that is so admired, that if it were provided within your industry, it would serve as a magnet to potential buyers?

I like what Steve Jobs said: "Your brand is the single most important investment you can make in your business." Your brand can serve as a North Star, as a mission statement does. It just provides one more coordinate on your company's map to success. Your brand allows you to have a pillar to use in your marketing. If successfully marketed and established over time, it will bring monetary value, a collateral win for your efforts. Before anyone else realized his brilliance, Warren Buffett put a monetary value to a company's brand, which was unusual at the time. You will notice his early stock purchases of companies like Coke, American Express, etc.

BUILD A BRAND.

JUNE 13
THE LAW OF CULTURE

"Corporate culture is the only sustainable competitive advantage that is completely within the control of the entrepreneur."
—*David Cummings, cofounder of Pardot*

The law of culture recognizes that great companies each have a unique culture that fits their brand, mission, and values. I've talked about Nordstrom before, and Google, as they have well documented cultures that are unique to their companies. Do you have a winning or innovative culture within your company? Is there an attitude of above-and-beyond service that trickles down to every customer experience?

The Cleveland Browns had arguably the greatest football coach ever as their head coach, Bill Belichick. They had arguably the best college coach, Nick Saban. Both of them were on their coaching staff at the same time. One served as head coach and one as defensive coordinator, and they failed. How could this happen? You have arguably the two greatest football coaches ever to live, on the same staff, and the team loses! Sadly, the Cleveland Browns have a storied reputation for a culture where losing is expected by their fans.

Effective leaders know that changing the culture of an organization is a must when planning to turn a company in the right direction. Start-ups normally have a childlike energy and optimism and sadly lose this with time. However, a few capture this unbeatable force in a bottle and make it a cultural must.

CREATE A WINNING CULTURE.

JUNE 14
THE LAW OF PROFIT

"Profitability is the sovereign criterion of the enterprise."
—Peter Drucker

Charles Sawyer said, "Profit is the ignition system of our economic engine." I have learned that profit and its fruit, cash, solve a multitude of mistakes in business. It is like a get-out-of-jail-free card in Monopoly.

You are going to make mistakes, but if you have no cash, these mistakes can put you out of business quickly. Having no cash flow is like playing poker when you have the least amount of chips at the table. You can't bluff much, and you'd better have a royal flush when you go all-in. There is little margin for error, and I have personally learned that this is not a fun way to run a business.

Profit allows me to grow my cash reserves, which allows me peace of mind as an owner. I can leverage my strong cash position to take advantage of opportunities that others can't. I can consider buying my competitor or burying them under a relentless marketing effort. Profit gives the needed ability to hire the most valuable talent because you can pay them enough to attract and keep them. Finally, profit (cash) provides the fuel needed to support the innovation and research required to be an industry leader.

WITHOUT PROFIT, YOU HAVE NO BUSINESS.

THE LAW OF SYSTEMS

"In order for any business to succeed, it must first become a system so that the business functions exactly the same way every time down to the last detail."
—Rick Harshaw

The law of systems understands that any process that gets repeated needs to become a system. Systems are the bionics of a company. Systems provide consistency because nothing is left to chance. Having set procedures empowers average and even new employees to have consistent value. When an organization has a proven methodology, it enables a business to scale at an exponential speed.

What has made franchising so popular is that the failure rate is dramatically lower than that of a random start-up. Systems have become the golden goose in franchising, where the search is for the system, and the business becomes the by-product.

The law of systems increases speed, and thus productivity is the reward. Henry Ford brought the first system into the automobile manufacturing industry with the assembly line. Ford established an order and a process that increased car production significantly, which allowed his cars to be priced dramatically lower than those of its competitors. Speed creates more profit.

Michael Gerber in *E-Myth Revisited* advises, "Build systems within each business function. Let systems run the business and people run the systems. People come and go, but systems remain constant." A person only needs to visit a McDonald's or a Jiffy Lube to see the value of systems. Each business delivers a fast and predictable outcome because nothing is left to chance or individual talent. They remove all possibility of error and offer a formula so any new hire can become a contributor.

Stephen Covey said, "Management works in the system, leadership works on the system." As a leader, you're always trying to create systems within your company, so you can consistently deliver what your customers expect.

CREATE SYSTEMS WITHIN YOUR ORGANIZATION TO SIMPLIFY PROCESSES.

JUNE 16
THE LAW OF CHANGE

"Change or die."
—Alan Deutschman

The law of change states that if we're not changing, adjusting, adapting, and improving, we are becoming obsolete and will be overcome by our competition.

In both of my books, I talked about the need to constantly change, and I even made it a pillar of my book, *The Greatest Entrepreneur in the World*. This is a spoiler alert.

The list of companies that once stood tall and now lie in the corporate graveyard is endless. Cause of death: inability to recognize or implement change at a speed equal to or greater than their competition.

May I read you some "headstones"? Compaq Computers, Kodak, Radio Shack, MCI, Enron, and Toys R Us just to name a few. The list of those on life support is Chrysler, Sears, and General Electric. I can rattle names off in a cadence if needed. They all have only one thing in common with their demise: failure to change at a speed equal to or greater than their competition.

If you have become comfortable, you probably need to change something. Charles Darwin warned, "It is not the strongest of the species that survives, not the most intelligent that survives. It is the one that is the most adaptable to change." Your competition, which may only be on the drawing board, or even in infancy, spends every waking hour charting the course you have failed to embark on.

ALWAYS BE CHANGING, ADJUSTING, ADAPTING, AND IMPROVING.

JUNE 17

THE LAW OF SHOULD, NOT COULD

*"I'm actually as proud of the things we haven't done
as the things I have done."*
—Steve Jobs

The law of should, not could means we will have endless opportunities, but we do not just chase after them all because we can; we stalk the one thing that will have the greatest payoff for the organization.

I don't know if you've ever seen the epic film *Jurassic Park*, but Jeff Goldblum, the lead character says, "Your scientists were so preoccupied with whether or not they could, they did not stop to think if they should." They created dinosaurs without ever considering the impact this would have. Their creation would be their greatest threat to survival.

Organizations will be presented with countless good opportunities, but great companies focus on and execute the best opportunities. You can do a lot of things within your business, but should you? Are they the best available? I want to go to the full thought Steve Jobs shared because it is an axiom that all entrepreneurs would be wise to read slowly. ""Focus means saying no to the hundred other good ideas. I'm actually as proud of the things we haven't done as the things I have done. Innovation is saying 'no' to a thousand things. You have to pick carefully."

BECAUSE WE CAN DOES NOT MEAN WE SHOULD.

MARKETING 101

Many people get marketing confused with advertising, but advertising is just one spoke of the wheel of marketing. Marketing is the complete selling process, the entire process from creating to communicating (advertising) and delivering products and services that have value to customers, clients, partners, and the public at large.

It is a good idea in your business plan to use the components of marketing in your comprehensive strategy.

- **Product Creation:** What are you going to sell, and how are you going to manufacture it?

- **Communication:** How are you going to tell the world what you are selling and why they should buy from you?

- **Delivering:** How are you going to put your products into your customers' hands?

- **Servicing:** How are you going to provide the service after the sale?

To be a great company, you need to have each of these mastered at the most affordable price possible.

MARKETING IS FAR MORE THAN JUST ADVERTISING.

JUNE 19

INNOVATION

"Changes call for innovation, and innovation leads to progress."
—Li Keqiang

Innovation is change on steroids. It is transformational. It causes upheaval in an industry as it disrupts all the traditional players. If done well, it anoints a new champion of the marketplace. Innovations don't respect stalwart companies. Their mission is to displace them.

Innovation is obvious when you see it, and it is the complacent entrepreneur's greatest enemy. The safest way to avoid the attachment of complacency is to become an innovator yourself. Build a culture that seeks innovation at every turn. It has been said, "Innovation is the child of collaboration." When you have a culture of bright and creative minds, the outgrowth is innovation. Consider taking change to a level that requires imagination and has no limits.

Great innovation is what has made the world we live in so improved—from the Wright Brothers' airplane to Edison's lightbulb, from Alexander Graham Bell's telephone to Bill Gates' software that made the home computer practical for the everyday person, and let's not forget Steve Jobs's iPod and iPhone. Each of these innovation icons took an idea further than anyone could have imagined.

TAKING AN IDEA FURTHER THAN YOUR
PREDECESSOR EVER IMAGINED = INNOVATION.

JUNE 20
DELIVERY

Let's take a close look at the power of delivery. Delivery brings two strong appeals to customers—convenience and meeting their wants without delay. This is an unstoppable one-two punch. It was Domino's who teased us first with a "hot pizza in 30 minutes or less." This bold delivery commitment made Domino's our first choice for pizza delivery.

Blockbuster required us to drive and walk into the store, stand in line, check out, and drive home to watch a video. Redbox eliminated half of these encumbrances and quickly made its presence felt. But it was Netflix who took the speed of delivery to a whole new level, allowing someone to stream a movie online, making Blockbuster (and I believe Redbox) obsolete.

Amazon has invaded retail stores like the Grim Reaper with its buying simplicity and overnight delivery on nearly everything. This speed of delivery has now brought Amazon into the home delivery grocery market with its purchase of Whole Foods. Whole Foods had a traditional retail business model that Amazon will merge with its online and delivery genius that is sure to make this combination a windfall.

Consider how you're currently delivering your product or service to your customers. Can you do it faster or more conveniently?

HOW CAN YOU IMPROVE YOUR DELIVERY?

JUNE 21

SPEED

"Speed has become an important element of strategy."
—Regis McKenna

We talked a little bit about Amazon, but look at FedEx. They made the very bold promise early on that they could get you a product nearly overnight, and they've done a pretty good job of it. It's made them billions and billions of dollars. For production speed, let's not forget Ford and the assembly line created a less expensive product to make and thus a less expensive product to sell, by choice.

As a business owner who has made millions providing services, I know the value of speed, and it is irreplaceable. It is very simple math. If John and Dave can build a 20-foot by 20-foot deck in four days, and this same job takes Bill and Steve eight days, my costs are doubled, and I lose out on four days' profit on another job. Speed is a force multiplier and is a business owner's strong ally in creating more profit.

Speed allows you to potentially fulfill an order that your competition cannot meet; this is a significant competitive advantage. Restaurants that can turn over a booth in forty-five minutes (getting a customer in, taking their order, and getting them fed and out) as opposed to sixty minutes allows them to serve 25 percent more people in a day.

SPEED IS PROFIT.

JUNE 22
PRICE

"Only one company can be the lowest priced."
—Anonymous

One of the biggest mistakes new companies make is trying to compete on price, specifically to become the lowest priced. This is common and is sadly a kiss-of-death move for a start-up. For one, you can rarely enter the market with enough established vendor relationships, expertise, and buying power to actually be able to provide anything at the lowest price with enough margin to be profitable.

Pick a price that you can actually make a profit on, and "justify" the price with your value offerings. Provide products and services that your customers believe are worth the price you are charging. There are many ways for a customer to find your price fair and even low if you are creative about how you offer them.

Restaurants, which typically do not have the same high level of traffic on Monday through Wednesday evenings as they do on weekends, may decide that since they have their staff there anyway, and waitresses need to make tips, they will have an aggressive dinner special on those nights.

If you own a service company, you can offer packages that in reality don't require your technicians much more time to offer, and so give added value to your pricing. One example is a free oil change with any purchase of four new tires.

Be careful pricing so low that your margin does not allow for enough profit to be able to sustain your business with advertising, hiring, and paying competitive wages for talented staff and allowing you to create reserves for a rainy day or new opportunity.

CAREFULLY CONSIDER YOUR PRICING STRATEGY.

FILLING A NEED

Every business I have started except one was based on filling a need. I saw there was a need in the marketplace that was not being met in a way that I felt was effective or maximized. What do I mean? Just because one company in your area is offering it (the need you have identified) does not guarantee that they are doing it well.

A need to fill has always been the first voice that has grabbed my attention when I am looking for a start-up. When I experience difficulty getting something done well in my area, I begin the research process of what it would cost to offer a company that could do this proficiently and at a price that would make it worth my investment.

It doesn't necessarily mean I had all the expertise to fulfill that need, nor was it a passion I had. There was a need, and I felt like I could create a business and put together a team that could fill the need repeatedly and skillfully. Finally, I could create clamoring ideal customers because of my effective advertising. That has been my formula for more than fifteen of my companies.

Look for needs that are not being met effectively in your community or area of interest, and you will find a business opportunity. Ask yourself continually, "Did I have enough choice of companies the last time I tried to get (fill in the blank)? Of the companies available, did they provide great service from beginning to end?" This is where you may find a need is being met but with a significant lapse in customer service or proficiency. Finally, if this company was like finding a needle in a haystack, then you know there is a need but not a company committed to advertising, which is always easy pickings.

START BEING ALERT TO NEEDS THAT ARE NOT BEING MET EFFECTIVELY.

JUNE 24
WOW FACTOR

Somewhere in your marketing plan, something needs to make people say, "Wow, that's a great product, service, or company." They deliver it fast, or the product is so incredible, or the customer service was unbelievable, or the warranty was so good and clear it removed all risk or skepticism. These are just a few areas and ideas when it comes to creating a "wow" somewhere in the buying experience.

Crutchfield carved a nice niche in car stereo sales through their catalogs when they offered the most detailed instructions at the time with customer support for how to do your own installation of their product. They took the guesswork and aggravation out of the installation process, which is one of the spokes in the wheel of effective marketing: customer experience.

A play such as a Broadway musical has choreographed times that they grab the audience, prompting a predictable response (gasp, applause, laughter). An effective marketing plan choreographs a "wow factor" into the customer experience.

DOES YOUR PRODUCT, SERVICE, OR COMPANY
DELIVER A WOW?

JUNE 25
EXPERIENCE

"Experience is simply the name we give our mistakes."
—Oscar Wilde

I have often shared, "Failure is best learned through a secondhand story." This is what experience offers. There are very few substitutes for experience—someone who has done what you are attempting to do and done it well for a length of time. This is called a proven track record. I have shared that if you want to get me to open my checkbook fast, help me to do something faster or take it further than I can by myself. Experience is the best weapon against failure that I have found.

Let me share a simple illustration. I have an idea or interest in starting a business in an industry that I have very little experience with—and for me, this is 95 percent of all the start-ups I have had. Let's say it has a manufacturing component, and I have no previous experience in manufacturing. I would seek someone who has great experience and success in manufacturing what I am planning to produce. At this point, you may have picked up on the way I put success after experience because experience alone is not enough. You want experience *with* success, this is the one-two punch that knocks over a lot of dominoes.

I recently went whitewater rafting with my family and the families of my college buddies on an annual trip. None of us had any experience going down the level of rapids we were attempting on that day, but our brash guide was a twenty-year veteran of this river and led inexperienced groups safely through. He boasted that he had never had a casualty on his watch. This is called experience with success. Once he finished this declaration, we had a newfound confidence and excitement for the challenge ahead.

LOOK FOR EXPERIENCE WITH SUCCESS.

JUNE 26
OBTAIN COMPETITIVE INTELLIGENCE

An in-depth analysis of your competition is required in every business plan. I spend more time studying my potential competition than on any other item in my preparation while starting a new business. I am like a general preparing for war. I want to know all their pricing. I want to know how they answer the phone and how they respond to leads. I will buy their product or use their services to gauge their quality. I know of no better way to establish what my competitive advantage will be until I know my competitors' weaknesses and strengths.

I have also had what I believed was a good potential business idea, but after obtaining my competition's pricing, I realized I could not make the net profit required to meet my income objective.

Do your due diligence in this area. The more you know about your competition, the better prepared your company will be to capitalize on their weaknesses.

Author John Christopher makes crystal clear the importance of military intelligence: "The secret of success in battle lies often not so much in the use of one's own strength but in the exploitation of the other side's weaknesses." The same could be said for competing in business.

YOU CANNOT GAIN AN ADVANTAGE OVER AN OPPONENT YOU DO NOT KNOW.

JUNE 27
ONE BITE AT A TIME

We have all heard the quip, "How do you eat an elephant? One bite at a time." I have to tell you that the timeless secret that all who have accomplished something grand will share is the formula for any great achievement.

People have asked me, "How do you start twenty companies?"

"One company at a time."

"How did you write your first book?"

"Getting up an hour before sunrise to write one page every day."

My formula for achieving anything seemingly insurmountable has been "It's a cinch by the inch." Do something every day to bring about the goal you have set.

I know you are thinking, I already know this, but what I am telling you is proven. It's the no-fail plan of all noted achievers.

Think of a goal you have now. What bite-size steps can you take daily? My fail-safe method is to create a daily habit to achieve this goal. Again, to write a book, complete a page every day. To lose weight, exercise for twenty minutes daily.

This may be too simple to grab your attention, but it is the secret to success. Mark Twain believed in this strategy: "The secret of getting ahead is getting started. The secret of getting started is breaking your complex, overwhelming tasks into small manageable tasks, and then starting on the first one." When I have a big goal, I try to identify the one habit that I can implement in my daily routine that will get me started.

ONE SMALL THING DONE DAILY EQUALS
MASSIVE ACTION.

JUNE 28
TEACHABLE MOMENTS

It is my goal to improve my team, so when I can offer some helpful advice to one of my business partners or staff, I don't want to miss the opportunity to teach. I don't sit down with them for an hour a week in a formal teaching setting. Initially, when someone joins my team, I share with them the systems I have in place, the culture we want to build, what I expect of them, and how to plan for a weekly win. But once we get into it—typically after the first couple months— teachable moments just happen.

Something happens where I'll ask, "Hey, next time, knowing what you now know, how would you do that differently?" They may provide an acceptable new strategy, or they may still not have a plan that I think works. I will then share, "You may want to try to do it this way."

Or I may assign them a project and see a lost look on their faces. I would then ask, "Are you understanding what I am asking you to do?" or "Do you need any help with this?" I am always looking for teachable moments.

Sometimes they make big mistakes, and I say to them, "What did you learn?" My team knows that when they're in doubt, they should not hesitate to reach out to me. I tell them I have made every mistake at least once already.

I have found that if you want your team to be receptive to teachable moments, be brief with your wisdom, and respect their plan if they believe in it. And finally, when they screw up, instill some insights to prevent this from happening again, but don't bring the failure or event up again. Let it go.

BE ALERT TO A TEACHABLE MOMENT.

INFRASTRUCTURE

Within a business, you have the infrastructure, which is the basic organizational structure (building, fleet, software, machinery, facilities) of the company. I go into too many businesses that are outdated or decrepit. They are using ancient computers. You can see the keyboard changing colors, and the monitors are the size of TVs from the1980s. Their fleet is beat up, with faded or missing lettering. The very building they operate from is embarrassing due to the way it is kept, and they wonder why they don't attract high-level talent or have not experienced growth in a decade.

I spend money every year on my company's infrastructure. I ask, "Is there a software program that can allow us to do something better or faster? Is there a new-and-improved phone system that we can use? Do we need more storage? What do we need?"

After asking my team, I am also on the lookout for ways to stay current at a minimum, but my ambition is to stay ahead. "Do we need to expand our facilities? Is our fleet in need of some new vehicles?"

You need to constantly put money back into the infrastructure of your company. If not, you're going to be out of business. You are not going to be able to respond quickly to a new competitor, or you're going to have a huge capital expense that you cannot afford. So again, spend money every year on infrastructure. This should be a part of your annual budget.

SPEND MONEY ANNUALLY ON IMPROVING INFRASTRUCTURE.

GUARDRAILS

I can remember numerous birthday parties for my children that involved a bowling party. What made the event fun for all were the bumpers or guardrails that kept the ball from being a disappointing gutter ball. Before beginning the game, these rails would magically appear, from what seemed like nowhere, preventing any wayward ball from scoring a big zero. In business, I have learned to create the same guardrails for myself, my partners, and my staff.

I try not to put myself in situations where my personal integrity could be questioned. I also use payroll services to keep employee tax money and withholdings set aside. I have seen too many small businesses get into trouble handling their own payroll. Finally, I have an accountant in my main office who handles all payables and receivables.

I also have a veteran accountant who comes into the office twice a week to oversee all transactions. She is my extra set of eyes and knows she does not work for any of the companies; she works for Sean Castrina. She reviews all bank accounts every morning and sends me a spreadsheet by 5 a.m. with any notes about items that I may want to explore further.

I'm constantly creating guardrails. Why? Because guardrails keep you from veering off the road. My partners have guardrails in place as well, so I know things are systematically getting done the way I want. I found that some partners were quick to delegate customer service issues in their division, which ended up with the issue being dropped. I put a guardrail in place that all customer complaints will receive a phone call or email within twenty-four hours, acknowledging we are aware of their issue. The issue must be completely resolved within five days. I have defined resolved as "The customer is satisfied and would use our company again."

I have learned guardrails keep good people from making dumb mistakes, and that's why I use them. Every one of my partners is fantastic, but I have a couple of guardrails in place, and they're all different for each of them because I know their weaknesses.

CONSTANTLY CREATE GUARDRAILS TO KEEP YOUR BUSINESS FROM VEERING OFF THE ROAD.

JULY 1
CHARACTER

"When wealth is lost, nothing is lost; when health is lost, something is lost; when character is lost, all is lost."
—*Billy Graham*

Character is who you are when nobody's looking. You need to develop character because if you lack character, you're going to start attracting people just like you. Your staff will know if you're truthful and have integrity. You will never keep a high-level leader with character if you lack character.

James Allen, author of *As a Man Thinketh*, spoke a great axiom over a century ago with, "You will become as small as your controlling desire." This is so powerful, as it shares that if you are controlled by a dominating weakness, that is all it takes to bring you down. We have all seen the actor or politician who ruined their reputation and life's work in minutes. Warren Buffett cements this with, "It takes twenty years to build a reputation and five minutes to ruin it."

The next time you have a character challenge like those below, pretend you are in full view of everyone (coworkers, family, and clients). This simple exercise might make a difference in what you choose to do.

Some Common Character Challenges:

· Telling a client the truth during a sales pitch

· Filing that tax return

· Sharing your opinion of a former employee

· Getting dangerously close to a coworker

WHAT WOULD IT TAKE TO DESTROY YOUR REPUTATION?

SELL THEM MORE

Once you have developed your "Venus flytrap," you would be wise to figure out what else you can sell them when you have them in your hold. More than any other retailer, Walmart realized that they have an ideal shopper, which to them is someone who would like to do all their shopping at one time, in one location, and get a great price. This is not scientific research, but my family members who swear by the store all sing the same chorus. This became even more apparent when they added their grocery store to all already attractive sales models.

Inside a Walmart, you can typically find an eye doctor (who, of course, will sell you glasses) along with a fast-food restaurant, so you don't need to leave when hunger takes over. Soon they may offer cots for weary shoppers to take a break and then start the shopping all over again but with a touch more energy.

Online shopping has taken "Sell Them More" to a whole new level, actually suggesting to you more products that you may like. They use pop-up ads and make new items appear on your shopping screen, and finally, at checkout, they may show you one final round of suggestions. Another technique used is for monthly memberships with a paired upsell. For example, my razor membership now has me also receiving my shaving cream from them. It's brilliant, and the two go together like peanut butter and jelly. They are now working on getting my skin conditioner and after-shave purchases as well.

I have used this secret in my direct mail coupon magazine that I later broke up into three niche magazines, allowing me to have one customer now buying three times the ad space.

Twenty years ago I started a handyman company because I could not get anyone in our area to reliably show up and do small home projects, as I am helpless and should not have a tool within twenty feet of me. With that said, this company now has eight unique divisions offering every home improvement you could ever want, resulting in our tagline, "The leader in home repairs and projects."

KEEP ASKING "HOW CAN WE SELL OUR CUSTOMERS MORE?"

JULY 3
MAKE AN EXHAUSTIVE LIST OF PRE-LAUNCH TASKS

The father of modern education, John Dewey, wrote, "Arriving at one goal, is the starting point to another." And now that you have a business plan that has confirmed that you have the potential to make the income you wish, the next step is actually starting the business. I have started businesses from retail to service and many in between. Without exception, the next step was to formulate an exhaustive list of every possible thing that needed to be done prior to "turning the lights on" and serving the first paying customer.

Here are some key areas, each of which will contain multiple tasks. Each industry will contain different items on this list, but this is a general list to get you on the right track.

- Name, Tagline, Domain
- Incorporating
- Licensing and Permits
- Banking
- Website
- Physical Location
- Signage
- Phone Number
- Forms, Stationery, Office Supplies
- Machinery, Tools, Products, etc.
- Professional Needs
- Staffing Needs
- Uniforms
- Miscellaneous

The first man to reach the South pole, Roald Amundsen, said, "Adventure is just bad planning," so roll up your sleeves and sort out the nuts and bolts before you launch. Never forget: "The goal is not just to launch a company, but to launch a *successful* company."

THE GOAL IS NOT JUST TO LAUNCH A COMPANY, BUT TO LAUNCH A SUCCESSFUL COMPANY.

JULY 4
CREATE A START-UP STORY

"If you don't give the market the story to talk about,
they'll define your brand's story for you."
—David Brier

I love being involved in start-ups, and one thing I tell whoever is in this business with me is that we've got to get the customers to cheer for us. We want them to want us to succeed. We've got to create a story that makes us the underdog. If there's a big competitor in our area, we want them to want us to win. What has our competitor failed to offer that we will make paramount? We will also weave this into our start-up story about why we started this business.

People want to do business with people they like, so what story would get them to like you, the owner, or your company? Advance a true story that they can get behind. I encourage you to consider developing a story with your start-up or your existing business. Look at your current advertising. Do you give the public a reason to like you? You should share a story or allow others to share a story of their experience with your company that makes you the hero in their buying experience. "I chose company A because I could not find anyone who could do B, and they did the most amazing job." OK, this is pretty simple, but you can have friends experience your company prior to opening so you can have these testimonials already on your website or in your advertising when you open.

DO YOUR CUSTOMERS LOVE YOUR STORY?

EMPLOYEE VALUE PROPOSITION

What do your employees get for what they're giving you? If your answer is, "I pay them," that is not nearly enough. You might say I pay them very well, and yes, that is a start in the right direction, but it takes more than pay to keep talent on staff and happy. Why do I say "happy"? Because without happy employees, you will have an unhappy culture that is not productive.

I had a secretary who loved to ride horses, so when the time change happened, I'd let her leave early so she could still ride horses. She would work what I believe was twice as hard for half the year in appreciation for this small adjustment I made.

I had another one of my staff who was taking a college course on Fridays right in the middle of the day. She worked full-time for us, but this was the only time this class was offered. What I could have done was to let her leave at lunchtime and take the class during lunch with the hope of squeezing the most out of her. However, after talking with her and learning this was a very demanding, high-level course with taxing assignments and tests, I chose a different course. I told her to take Friday mornings off and just come to work after class for a couple of hours to wrap up the week.

Whatever the case may be, your employee value proposition is what you give to your employees for what they're giving to you. I would encourage you to be creative. I would encourage you to give more than what they ask for or expect.

GIVE YOUR EMPLOYEES A REASON TO
COME TO WORK.

JULY 6
GREAT PEOPLE SKILLS CAN MAKE THE DIFFERENCE

People do business with people they like and trust. This sounds simple, but I meet business owners all too often who have little or no people skills. They do not look you in the eye, or they interrupt when you are talking, just to name a few unwelcome characteristics. If you could only improve one thing about yourself that may have the greatest impact on your success, it would be having great people skills: the ability to have those who meet you like you and have confidence that you are trustworthy.

I look back on my direct mail magazine success and attribute it to my people skills more than any one thing. I had a direct mail magazine that featured Domino's Pizza and McDonald's franchises. What made their advertising special was that the Domino's owner had been in litigation with the former magazine owner before me, and McDonald's did no local print advertising other than mine. For the record, the magazine had failed and was not being printed when I acquired it.

Later it became clear that they advertised with me because they liked me personally. I quickly earned the trust of the Domino's franchisee with free advertising space to make amends for the previous owner, and persistent friendliness on the phone allowed me to break the ice of the McDonald's franchise owner. I would later play golf with both owners. It was my people skills that won their business.

People skills let employees want to work for you and be loyal. Your associates will want to network with you if you are likable and trustworthy. And of course, the customers you meet will trust your business if they trust you. However, if you aren't honest with people, business writers Michael Copeland and Om Malik warn, "They'll eventually learn the truth, and when they do, your credibility will be compromised. Permanently."

If you could only read one book in the next year, I would encourage you to read Dale Carnegie's *How to Win Friends and Influence People*.

IMPROVING YOUR PEOPLE SKILLS CAN HAVE A TREMENDOUS PAYOFF.

JULY 7
ACCOUNTS RECEIVABLE

Accounts receivable is money owed to your company by your customers and clients. One of the biggest problems I see with small businesses is that they do invoicing. They are always owed money.

I have a flooring company that I deal with. The owner was stuck for around half a million dollars when the recession happened. I would never extend that much credit to a locally owned business. I am sorry, I don't have that level of confidence that the owner is always going to be in a position to pay me back. I also find that the businesses that require lines of credit are usually run poorly or they would pay you immediately if you stood firm or requested it. I am aware that in some cases you have government contracts and large-scale projects as the norm, but read my lesson on client concentration because I have seen more than one friend get stiffed for an obscene amount of money, causing them to go out of business.

I own a company that would traditionally be paid by invoices, hoping to be collected in a timely manner. However, we demand and expect to be paid at the time of completion. Customers will say, "I thought you could mail an invoice," to which we reply, "The service has been provided. Why would we wait to get paid?" The payment expectations are clearly spelled out in our agreements but would be "when they get around to it," if allowed.

Why would we not collect it immediately? Service has been provided. I view it like buying gas or groceries, when you receive the goods, you pay the bill. If not, I would need to hire and pay staff to collect past due money and you never end up getting 100 percent of what is owed. Even if you were to get paid in full, you would still only get a fraction of what you earned because now you have accounts receivable costs related to invoicing and collection. Totally unnecessary!

SEEK TO HAVE NO OR MINIMAL ACCOUNTS RECEIVABLE.

JULY 8
TOP DOG

Give your employees a target standard to aim for that challenges them to be better. Don't make your expectations broad like, "I want you to be a good employee." I recently had a new employee say to me, "I want to be your top dog." Clearly setting an ambitious goal to be our best and what I would view as our most capable and profitable team member. So, I went out to his job, and I gave him an index card on which I had written a detailed list of what it would take to be my top dog.

I said, "You must be exceptional at your work as well as fast. Customers will brag about your quality of craftsmanship and request you in the future. Other employees who work with you will also tell me you are the best they have seen or worked with. And finally, I should not have to manage you other than to give you the work order."

He was surprised, to say the least, when I brought him this detailed list of what it would take for him to be my "top dog." His request did not catch me off guard, and I liked the ambition. However, once he saw the list, he knew there was a mountain to climb.

Provide an ambitious target that is measurable for new employees. Challenge existing employees who may be getting a touch complacent. Tell them what great looks like on your scoring system. If you can make it measurable with specific numbers, that is always helpful.

GIVE YOUR EMPLOYEES A TARGET.

JULY 9
SELL AND STAY

If you want to sell your business, I encourage you to start looking to work on this between three and five years beforehand. Selling your business for the price you want or need requires a strategy. This strategy requires justifying your sales price. This is done through detailed banking and accounting records that support your stated profit over a sustained period of time. Customer records must not only show a robust customer base but also one that can be seamlessly transitioned to a new owner. Finally, you should have a staff that will ingratiate itself to the new owner. Each one of these qualifiers needs to be met for a successful sale, and thus each needs to be accompanied with substantial proof.

I encourage you if you're looking to sell your business, not to think you're going to sell and sail off because that's not realistic. You're probably going to sell and stay, and that's going to give you much more of a return on your hard work and investment. It's going to make the entire process much more comfortable for the buyer, knowing you will be there to introduce them to key clients, contractors, and vendors of choice. There is no substitute for a tour guide, and astute buyers know this.

So again, consider looking at the selling process three to five years out. Begin creating a paper trail to support your claim of profitability, and finally, consider being their tour guide for a pre-agreed period of time.

BE READY TO STAY A LITTLE WHILE AFTER
SELLING YOUR BUSINESS.

JULY 10

DIFFERENTIATION

"Branding is deliberate differentiation."
—*Debbie Millman*

What will make your company different from your competition? Differentiation is the process of determining—and more importantly the strategy of distinguishing—how a product or service differs from others. When you're setting up a business, it is so important that you carve out a space that makes you different from your competition. Without differentiation, you offer no compelling reason for a customer to choose you.

Fox News is an example of a company doing this very well. You are probably familiar with MSNBC and CNN, but Fox decided to clearly differentiate itself from the other cable news outlets with a direct appeal to the conservative Republican position. The others I mentioned have a clear progressive Democratic bent and attracted viewers who shared their position. Instead of following the trend, Fox strategically marked out a unique niche that wasn't being filled. This model has made it the most-watched cable news network.

You must differentiate yourself from your competition. Implement this strategy from the inception of your company, and keep a contrast between what you offer and the crowded field of opponents.

BE DIFFERENT BY CHOICE.

JULY 11
PROTECT YOUR
INTELLECTUAL PROPERTY

Intellectual property in business usually refers to a name, logo, trade secret, or invention. It is the result of someone's creativity. It has value and must be protected. You can look at nearly any product to see trademarks. For example, Coca-Cola's "Coke," shown with a small "r" inside a circle, is a registered trademark. The Coca-Cola brand and the word Coke are recognizable and carry substantial value to its owner. This is a simple illustration of intellectual property (IP).

Other common types of IP include copyrights, patents, industrial design rights, and trade secrets, which apply in some jurisdictions. Trademarking, trade secrets, and patents seem to be the ones that apply most in businesses. There are subtle but important differences between these types of protection that you need to learn and apply to your specific business situation.

The vital reason to have IP protected is that it adds real value to your company—value that someone can invest in. We all recognize the value of real estate, but IP is equally valuable. Zwilling emphasizes, "Intellectual property is also often the largest element of early-stage company valuations for professional investors." IP rights protect unique aspects of your company that give it a competitive advantage, especially while trying to keep an edge against bigger, more established competition. They make it possible for you to license or franchise part or all of your operations, should you choose to. IP rights prevent others from unfairly encroaching upon you.

The process of applying for IP protection is simple and can start with an internet search of "how to trademark" or "how to patent." Sometimes it is as simple as paying a fee and registering your IP with the proper authorities. Make sure you add the appropriate trademark ™ or copyright © symbols to your business communications, including your advertising and signage, to discourage unscrupulous copycats. It will also lend public credibility to your business.

FAILURE TO PROTECT INTELLECTUAL PROPERTY MAY COST YOU MORE THAN ANY ONE MISTAKE.

JULY 12
BE THE BANK

I remember during the economic downturn in 2008 I had my bank call in a few loans. I didn't even know this was possible but somewhere I signed that if at any time they wanted to call in (collect in full) the balance they could. Well, in 2008, they viewed me as a risk not worth taking.

This forced me to view loans as well as debt and lending institutions in a new way. I decided that I wanted to be the bank. I was going to pay off all debt and move forward without having what I view as unacceptable debt.

Acceptable debt to me is a debt with an interest rate so low I would rather stare at cash in the bank then rush to pay this off or any loan balance I could write a check for at any time. I call this *selective debt*.

I have now amassed massive cash reserves and eliminated all local credit accounts in an industry known for financing materials paid as you perform a job. After we amassed an arsenal of cash, we were able to offer in-house financing to our customers. This gave us a considerable competitive advantage, enabling us to get jobs that other people couldn't get. Having cash on hand allowed us to leverage this strong position—buying in bulk, pre-buying, and even paying upfront for large advertising campaigns. This buying power always provided us more return on our dollar.

Selling a business when you do not need the cash is a tremendous luxury to have. I was also able to sell off businesses, providing financing for the buyer and allowing a more advantageous price. I believe the Good Book encourages us to be the lender, not the borrower.

BE THE BANK, NOT THE BORROWER.

JULY 13
BUILDING YOUR CABINET

In my book, *The 8 Unbreakable Rules for Business Start-up Success*, I talked about protecting your business. Not enough small-business owners do this. Much like the president has a cabinet of advisors, you would be wise to have a group of trusted professionals from whom you seek advice.

This is the cabinet that I recommend:

- **A payroll company**—I don't think any small business with three or more employees should do payroll themselves, so I recommend using a payroll company. It is tempting for a new business owner to borrow from money that is not theirs, and a payroll company will eliminate that temptation. They'll also keep your tax payments current and provide all needed tax documents for your employees at year-end.

- **A bookkeeper**—The next professional on the team would be a bookkeeper, someone who keeps all the financial transactions current, so you know exactly how much money you have.

- **A lawyer**—A lawyer you can get trusted legal advice from, whether it is preparing a contract template to drawing up partnership agreements.

- **A marketing professional**—You may bring on a marketing person. I have recently added a digital marketing professional to my cabinet. Digital marketing is new on the scene, and I don't have the time to learn it, so I brought this person into my cabinet.

A few years back, I also brought on an engineer because in one of my companies it is critical to be able to get immediate advice that only an engineer can provide. This person has kept us from underbidding jobs with potential structural problems we would otherwise have missed.

I would start with payroll, bookkeeper, and a lawyer and expand to the professionals who would best help *protect* your business. Then move on to professionals who will help *grow* your business.

BUILD A CABINET OF TRUSTED, EXPERIENCED PROFESSIONALS.

JULY 14
ACTIVE BUSINESS PLAN

"The wise adapt themselves to circumstances, as water molds itself to the pitcher."
—Chinese Proverb

Your business plan cannot account for everything that is going to happen. Behavioral investigator and author of *Captivate: The Science of Succeeding with People* Vanessa Van Edwards advises, "Don't plan everything. Listen to your customers and make changes as needed." What I have found with regard to a business plan is that it becomes a document that, once written, is never looked at again, or, even worse, followed with no variation even though the battlefield has changed dramatically. I put together a business plan for every venture I would like to pursue. I admit my business plans would not be thought highly of by the *Harvard Business Review* because I know there are only a few questions I really need answers to. What I have learned is that my plan needs to be active and by that, I mean fluid. It can change overnight as conditions I had not taken into account change.

I agree with Richard Branson when he declares, "Every success story is a tale of constant adaptation, revision, and change." A business owner, much like a general in battle, must be able to make adjustments as conditions require. After one great victory, Napoleon Bonaparte, one of history's foremost military leaders, said to his defeated foe, "You draw up your plans the day before battle, when you do not yet know your adversary's movements." Entrepreneurs make the same mistake.

HAVE A PLAN THAT IS FLEXIBLE ENOUGH TO BE CHANGED.

JULY 15
NINE C'S OF LEADERSHIP

In Leadership Forces, they instill legendary Chrysler CEO Lee Iacocca's *9 C's of Leadership* that I have condensed. These are so good that they have to be shared. I would highly recommend reading his book, *Where Have All the Leaders Gone?*.

1. **A leader must show curiosity.** You have to listen to people outside of the 'Yes, sir' crowd in your inner circle. You have to read voraciously because the world is big. It's a complicated place. The inability to listen is a form of arrogance. A leader shows great curiosity.

2. **A leader must be creative.** You have to go out on a limb, and you've got to be willing to try something different, thinking outside the box. Leadership is all about managing change. You must adapt.

3. **A leader must communicate without question.** I'm talking about the ability to facilitate, to talk truth and reality to people. I don't think there are many skills more needed in a leader than the ability to communicate.

4. **A leader must be a person of character.** That means knowing the difference between right and wrong and having the guts to do the right thing.

5. **A leader must have courage.** Swagger is encouraged; tough talk is encouraged, and courage is a commitment to sit down at the negotiating table and talk.

6. **To be a leader, you've got to have conviction.** Have a fire in your belly. You've got to have that passion. You've got to really want to do something to get something done.

7. **A leader should have charisma.** I'm not talking about being flashy. Charisma is the quality that makes people want to follow you. It's the ability to inspire.

8. **A leader must be competent.** You've got to know what you're doing. More important than that, you've got to surround yourself with people who know what they're doing.

9. **You can't be a leader if you don't have common sense.** Some people just cannot make what seem like obvious decisions. I'm often shocked at how people are paralyzed over a decision when the solution seems so obvious to me.

MASTER THESE AND YOU ARE A LEADER.

JULY 16
INTERVIEWING PEOPLE—PART I

I want to talk about the interviewing process because this is one area of my company that I take very seriously, and I get very involved in all high-level hires. The way it works is I tell my partners, "You do the first interview, but I want to be involved in the final one that gets them hired." They do not have the authority to make a final hire, and nobody ever fights me on that because my partners realize that collaboration is always better. I tell them, "Best case, I will confirm what you think, and you will bring them on with more confidence, and they will be an asset. Or I will pick up on something you may have missed that will save us from a disappointing new hire."

Some Interviewing Tips:

1. **Pre-Interview.** Before we interview anybody, now that my partners know that I'm going to be involved in the process, they are forced to do due diligence.

2. **Which need are we filling?** I want to know the job. What's the need here? I want to know if they're qualified. I want to know their experience. In less than thirty seconds, give me why you think this person would be a good fit.

3. **Make sure there are no red flags.** Do they have a DUI? In our business, that can be very expensive because we provide vehicles. I need a little bit of their background because, in one of our businesses, we send our team into people's homes. So, we must have some background information on them.

4. **Where do you see this person fitting, based on their talent?** We also want to see what their potential is long-term based on their skill and experience.

There needs to be a reason for the interview, and there needs to be some due diligence. I don't want to sit down with somebody who's not qualified. I don't want to sit down with somebody who has immediate red flags. This vetting process has saved me countless hours with someone who would not make the final cut.

DO SOME DUE DILIGENCE BEFORE ACTUALLY
INTERVIEWING ANYBODY.

INTERVIEWING PEOPLE—PART 2

The Interview.
This the typical content and flow of the actual interview:

- **I tell them about our company.** Why do I think our company is a great company to work for? I share that I have high expectations for any hire. I share our mission statement. I share our company history: why I started the company, some critical decisions that we've made along the way that has made the company what it is, and where the company is today. I share company accomplishments and awards. I assume I am sitting with someone who is considering multiple opportunities and I am pitching them on our company.

- **I share our culture.** We have a great culture, but we have very high-end clients and what might be accepted in most companies may not be acceptable for us. I will share with them what our customers expect of us.

- **I try to pick up on red flags.** So, I lay a couple of little hooks out there to see if they bite. One is called "too broke." What does that mean? There are certain people you're going to interview that are too broke to hire. They need to get paid immediately. They couldn't miss a day's pay; they would go under. I'm not trying to criticize, but there are situations where some people are always going to be trying to borrow money, and broke people sometimes do stupid things like trying to work directly with a client.

- **Is their personal situation a distraction?** What do I mean by that? I look at how they got to the job interview. When I see that somebody else drove them, well, I know there is a transportation issue. They're just red flags people will openly share with little prompting. I have learned that people with personal baggage are not a good fit.

Your goal is always to staff up, and you can't do that if you can't interview, assess talent, and make a great hire.

TAKE YOUR TIME, INTERVIEW, AND GET THE BEST EMPLOYEE.

JULY 18
QUALIFY YOUR LABOR MARKET

When you are deciding what kind of business to start, think twice before you pick a business where hiring is harder than finding a rocket scientist. What do I mean? If you choose a business that requires an expertise or skill that you don't have, obviously you will need to hire someone who has that skill. Make sure you can find and hire such a person within no more than three days. If you can't, the employee has you hostage and will eventually know it. As a rule, it is hard to grow when you cannot hire quickly. HR expert Carolyn Hughes of SimplyHired.com insists that hiring qualified employees on the fly is the key to sustained growth: "A company can only grow as fast as it can hire great people. Your success as a business depends upon your commitment to the hiring process. The benefits of finding great people who fit with your company culture, share your vision, and make an immediate and lasting impact cannot be understated."

Also, beware of any professional certifications that the business you are entering may require. In simple terms, if you are starting an electrical service company, you need an electrician on your staff.

I recently wanted to start an appliance repair business. I knew there was a need, as there were very few companies to choose from in our area offering this service. I was as excited about starting this business as any in the past. Then I ran some help-wanted ads. It was nearly impossible to find someone with the manufacturing certifications needed to work on the various brand appliances. I knew from experience that I would not start this business when hiring an appliance repair person was such a huge stumbling block.

Be aware of possible labor supply issues when it comes to lower-skilled workers, too. In some labor markets, you may encounter shortages of these workers, especially during particular seasons. Above all, be aware of what your labor pool actually looks like. Placing ads will give you some indication. Online ad placement is effortless and will allow you to get a very good idea of how easy it will be to staff your company.

CAN YOU PUT A TEAM ON THE FIELD?

JULY 19
BLUE COLLAR BUSINESS PLAN

People pitch me business ideas all the time, and I have learned to streamline the information I need to decide if this is worth taking to the next level. There was an old show—yes, I believe in black and white—called *Dragnet* about detectives solving a crime. One was a straight-and-narrow thinking guy called Joe Friday, who would always say, "Just the facts." He did not want a commentary or your opinion; he wanted only the pertinent facts that applied to the case he was investigating. I am very much the same way. Don't distract me with your passion for the idea and your optimism. Share with me the critical information I need. Here is what I call my "Blue Collar Business Plan," and if you can successfully answer these, in many cases, you have something worth chasing.

Ask:

- What are we offering (selling)?
- Why are we selling this? Show me there is a clamoring buyer waiting for this.
- Who specifically is this customer who wants to buy from us?
- How will we reach them? (Advertising strategy)
- Who is our competition? How will we be different and better?
- What is the cost to get this off the ground? Ongoing monthly operating costs?
- Who and what do I need to launch?
- What is the payoff? What will make this worth the time, risk, and resources? These are my pillars of a business plan.

START WITH WHAT, WHY, WHO, AND HOW.

JULY 20
FARM SYSTEM

If you've ever played baseball or followed a Major League team, you know what a "farm system" is. It is the minor league system of the MLB where they develop talent. If you want to have a great company and you want to have depth in your staff, you need to build a farm system. This means that you start getting young raw talent that can be developed.

You may consider interns or an apprenticeship program. It is a simple formula: find younger talent that has the potential to be developed into a starter (valuable contributor) on your company roster. I have learned that when you have an eye for talent, this can save you a great deal of money.

If you've got to hire everybody ready-made who has twenty years' experience, it gets very expensive. Now, I understand in some key positions you may need to do that, but you also need to develop a farm system within your office staff, within your technicians, within your technology. You want to get some young talent in your company who understand your culture and let them have opportunities to grow and develop.

Any Yankees fan or a fan of their bitter rivals, the Boston Red Sox, knows the value of identifying and growing talent through a farm system. Remember the names Derek Jeter and Mariano Rivera were homegrown talent who led the "Pinstripes" to four World Series Championships.

DEVELOP A FARM SYSTEM.

JULY 21
SCOREBOARD

I've shared with you that I have a dashboard system where I get critical numbers and information at the end of every day, but you also need to create a weekly scoreboard. You need to develop a scoring system where a win is easily recognized as well as a defeat.

We really run week-to-week, and certain numbers define the week with a win or loss. So, with all my partners, I create a number and tell them, "You turn in a sheet at the end of the week, put it on my desk, and write the number I requested with a W for a win you hit (or exceeded the number) or *L* for a loss and that number." When they first start, I let them know we're going to chart this for fifty-two weeks. Not only do they put this weekly score sheet on my desk, but they also have to write it on a large whiteboard where these weekly scores will stare at them.

My point is this, you've got to simplify things. In business, it's competition. Are you winning or are you losing? If you're profiting, you're probably winning. Create a scoreboard for your key managers and partners so they know when they have a win and, more importantly, they know when they have a loss. I have found that this visual exercise creates self-accountability; the numbers speak for themselves, so I do not need to say anything.

HAVE A SCOREBOARD SYSTEM IN YOUR COMPANY.

JULY 22
RECALIBRATING

Do you remember the telephone game from when you were in elementary school where you'd whisper a short sentence in the ear of the person next to you? This chain of events would go on for five or more whispers, then the teacher would ask the last student to share the sentence they just heard. Without fail, it did not replicate the original phrase.

This is what happens over time in your company. You start with this bold mission, these key initiatives, and five years into it, you're not doing anything even close to what you originally intended to do. This is not always a bad thing if you have innovated and made the changes needed to outpace your competition.

Sometimes you need to go back and get back to the original settings. Why did you start the business in the first place? What was your value proposition? What value, if any, are you currently providing to your customers? What were your original goals for this company, and have you met or exceeded them? Have you become complacent with no strategic initiatives? You need to have key metrics that you can measure and see if the organization has veered away from what it was doing that made it the customer's favorite. Are you still efficient and effective? What systems need to be reviewed and updated?

Again, you need to recalibrate. I encourage you to look at what you're doing every year and see if you need to make some adjustments to the way you're currently doing business. Do you have a culture that in no way reflects your core values? A tune-up might be in order.

SOMETIMES YOU NEED TO RECALIBRATE.

PERSONAL BRANDING

"If you're not branding yourself, you can be
sure others will do it for you."
—Unknown

Lebron James and Tiger Woods are athletes who are always worrying about their brand because there's value in their brand. As an entrepreneur and leader, you have a brand whether you realize it or not. You have a reputation with your customers. They either believe you are trustworthy or not. Clients and partners are either confident in you or they are not. Employees have an opinion of you, either good or bad.

Tom Peters in *Fast Company* gives great advice: "All of us need to understand the importance of branding. We are the CEOs of our own companies: "Me, Inc.". To be in business today, our most important job is to be the head marketer for the brand called *You.*"

You need to build a personal brand. You don't need to overthink this. In essence, a personal brand is your reputation. You want an authentic brand you can deliver on every day. What qualities are just innate? They flow from who you are. You need to make your behavior fit this brand. When you're talking to clients, maybe you repeat certain words or certain qualities that you bring to the table.

Gary Vaynerchuk emphatically exhorts, "It's important to build a personal brand because it's the only thing you're going to have. Your reputation online and in the new business world is pretty much the game." If you want to be a successful entrepreneur, find some qualities that your customers would love to have in a business owner and adopt those and then reinforce them by your actions.

ALWAYS LOOK TO CREATE A PERSONAL BRAND.

JULY 24
VALUE PROPOSITION

This is normally in your business plan, and you need to constantly review this. Simply put, let's look at it from a marketing statement. Why do customers buy from you? That's it. What is it that you offer that your customers find valuable and your competition does not offer? What makes your company or products attractive to customers? If it's a service, (e.g., plumbing company), there are a lot of people who do plumbing, but do you do 24-hour plumbing? Maybe if you have an existing client, you don't charge for emergency hours. This is your value proposition.

You need to have something that's valuable to your customers. It's a value proposition, and you need to constantly review it and make sure you're still delivering on it. You need to make sure that you actually have something that people want and thus consider of value. What may have been a value proposition ten years ago may not matter today. Your value proposition will change with new competition. You either need to match or exceed what they are offering. For example, free shipping is now often standard for online retailers to provide, but this is the result of Amazon.

Here is my tip to creating your value proposition: Keep it concise and communicate to customers why they should buy from you and not from your competition.

Here are three ways to communicate this:

1. The problems you solve.

2. The benefits your product or service offers.

3. Why you are better than the competition.

REVIEW YOUR VALUE PROPOSITION.

JULY 25

HARD WORK

"Good ideas are cheap. Success comes from hard work,
not a stroke of genius."
—*Nire Yal*

I have said on countless occasions: "It is not the idea that matters; it is the person who has the idea." Ideas are a dime a dozen in business. Google was a great idea, but I am telling you that idea could have been in the hands of a million other wannabe entrepreneurs and would have either sat dormant with no action or someone would have quit during the painful start.

I always bet on the person with the idea, not the idea itself. The person is always the engine of the start-up. Tony Robbins lends support to this: "The most painful mistake I see in first-time entrepreneurs is thinking that just having a business plan or a great concept is enough to guarantee success. It's not. Business success is 80 percent psychology and 20 percent mechanics." In other words, "You gotta want it so bad that you are willing to do whatever it takes to make it happen."

I often joke that I get a "good idea," as you never really know how good it actually is. The marketplace answers that question for you. I beat my idea into submission. I am going to do whatever is needed to make it work. Sometimes I have to bang a square peg into a round hole because I was off on a calculation or an initial assumption.

The illustration I share over and over with would-be entrepreneurs is that the start-up journey, and success in general, is like a roller coaster. You always begin with the slow ride to the highest point. Then a few curves present themselves (obstacles) that will propel you through the rest of the ride you'll remember as being awesome. I find my journey starts slowly and often painfully with a few curves but, looking back, the ride has been priceless. But let's be clear: there is no substitute for hard work initially. I say initially because in time, you can share the burden.

Initially, no one will see or understand your idea as you do. You will have to be the engine behind it.

THERE IS NO SUBSTITUTE FOR HARD WORK.

JULY 26
TARGET MARKET

"There is only one winning strategy. It is to carefully define the target market and direct a superior offering to that target market."
—Philip Kotler

Your target market is the perfect customer for you. This is the one who is most likely to buy from you. They love what you sell and how you sell it. If your target customer is male between ages 25 to 35, you would market a product to that person far differently than you would a product that is for someone ages 60 and over. For the younger buyer, I would consider using digital ads or TV commercials during UFC fights or ESPN. For the older audience, I would consider using TV advertising during shows like *Wheel of Fortune, Jeopardy!,* and *60 Minutes.* These are two completely different customers, and to target them effectively, you need to know that.

Let me help you find your target market:

- Male or Female
- Single or Married
- Incomes: Lower, Middle Class, Upper Income, Wealthy
- Conservative or Progressive
- Race: Nobody wants to admit the elephant in the room, but there is a reason why BET (Black Entertainment Television) made its founder a billionaire because he was smart enough to know that black and white viewers have different wants regarding entertainment.
- Age Category: Teenagers, 18–25, 25–40, 41–55, 55 and over. Clearly, this will be broken down based on what fits your business, but you should get the general idea. You market to each of these age groups differently with different vehicles and messages.

The list can keep going and going, but I hope you get the idea. The better you know your target customer, the better you will be able to craft messages in your advertising that appeal to them. If you don't know your target customer, you will waste your advertising dollars on vehicles that have no chance of reaching or appealing to this person.

WHO'S YOUR TARGET CUSTOMER?

TURNAROUND

Sometimes your business needs a complete turnaround. It's absolutely going in the wrong direction. What's worse is that you may not realize it. Some people think they just need to make minor changes or increase morale and possibly set a new company initiative. Too often you hear a failing company talking about going back to basics. However, the basics get redefined by new, innovative companies every day, so what was "the basics" twenty years ago is archaic today.

When is it time to do a complete turnaround?

- You're losing market share to competition for a sustained period.
- You're losing customers.
- You're in a dying industry.
- Your products that once were leading sellers are no longer selling.
- Your profit margins have dropped at an alarming rate.
- You've lost key employees to a competitor.
- You're running out of cash at an alarming rate.
- You're scared you may be out of business sooner rather than later.

You are the leader of the company. As the owner and founder, you need to be alert to the above signs of trouble and make the massive course change required so you don't hit the iceberg.

SOMETIMES A COMPLETE TURNAROUND IS WHAT YOUR BUSINESS NEEDS.

JULY 28
HOW UNDERDOGS WIN

At the time of this writing, the last five days have been "the week of the underdogs." The LSU Tigers (college football team) went into Tuscaloosa and beat Alabama where the Tide had a thirty-one-game winning streak under Nick Saban. Minnesota upset mighty Penn State, and Kentucky—the number-one-ranked college basketball team—got beat by Evansville at home in Rupp Arena. Yes, I said Evansville. This was the first time a number-one-ranked Kentucky team has ever lost to an unranked nonconference opponent.

When you are a start-up, you are the underdog. It has some advantages, and as you read above, underdogs can win. Normally underdog teams are led by a compelling leader who gets them to believe they can win. All three coaches above fit that mold, and—a little known secret—the coach of Evansville played on the 1996 Kentucky National Championship Team. He was able to prepare his team for what Rupp Arena would be like. The Minnesota coach shared, on the night before the big game, how pressure turns coal into diamonds, convincing his players they were diamonds and ready for Penn State. Coach O from LSU, with his gruff voice and Louisiana accent, barks motivation like no other, and his players responded. You as the leader need to learn from these coaches and motivate your team to believe that your company will prevail and be a great company.

I like being the underdog as a start-up because it allows us to feel like we have everything to gain. Since we were at the bottom, we knew who our competition was, and we reveled at the opportunity to overtake them. I used to go by my competitors' place of business and take pictures and hang them up to motivate me and my team.

UNDER THE RIGHT LEADER, UNDERDOGS WIN.

HAVE A SUPPORT GROUP

If it makes you feel better, call it a network. We have all seen the value of support groups to help us get to the gym more regularly, lose weight, or meet other personal goals. The same is true in business. It's important to have one or more people in your life who can help you achieve your business dreams. We all need mentors and cheerleaders.

Your support group should consist of people who can encourage you, confront you, and at times, guide you. It is possible that one person can do it all, but more likely, you will need a few people whose opinions you respect and listen to. As a rule, I do not take advice from someone who has not accomplished the thing I am asking his or her advice about. For example, I do not take financial advice from someone who means well but is broke.

A great organization from which to obtain business mentoring at no cost is SCORE, a nonprofit association dedicated to helping small businesses get off the ground, grow, and achieve their goals through education and mentorship. It is comprised almost entirely of retired businesspeople, including former or active company CEOs. The group has been around for over fifty years. You can apply for a local mentor at www.score.org.

In addition to a mentor, some business owners also seek out—and pay for—a business coach. A coach is someone who can work with you in a more hands-on way to develop badly needed leadership or management skills. Accepting the help of a coach can take great humility, but the personal and financial rewards are often well worth it.

Bob Nardelli, the former CEO of Home Depot, wrote, "I absolutely believe that people, unless coached, never reach their maximum capabilities." Studies have documented extraordinary gains in leadership performance in companies in which the top executives are coached. Depending on your budget, and your possible shortfalls, you may want to explore this option, too.

THERE IS A REASON TEAMS HAVE ASSISTANT COACHES AND CHEERLEADERS.

8 ROLES OF AN
ENTREPRENEURIAL LEADER

I have learned over my business career that there are many positions people play on the team that help a business function and grow, but no one can perform the 8 Roles I believe each founding entrepreneur needs to fill to build a company of significance. I define this as growing, profitable, and revered by your competition

1. **Dreamer:** It is the founder who begins the enterprise with nothing more than a dream that their business can provide value to a target audience.

2. **Innovator:** The dream will manifest itself in innovation that will become the business.

3. **Gambler:** There is always a bet that is made that the time and money initially invested will pay a worthy return. The payoff is not just money but flexibility of schedule and significance.

4. **General:** Someone will have to craft the strategy and implement its execution.

5. **Coach:** A coach has multiple roles (recruiter, motivator, talent scout, etc.) and the combined sum of these roles endears this leader to their team.

6. **Networkers:** The ability to not only hire staff but to surround yourself with a cabinet or professionals, advisors, partners, and mentors to assist in expansion, decision making, and protecting you and the origination.

7. **Salesman:** A pied piper will launch this venture and spend every day forward selling its value to all who will listen.

8. **Learner:** To become a great entrepreneur, you will need to expand your understanding and competency of your industry, business, economics, and leadership. This thirst for knowledge will become a lifelong pursuit.

GO FROM LAUNCHING TO BEING A LEADER.

PREPARATION MEETS OPPORTUNITY

"Luck is what happens when preparation meets opportunity."
—Seneca

You always need to be preparing for success. That's why I'm so big on reading; that's why I'm a proponent of going to seminars and listening to podcasts. You will be shocked: if you prepare for success, it will meet you halfway most times. You'd be surprised how many opportunities I get within areas that I'm studying. I'm big on real estate, so if I'm constantly reading about real estate, I expect real estate opportunities to present themselves.

It's somewhat like the law of attraction. You know, when you buy a red car or start wanting to buy one, and all you start seeing is red cars or the model you want. I think what happens regarding such preparation is, for one, that you are much more alert to things you are studying or focusing on, and, two, because your knowledge is increasing, you see opportunities that are three levels deep that you would not have noticed with your previous lack of knowledge.

You want to prepare yourself for opportunities. If you do, don't be surprised when favorable circumstances present themselves. Expand your knowledge level within your industry or business in general. Find something within these two areas in which you can become an expert. There is a principle of sowing and reaping, and this the same thing. Preparation is the sowing!

ALWAYS BE PREPARED; YOU NEVER KNOW WHEN OPPORTUNITIES WILL COME KNOCKING.

AUGUST 1

PERFECTION

"Instead of waiting for perfection, run with what you do,
and fix it along the way."
—Paul Arden

I can be a perfectionist, but I've learned not to worry about it quite so much because it's hard to hit. It's hard to expect that from your employees. It's very daunting to work for somebody who is a perfectionist, and it's very expensive to try to shoot for perfection.

I've told my employees this. I have found that realistically our clients are willing to pay for "B" work because I think our "B" work is "A" work, but they're not willing to pay for perfection. So, don't give it. Do the very best job you can, but don't spend forever on something.

I like what George Fisher says, "When you aim for perfection, you discover it's a moving target."

Perfection sounds great in theory, but it's very expensive. You need to find a realistic expectation that your employees can meet that satisfies 95 percent of the customers. What I found is 5 percent of customers are never happy anyway, regardless of what you do.

Finally, perfection is the unnecessary speed bump of progress. Why do I say this? Because again, if perfection is the only acceptable outcome of every project, it will take three times longer than it should, frustrate 75 percent of your team, and cost twice as much. Don't get me wrong; I like things to be done exceptionally, but at some point, the baby has to be delivered.

NEVER WORRY TOO MUCH ABOUT PERFECTION.
JUST DO YOUR BEST.

AUGUST 2
SCALABILITY

A lot of companies want to grow, but are they able to grow? Do they have a ceiling? Can they withstand a stress test? Can your company meet the increased demand for what you are selling? An example of not being scalable initially was FedEx. When they first got started, they put the company through a stress test and shipped out 157 packages and only five were received. Obviously, this test revealed glitches that had to be solved before going to the market with this business model.

You have got to test your company's current systems and business model. You may not be ready for growth. You need to see it at maximum capacity. What could you handle? Does your infrastructure support it? Do you have the office staff to support it? Do you have the labor to support it? Again, growth is great, but you need to make sure you have the scalability to be able to do that.

I have started businesses that I believed were scalable but realized our ceiling was much lower than I thought. This became clear when either demand increased or when we tried this business in another area, which often revealed staffing problems. Other times, we did not have the office support in place to meet the stresses of serving this level of demand. Finally, we found providing customer support, in areas other than in our main location, was not able to be handled at the same speed. These issues all revealed a scalability problem.

IS YOUR BUSINESS SCALABLE?

AUGUST 3
POLISHERS

Not everybody's going to come to you perfect. Some of them are going to come to you pretty darn good, and that's when all that they need is a little polishing. You've got to look at people and see what one thing you can help them with. And I have yet to meet anyone, no matter how talented or experienced, that did not have one thing they could improve.

Don't be intimidated just because somebody is really good, or even great, and feel like you can't say anything to them or suggest an improvement. I don't want anybody on my staff to whom I can't give a suggestion. I went by a job site the other day where one of our most talented and experienced guys was working. I noticed that he did not have a tablet with him to write things down. I threw out a piece of simple advice to him. I took out a spiral notebook and showed him how he should make a list of materials before he goes and buys everything. He claimed never to forget anything, to which I just said, "You are a better man than me." I went on to share with him that your brain can get cluttered with a list that you can write down and have a guaranteed 100 percent success rate every time you go shopping.

Later I would show him how to take five minutes at the end of the day to strategize tomorrow's work. I explained how his brain would spend his sleeping hours figuring out how best to get everything done since it now had a seed planted. I was speaking to a worker in his early fifties who was the most talented worker I have ever had. He then confided in me that nobody had ever shown him these few simple things.

Never stop improving. Even your most valuable players, such as Michael Jordan, had a coach.

BE A POLISHER AND BRING OUT THE BEST IN YOUR PLAYERS.

AUGUST 4
COURSE ADJUSTMENTS

You need to have a business that has a structure and a set of systems so that even when it goes off course, you can get back on track. This is why I love systems, dashboards, and experienced staff. With the three elements I just mentioned, when you are off course, you can easily be alerted to this, as well as have critical information to make needed adjustments. Finally, an experienced staff tends to see problems well in advance of them being fatal blows to the company.

Take profit. Profit can decline for one week or maybe two, but three and four weeks is creating a bad trendline. We know how our systems work, how our labor-to-profit ratio works, and if we have so many people working, we know roughly what we are going to earn each week. We also know that if we have so many phone calls or online estimate requests come in each week, we know our conversion rate and average size job, giving us a predictable cash flow number to work with. Even my digital companies have a blue-collar approach to keeping it simple and creating similar alert signals.

However you do it, I often tell people who are running a business—specifically a start-up—that it can go into cardiac arrest quickly. Without a surgeon (experienced staff) who has critical data to make a diagnosis, the business meets a fatal outcome. The sooner you get your business from being a kite to a battleship that can stay afloat, the better. That's when it gets fun and that's when you focus on growth. I encourage you to create systems and measurable numbers with alerts that allow for quick and minor adjustments to correct the course.

HAVE A BUSINESS STRUCTURE THAT ALERTS YOU WHEN THE BUSINESS IS OFF COURSE.

AUGUST 5
PICK YOUR BATTLES

"You can win the battle but lose the war."
—King Pyrrhus of Epirus

King Pyrrhus is credited with making the above statement after defeating the Romans, recognizing that in winning, he lost the lives of his best officers and many of his troops. He would go on to say, "Another such victory, and we are lost."

Early on in my leadership journey, I am embarrassed to admit, I made this mistake more than once. I have now learned a few rules of warfare that I adhere to, such as:

- **Is this battle worth winning?** Really? What will I gain, and is it worth it?

- **Will winning the battle destroy a long time personal or business relationship?** There are relationships and allies where a short-term win is a long-term loss.

- **Don't fight dirty.** Stick to the facts, and don't make it personal.

- **Don't say something you cannot take back.** Some statements do irreversible damage.

- **Pick a fair fight.** Don't argue with subordinates who cannot genuinely argue back for fear of losing their jobs.

- **Know when to walk away.** Some fights can spin out of control quickly with voices being raised, and the result of this is ugly.

PICK YOUR BATTLES SPARINGLY AND FIGHT FAIRLY.

AUGUST 6
KNOW WHAT YOU DON'T KNOW

It is not what you know that is important; it is knowing what you don't know that is the Achilles heel of many entrepreneurs. Sometimes they believe they can fill every role within the business, which is impossible and leaves them performing roles at which they are average and ineffective.

I have learned over the years that the employee who tells me they can do something is, in reality, often below average at best in this. What ends up happening is they either fail miserably at the task, or it takes twice as long as it should. But in either instance, their weakness is exposed. Now with new staff, I implore, please tell me what you don't know how to do. I am fine with that and will work around it. I am genuine about how I share this with new hires, and now they disclose areas of weakness. This simple exercise has saved me money and damage to our reputation.

I was recently in the office of an owner of a business who we use a great deal, and the owner could not be a nicer guy. With over sixty years of experience in business, he was telling me how he was learning digital marketing and sharing blogs he was reading. The problem was he owns a multimillion-dollar company that needs an outside company or full-time in-house person handling this responsibility. I looked at him and said, "You are wasting your time." I want to be clear: I love learning, but I strongly adhere to the idea that you will go from weakness or new area of learning and at best get to a five out of ten, which still makes you a liability. Or you do what I do, and what I recommended to him, which is to keep improving your strengths and get someone else to own that weak area, someone who is a professional who you can hold accountable for results.

**IT'S WHAT YOU AND YOUR STAFF DON'T KNOW
THAT GETS YOU IN TROUBLE.**

AUGUST 7
PEAK PERFORMANCE

Peak performance is the performance at the best level of a person's physical and cognitive abilities. What am I talking about when I talk about peak performance in business? Well, I don't work my team members on weekends if at all possible, which in our industry is very different from the norm. Our work is physically demanding, and in working outside in the heat or freezing cold, I have found there is a limit to how many productive hours I can get from my staff. I try not to call or text my partners over the weekends unless it is an emergency.

I want my team to be fully aware of the times and events on our calendar where I need them at their best. There are certain jobs and or periods within my various companies that are more critical than others. You cannot run a marathon every day. Much like a good coach, I want my players to be at their best when the seasons are on the line. When you are not pushing them every minute, they will respond in a big way to the crucial periods.

You can never get the best out of anybody if you're burning them out constantly. I know you want to make a lot of profit, but you might want to think about working people less but getting the best out of them.

IT'S ABOUT GETTING THE BEST FROM YOUR PLAYERS.

AUGUST 8
100-HOUR WORKWEEK

I recently had one of my closest friends share how his boss of twenty-five years sold one—yes, just one—of his companies this past year for *$151 million.* Yes, the million is correct. The tragedy of this story is that after the sale, this titan had three strokes in that year. Anyone who knows him well would say they are surprised he didn't have them earlier, as he worked twenty-hour days his entire career.

I remember interviewing with him when I was out of college, at 5:45 a.m.—yes, before the sun rose, as he never waited for the sun to dictate start time. Dressed in a power suit and a shirt starched so heavily it could stand up by itself, he wore cufflinks the size of golf balls and a Rolex that would consume my annual pay. He exemplified success and power, but it took me less than five minutes to know that I did not want what he had. I knew through rumors of his family's dramatics and his hundred-hour work weeks. Those clues gave me all the warning rumbles I needed.

At the end of our interview, he tried to close me. I said I needed to think about it. Yes, it was a fib, because there was no chance I wanted this life. In our recent get-together, my friend remarked: "You saw through him, and I did not." He was lamenting the twenty-five years he had served in purgatory under this tyrant in pursuit of wealth.

My friend noticed my morning was quiet, as I started with reading, thinking, planning, and exercise. I was present when my kids awoke and had dinner with my family that same night. He was shocked by how little I worked, to which I replied, "I have been doing this for twenty years. I would hope I would have recruited a team to do the heavy lifting by this point."

I went on to share with him the couple of events I was focusing on for the day, but neither required an entire day of energy. He remarked, "You have it made," at which I thought to myself, *This is just common sense.*

CREATE A BALANCE BETWEEN WORK AND LIFE.

AUGUST 9
BLOCKING BACK

If you want to be a great entrepreneur, you better get a few blocking backs for you. Every great running back has a fullback who will start a few feet in front of them. Once the play is initiated, this player has one and only one objective: to block someone on the opposing team in order to create a hole for the running back to dart through. Rocky Bleier provided these rays of daylight for Hall of Famer Franco Harris, as Daryl "Moose" Johnston did for Emmet Smith. Often, they go unnoticed, but guess what? Those great running backs would never have achieved their Hall of Fame status without those selfless players blocking for them.

You need to get some key people on your team who are willing to take a hit for you. These are the people who come to you every day and say, "What can I get off your desk? Is there something I can help you with? What do I need to do to help us get this goal accomplished?" They're called blocking backs, and they're critical. They are selfless and just want you and the company to succeed.

You may not be into sports, so let me give you a military analogy: the general is not on the front lines of combat. You cannot entangle yourself in everything going on. Much like a general, you need to focus on creating the strategies to grow your company.

YOU WANT PEOPLE ON YOUR TEAM WHO
BLOCK FOR YOU.

POWER OF PERSUASION

"I think the power of persuasion would be the superpower of all time."
—Jenny Mollen

Do you possess the power of persuasion? When you share an idea, do people get on board? To be persuasive is the ability to present your side of the story, to present your idea, your vision, in an incredible, compelling way that makes others want to join forces with you. Persuasion is not talking someone into doing something they don't want to do. That is manipulation. I have read all the tips about how to be more persuasive, but I personally think it's insulting, as this would never work on me. Things such as mirror the person's body language, which I would pick up on in about twenty seconds. Or mirror the speed and tone of their voice. Let me tell you what I have found that actually works on smart people who don't initially share your enthusiasm for an idea or opinion. Remember, if you don't have their respect, nothing you say will matter. Assuming you have their respect because you have credibility, these may help:

- Speak with passion for your idea or thoughts.
- Be realistic and not in a fantasy world.
- Share how they benefit from this.
- Be open to collaboration and criticism.
- Ask for them to support you even if they don't agree completely.

If you want to be a successful entrepreneur, you're going to need to bring others along with you. You're going to need to be persuasive.

LEARN TO BE PERSUASIVE.

AUGUST 11
KNOWING WHAT I NOW KNOW

I spend a lot of time each week sitting down and going over lessons that I've learned over the week. If I had to do it all over again, knowing what I now know, what would I do differently?

This simple exercise allows me to take mistakes in stride because I will learn from them and not repeat them.

Knowing what I know now, I ask myself:

- What would I do differently?
- What would I not do at all?
- What information do I wish I had at the time I made this decision?
- What resources do I wish I had?
- Was the timing ideal?
- What should I have said?
- What should I not have said?

Don't beat yourself up over mistakes and failures. You need to have a file of "knowing what I now know, I would do this differently or not at all."

TAKE TIME TO GO OVER LESSONS YOU'VE LEARNED.

AUGUST 12
BECOME A BETTER THINKER

"I've always been a big, bold thinker."
—Kelsea Ballerini

Becoming a better thinker is such a valuable skill and surprisingly, it costs nothing more than time, silence, and focus.

10 steps to becoming a better thinker:

1. Recognize the value of a great idea.

2. Recognize great ideas are the fruit of great thinking.

3. Great thinking is the result of regular thinking.

4. Schedule a regular time to think.

5. Bring a pad of paper or some method of recording your ideas and thoughts.

6. Find a place that allows you to do your best uninterrupted thinking.

7. Find others with whom you can share your ideas.

8. Become a sounding board for others' ideas.

9. Reading is a great primer for ideas.

10. Keep a journal of your best ideas and their payoffs.

NO GREATER SKILL DOES THE ENTREPRENEUR HAVE THAN TO BE A GREAT THINKER.

AUGUST 13
LEARNING FROM FAILURE

What can we learn from failure? For successful people, failure always pays a dividend in knowledge. Let me share some of the lessons I've learned from failure.

I changed my view of failure. I know now it's just temporary. It always has an equal or greater payoff in the future associated with it. Basically, if I lost $100,000 from that venture, I have saved myself $100,000 since then, or $100,000 in the future.

I mine every failure for gold. I learn every possible lesson this failure can teach me.

Failure will teach you three valuable qualities. Failure will take you through a three-step course that is a must on your success journey. It will teach you perseverance, problem-solving, and leadership. Most failures will require all three of these skills to make it through to the other side.

You get credibility and experience. Because I've gone through difficulties and I share these multiple experiences that I've navigated, it gives me credibility and experience with my team. They trust me when I say I can handle this.

Life has failure baked into it. I expect failure. I don't look for it, but I know it's going to happen. If I try ten things, some things are going to fail, so I have learned how to respond to failure. I get out of a bad situation as fast as I can with the least amount of collateral damage.

FAILURE IS SUCCESS'S CLASSROOM.

AUGUST 14
BUY EXPERTISE

"Never become so much of an expert that you stop gaining expertise."
–Denis Waitley

An article in *Recode* shares a story of why struggling personal care company Edgewell, which owns brands like Schick, Playtex, and Wet Ones, decided to buy its direct-to-consumer competition, Harry's, in 2019 for $1.4 billion. It wasn't just about gaining online market share. Edgewell wanted Harry's marketing prowess for its own products. It wanted the expertise of Harry's cofounder Jeff Raider, who incidentally also founded the billion-dollar online eyeglass retailer, Warby Parker.

Raider remarked, "We actually get to take over responsibility for Edgewell's brands in the US. We'll run them ... They've (Edgewell) got some iconic brands with lots of awareness and great products ... Our opportunity is to actually get to think about how to reposition those brands to consumers and create great products that they want, which is very much the same mission as we had before."

Edgewell adhered to a couple of my key principles ("Know what you don't know" and "Pay the big money when someone can take you further and faster."), which were the pillars of this deal. Raider and his team will do what they do best, and Edgewell will stay out of their way.

IF YOU DON'T KNOW IT OR CANNOT DO IT, PAY FOR SOMEONE ELSE TO HELP.

AUGUST 15
MANAGE EXPECTATIONS

I have found managing expectations to be a critical component if you want happy and satisfied customers. Managing expectations starts first with clearly communicating what customers can expect. New business owners fall into this trap in their efforts to bring on an investor or to attract the account that could be a game-changer. What I will tell you is that if you do fail to deliver early on, you can irreversibly damage your reputation. It is possible that you go into this with your eyes wide open recognizing you have a challenge ahead of you and yes, there are times when you have to bet that you will meet the challenge. But this cannot be a day-in and day-out practice because it only takes one or two failures to deliver to bring the house of cards down.

There are often times I have to send an email to a client and kind of tap the brakes a little bit and say, "I want to make sure you understand what we can deliver," and I'll go through the bullet points on what we can deliver. There are just times in a conversation or correspondence where you can tell the other side has added a few deliverables that were not in the contract or implied indirectly. I have also found clients and customers alike appreciate this, and if for some reason they have expected something you cannot or do not intend to deliver, this allows all parties to make a clean break.

I'm trying to manage their expectations because sometimes I get a gut feeling that what they expect isn't what we're going to be able to deliver on, so I need to manage the expectations.

LEARN TO SET AND MANAGE EXPECTATIONS.

AUGUST 16
HANDLE WITH CARE

If you are not a superstar, you will not attract superstars, and you darn sure won't keep them. I am always looking for superstars, and they don't come around like an annual holiday. They are more like finding a unicorn. They also require being managed differently than the herd. For starters, they must respect you, knowing you bring something to the table that they view as valuable. This may be something they cannot do or an opportunity that only you can provide.

You need to learn what motivates your top players. You need to find out: Is it money? Security? A pat on the back? Flexibility? Autonomy? Opportunity for advancement or even a partnership? Not that a superstar wants to be underpaid, but I have learned it is rarely their top motivator.

After you know what motivates your top players, you need to be always improving them. This is a problem too many leaders create because of their insecurity. They are just so happy to have this person that they are afraid to manage, improve, and lead them. Superstars have no problem being led by a worthy leader but will run over a weak, wannabe leader.

Learn also what sets them off. Every superstar has a time bomb, and if you mess with it, they will go off. So, you need to know what their triggers are. You have other employees that have triggers, but they would not dare pull them. Alpha dogs—which superstars are—will be confrontational if put in a situation that requires it.

Warning: you can't have more than so many alpha dogs in one department on one project. They normally have the sharp elbows in the sandbox. In closing, never ever criticize or embarrass an alpha dog in front of anybody. If they need to be corrected, do it privately, and with kid gloves. Yes, you will bite your tongue, and why? Because, the 360 days out of 365 that they are on, they contribute more value than anybody else.

RECRUIT SOME SUPERSTARS AND WATCH THE PROFIT GROW.

NONNEGOTIABLES

The reason why I want to talk about nonnegotiables is that football season is ready to start, and a lot of football players find this is a good time to hold out, not reporting to training camp, hoping to have their contracts reworked with a sizable pay increase. Certain organizations quickly give in and sign that person to a new, more lucrative contract, and certain organizations will refuse. Why? Because they have a method of operating that says we don't allow one person to disrupt what we believe is an organization nonnegotiable. I have heard it said, "It's just how we do things around here."

In your business, you need to establish some guiding principles that allow you and your company to make hard decisions as well as take action without delay. One of the partners will say to me, "This person wants a pay raise," trying to be the advocate, to which I respond, "Are you prepared to give the other fifty people he tells a raise?" Giving random raises is just not good business. We also value reliability, so if someone—no matter how talented—starts displaying that they are no longer reliable, we let them go without delay. It's just one of our nonnegotiables.

We have a list of nonnegotiables, and they will reflect your core values as well as experiences, but you need them as they have allowed me to make what would be hard decisions quite easily.

YOU MUST HAVE A FEW NONNEGOTIABLES.

AUGUST 18
SUCCESS IS A PROCESS

Success is a process, a series of actions or steps taken to achieve a particular result. A well-done process will bring you to the desired destination. Author Malcolm Gladwell, in his book *Outliers*, shares the 10,000-hour principle. The outliers (the world-class achievers) put 10,000 hours at a minimum into their craft.

My son would put on his red Nike golf shirt and ask me to go play golf with him. He looked like Tiger Woods (at least he thought), but he did not play like his hero. Why? Because Tiger Woods did not just happen; he had been hitting golf balls since he could stand up. The Olympic gymnast did not start doing cartwheels as a teenager. Success doesn't just happen. It is the result of doing a few critical things daily that others choose not to do. The marathon you wish to run will require a daily run that will test your commitment to this objective.

I have also found that being exceptional at something also requires a passion to succeed.

Passion provides the energy required to do the process. I love creating a business. I never get bored with starting a business, carving a niche in the marketplace, developing the brand, and forming the team. I love the process and the result. A successful business is often the payoff. If you want to achieve something others struggle to reach, fall in love with the process or habits required to be great at this. If you start climbing the mountain and climb a little more every day, at some point you will reach the summit.

LEARN TO LOVE THE PROCESS.

AUGUST 19
MISSION STATEMENT

A mission statement is what you do, how you do it, whom you serve, and what results you deliver. It defines your purpose, why your company exists, what you plan to do, and, to some extent, how you're going to do it.

My company's mission was to provide workmanship that exceeds our customers' expectations in a timely and professional manner. We in contracting know that people are never timely. They tell you that they're going to show up, and then they don't show up. So that was huge to me. I had experienced that in the past. That's what made me want to start the company.

Examples of Great Mission Statements

Twitter, Inc.: "To give everyone the power to create and share ideas and information instantly without barriers."

Chipotle Mexican Grill: "'Food with integrity' is our commitment to finding the very best ingredients raised with respect for the animals, the environment, and the farmers."

A business plan should have a mission statement. It should be one that you look at regularly. It should be something that's posted. It should guide your company.

LET YOUR MISSION STATEMENT GUIDE
YOUR COMPANY.

AUGUST 20
INCREASE REVENUE AND PROFIT

This past year, like most years, I started another company and, using my go-to formula, I have a partner. He reached out to me yesterday saying he was working on the business plan for year two. To which I quickly replied (in almost a reactionary manner as it did not take me even one second to process my answer), "Just bring in more revenue and increase profit." Yes, to be clear, more revenue does not always mean more profit, so keep an eye on margins and costs if you wish to increase profit. Profit is the only number that actually tells the score of the game.

My point was that in the first two years of a company, there are only two goals: increase your revenue and increase your profit. Think about it: if you do both, you will have the needed cash to solve nearly every other problem that can present itself. If you do not have cash (which only comes from revenue that exceeds expenses) you won't have the only measurable that matters: profit. In your first two years of a start-up, keep the target simple.

Yes, I love building my team and company culture, but when you have no money and you are out of business, none of this will matter. These are targets you hit along the way to building a great company. Your focus needs to be on staying alive, and cash is the only remedy I have found for that.

SET YOUR GOAL TO INCREASE REVENUE AND PROFIT THIS YEAR.

AUGUST 21

MOMENTUM

"People with momentum can get so much done. Momentum is easy to lose and almost impossible to fake."
—Shaun King

The great thing about momentum is when you have it, all things are good, and when you don't have it, you can't get anything going your way. If you have ever played baseball, you are familiar with the power of momentum. Your team is winning by five runs, and your opponent starts getting a couple of hits, then the "Big Mo" happens, and they score six runs in one inning, winning the game in dramatic fashion.

You've got to create momentum in your business. What happens too often is you're just surviving to make payroll. Or at best, we get caught up in routine with nothing on the horizon that excites anybody. Are you familiar with this saying, "Same old, same old"? That means you are doing the same old thing you have always done.

If you want to motivate your staff, start creating some momentum within your business. How do you create momentum? Set a few goals for next year. I have learned to make some goals seem hard, but internally you know that with just a little work, you can hit them. This is called orchestrating an early win. Teams do this in sports, scheduling someone early on they can beat. It never hurts to schedule an easy win, followed by a few goals that will continue to stretch your team.

Some other things you can do to get a little momentum is to hire someone who can stir the pot a little. This person has some energy that positively disrupts things. Sometimes it's just getting new uniforms. Maybe you need a new sign out front or an update to your office.

Sometimes you have to create momentum within your business. Nobody wants to work for something that's just not moving.

CREATE SOME MOMENTUM.

AUGUST 22
GIVE BACK TO YOUR COMMUNITY

The PGA Tour has made it a staple of their events that each tournament gives proceeds to the host city. Building brand awareness in your local community is a great way to attract new business. I have personally been a sponsor of our city golf championships for all the various age divisions. We have been sponsoring the event annually for so long that they have allowed us to put up permanent signs announcing our support. Sponsoring the event was a no-brainer when I was approached. It fits a great demographic. All you have to do is watch a Sunday golf event, and you will see the most prestigious brands using the event as their marketing platform.

Why do you give back to your community?

- Your goal should be to become a business that has people cheering for their success, and this clearly accomplishes that.
- It raises your profile and brand awareness.
- It's just good business in that there is no downside to being generous to the community where your business resides or does business.
- It reminds people who may have not used you in years, or for whatever reason stopped using you to put your company back in the phone.
- It gives your company and its employees a sense of pride to be involved in a charitable cause.
- If it is an event, program, or school you have a target audience to cross-market to. Your priority is being charitable, but you are smart enough to know there is also an audience who recognizes and appreciates your support.

I can think of no downside to attaching your business to a community event or cause that your support. Make sure if you are involved, you put your best foot forward: look and act like the brand you want people to like and buy from.

CONSIDER SPONSORING A COMMUNITY EVENT.

246

AUGUST 23
NUMBERS DON'T LIE

I am consumed by numbers. Why? Numbers don't lie. You can't manage what you can't measure. I have shared that I have a dashboard system that gives me critical numbers that I want to see daily and weekly to notice if any negative trends are developing. Start-up businesses need to establish baseline numbers that must be met, in a given time period, to provide justification to keep going with this venture. I say numbers are the truth serum for a business owner.

I don't start businesses without setting an income number that I want the company to achieve in a given time period. This is one of the hurdles I set for a good reason: this number provides accountability as well as a reality check. What do I mean by this? You can get so excited that you got your business off the ground, but it is not making money six months in. In fact, it is requiring you to use a line of credit to keep this dream afloat. Only numbers can give you this slap in the face.

I create numbers that I want my team to meet. If you get a blood pressure test, certain numbers will alert a doctor to a problem. I want the same effect. It might be income brought in, profit margin, traffic to the site, requests for estimates, or cost to acquire a customer. Whatever it may be, certain numbers reveal whether this business has legs (it will be able to walk and stand on its own soon).

You should be consumed by numbers. I would encourage you to make decisions based on the numbers, not emotions or opinions. Establish some hard numbers with a deadline to update you on how this business is actually performing.

NUMBERS ARE THE TRUTH SERUM FOR A BUSINESS OWNER.

AUGUST 24
NURTURE IDEAS

As an entrepreneur, you want to nurture an idea and make it grow. Every idea does not come out of your mouth perfectly. It needs to be put in the soil. What does that mean? Maybe you run it past some employees and partners and people that you just have a high regard for. Run it by them and get their criticism. In my twenties, I thought all my ideas—at inception—were brilliant and ready for public consumption.

Ideas taste best after being in a crockpot. Most ideas need time to draw out the best outcomes. I used to think that the second I had a good idea, it was ready to be served to the marketplace. I have since learned to allow my staff to add some spices (criticism and improvements) and, occasionally, a request to throw the dish in the trash because it is inedible. Some ideas are just not good after another person has run it through the lens of reality.

You need to test your ideas, vet them. You need to bounce them off of other people. You possibly need to work them through a little bit longer on your own. Maybe you don't go full bore with the complete idea initially. You try it in phases. Sometimes if you go too fast, too hard with it, it just dies an ugly death.

Now, my team and family will hear me say, "I have a good one," of course implying I believe I have a good idea, but I need to stew on it for a while. I need to just roll it around in my head for a time. This is my way of marinating an idea to draw out its flavor. Then I will bring it to others to allow them to spice it up a bit.

AN IDEA NEEDS TO BE NURTURED TO REACH ITS FULL POTENTIAL.

AUGUST 25
OPPORTUNISTIC

True entrepreneurs are always looking for an opportunity. They're always looking to expand something, to start something, to be a part of something. They're looking around at all times to turn an idea, business, or deal into something great and always something profitable.

If you want to be a great entrepreneur, you might want to start being more opportunistic.

Starting today, start being very alert to opportunities around you. They'll come dressed up in many, many forms, sometimes in disguise, but if you start looking for them and taking advantage of them, you'll be shocked every year on how many new profit streams you add to your empire.

I have found making money at this point in my life to be a game. When I buy an outrageously expensive car, I have zero intention to pay for it from existing wealth. I made this purchase an end goal, forcing me to look for new ventures to pay for it, and guess what? I always find an opportunity that indeed pays for these luxuries. Of course, twenty-five years into being opportunistic, I have a quick method of vetting opportunities. Let me share them with you:

- Quick money is a red flag.
- It will pay a return in a reasonable period.
- Unproven ideas make me nervous.
- Is it in my strike zone (area of expertise or previous success)?
- Do I see a payoff that makes the opportunity worth it?
- Do I have a good feeling about it?
- I have a fixed small amount I am willing to put into opportunities.

WARNING: The older you get, the less time you have to recover from a failed venture.

BE ALERT FOR VETTED OPPORTUNITIES.

AUGUST 26
PARADIGM SHIFT

*"Positive thinking will let you do everything better
than negative thinking will."*
—*Zig Ziglar*

It just means a change in thinking. It's one of the first things I do when I mentor one of my business partners. I try to start getting into how they think immediately. You've heard me talk about being positive or negative. I've never met anybody successful—really successful—with a negative mindset. Clement Stone believed, "There is little difference in people, but that little difference makes a big difference. The little difference is an attitude. The big difference is whether it is positive or negative."

A paradigm shift means you've got to change the way you're thinking, and as an entrepreneur, let me just give you a few paradigm shifts to consider:

- Negative to Positive
- Pessimistic to Optimistic
- Small Thinking to Big Thinking
- Poverty to Abundance
- Stingy to Generous
- "I can't" to "I can"
- "I won't" to "I will"

One small example of a paradigm shift is when I lose a good employee. I hear it is supposed to be so difficult, but I love hiring employees. I'm always talking about the opportunity to staff up to improve my team, and this allows me to do just that. It's a paradigm shift. So, when we lose somebody, I always share, "This is a great opportunity to get somebody even better."

MAKE A PARADIGM SHIFT.

AUGUST 27
PARTNER INTANGIBLES

I'm a talent scout. I identify people I believe would be a good fit years before they become partners of mine. I just kind of keep a mental Rolodex of people that I've met over the years that I think have the qualities that I like. When I have an idea for a business, the two most important hurdles I want to get over are is there a need for what I am selling, and do I have someone I can partner with who has the expertise, experience, and time to run it for me.

So, the first thing I do after I get an idea is to identify a partner who has an interest in going on this journey with me. I don't run the day-to-day of any of my companies, so I have a mental Rolodex of people that I think would be great partners based on the qualities I like. On average, I start one new business per year, and that requires at least one good new partner that I need to identify and recruit.

What do I look for in partners?

1. **College graduates or military service when possible.** This is not the only fit, but I do believe both candidates, by finishing school or military commitment, have shown perseverance and discipline.

2. **Integrity.** Why is integrity so important? Because I let them run their own division or company. I give them incredible autonomy. They can write checks. Don't get me wrong, I have a CPA in my office and then I have a CPA who oversees my CPA. So, you're not going to rip me off for very long before we catch you, but the point is clear: I want people I can trust.

3. **Likeability.** I want to work with people who I enjoy being around. I don't necessarily need to be buddies with you, but we need to be able to talk. Since I am the one forming the team, why wouldn't I want to surround myself with people I like? It's just common sense.

4. **Great communication skills.** This person is going to be your voice to the team under them, and they need to be able to motivate and articulate the strategies you have established.

5. **Problem solvers.** I do not want to have to solve every problem for you, so you need to be able to solve problems and resolve conflicts.

6. **Leaders.** They have to be able to lead other people. If they can't lead other people, how are they going to run the company?

WHAT QUALITIES WOULD YOU WANT IN A PARTNER?

AUGUST 28

PERSISTENCE

"Ambition is the path to success. Persistence is the vehicle you arrive in."
—Bill Bradley

What is persistence? The definition says it's a continuance on a course, despite obstacles or interferences. This is the life of an entrepreneur: obstacles and interferences.

As entrepreneurs, we don't even see persistence. We don't even view it as something we need to worry about. We know there are obstacles, and we constantly persist. Persistence is the difference between being a success and not being a success.

If you have any intention of building a company of any relevance, you will face obstacles that, if you had known about them in advance, would have made you avoid starting the business in the first place. When I look back over my entrepreneurial journey, I have persisted against obstacles, that, looking back, seemed like climbing Mount Everest. But when I face something extremely daunting, in the back of my mind I always think, "Would my competitors battle through this?" This motivated me because I think the ability to survive through relentless challenges is what separates good from great.

If you want to add one quality to your personal makeup, consider adding persistence. Other than luck, I am not sure if any other quality will serve you better as an entrepreneur.

MAKE PERSISTENCE YOUR DAILY HABIT.

AUGUST 29
PLAY RISK, NOT MONOPOLY

Why do I say you had better be good at the game Risk and not Monopoly? Well, let me share the different strategies used to be successful in both games. In Monopoly (while a great game and I love it), you spend everything you have as fast as you can to own everything in sight and then hope for some good fortune. You don't land on other people's properties, but they land on yours. True or untrue? This is how too many people operate their businesses: spend too much, too fast, expanding and hoping for some luck along the way.

Risk, the game where your objective is to take over the world through battles and expansion, is the opposite. If you expand too quickly and do not fortify your territories, your competition will defeat these vulnerable holdings. In Risk, you learn the value of slow growth and fortification, two critical skills in growing a business.

So back to Monopoly:

You spend too quickly.

The biggest problem entrepreneurs have is that they run out of money because they burn through cash too quickly. Cash has a finite supply in every business, and once it is exhausted, you are out of the game.

You expand too quickly.

You can't expand too quickly because you've got to build to scale. Scale is quite similar to being fortified in that you must be able to withstand an attack. You need to build a sustainable model, as your objective should be to have a durable company.

You depend on luck.

You don't call it luck, but you assume everything is going to go your way, and I have learned that it is just not reality. You need to be able to afford to make a few mistakes along the way.

BE SMART AND PLAY RISK, NOT MONOPOLY.

AUGUST 30
WHAT I DON'T DELEGATE

I would think that at this point in the book, you have drawn the conclusion that I like to delegate, and this is true. However, there are things you cannot and should not delegate most of the time. There is an outlier situation for all of these I am sure.

Eight Situations Owners Shouldn't Delegate:

1. Terminating an employee that is anywhere under your purview of leadership

2. Signing contracts that you have not personally reviewed and authorized

3. Setting the course for a division or company

4. Solving problems with major consequences

5. Audits where your input is critical

6. Decisions that you should be making

7. High-level hiring

8. Taking responsibility for a failure (The buck stops with the owner.)

As I like to say to my team, "I get paid the big money to solve the big problems." The truth is, as the owner, numerous things are my responsibility. I once delegated a worker's comp audit to someone not suited for this and got a year-end bill that still makes me shiver. I don't mind getting advice, but I need to make the final call on the solution to a problem. When making a final call on hiring, if the potential hire is so good, I will only confirm this. Failure always starts at the top.

Leaders set the destination. It is managers who help get you there.

SOMETIMES YOU HAVE TO BE THE ONE
TO TAKE OUT THE TRASH.

AUGUST 31
POSSIBILITY THINKING

*"I am looking for a lot of men who have the infinite capacity
to not know what can't be done."*
—Henry Ford

What if we did it this way? What if we tried it that way? Thomas Edison is said to have failed 10,000 times in his effort to invent the light bulb, but he would tell you he found 10,000 different ways that did not work, implying that this is what actually led to his monumental discovery that we all are grateful for every evening. Innovation is the by-product of possibility thinking.

Possibility thinking is just looking for a different way to do things. What if we did it this way? What if we tried it that way? Are there more ways we can use this product? Are there more markets that our service can be used in?

In one trip to the grocery store, you can see the power of possibility thinking. Cereals that have now become breakfast bars. Cookies that have turned into multiple iterations—smaller versions for snacks, lunch-size servings, in cereal form (this is how you know you're not having a nutritious breakfast) and into ice cream.

Another good example is Post-it notes, as 3M has made a fortune—actually over a billion dollars—with an initial idea that failed, glue that was not strong enough. Someone said, "What if we used it for this?" This question has now been turned into more than six thousand Post-it products.

Just to get you started:

- Can we make it smaller?
- Can we make it bigger?
- Can we mix it with something else?
- What other uses can this product be used for?

Learn to add "What if" to your vocabulary!

CAN WE MODIFY THIS A LITTLE BIT TO EXPAND OUR POTENTIAL USERS?

POWER PHRASES—PART I

"A word fitly spoken is like apples of gold in settings of silver."
—Proverbs

I believe that as an employer, as a leader, there are a number of languages that you'd better have, and money is not the only one. What I mean is, some owners have a default mindset that says, "I give them a paycheck." Implying that this is all I need to do for a worker to do what I ask. Smart leaders know the power of the tongue and how a well-chosen word or cluster of them is the lubricant often needed to get teammates to do more and better.

These are so simple, my friend, but I cannot implore you enough to add these to your leadership quiver. They each cost you nothing but awareness and a little humility.

"Thank you." It's so simple and it should flow like breathing from a leader's mouth. Appreciation for a job well done, or for just being on the team. The list of well-timed "thank yous" can be endless.

"You did a great job." (with specificity)

The secret to this being powerful is not just the phrase "great job," though there are times when that may be sufficient, but I have learned it has a greater effect when you go into detail. I tell you why I think you did a great job. Let me just relate to you a hypothetical situation that shows how I could do this: "Dave, the way you got that proposal done two days ahead of schedule means a lot to our company, and to our client, and also specifically to me as well. The additional ideas and solutions you offered were creative and added a lot of value to your proposal." That is how you communicate, "You did a great job."

"Tell me more." People love to talk about themselves. If somebody starts sharing something with you, get them to talk a little longer. What we as people tend to do is interject our own story. Our story's always a little bit better. We've all done that. So just encourage people to tell you more. Let them have the stage!

"What would you do?" This phrase shows that you think that the person has great insight and that they have more experience in this subject. So, you say to them, "Hey John, what would you do? Susan, what would you do in this situation?" It shows that you value their input.

TRY ONE OF THESE TODAY.

POWER PHRASES—PART II

"**Do you have any ideas?**" This gives somebody a seat at the table. This again shows you value their input.

- **"How can I help you?"** This is the owner or a high-level leader saying to a staff member, a subordinate, "How can I help you?" It shows that they are more than a body in the building. I recently had an employee have a death in the family who was going to drive from Virginia to Florida for the funeral. I knew this person had a vehicle that I would not want to drive or trust for such a trip, so I offered my Mercedes for his family. I meant it, and he knew it. Why? Because it was not the first time I had lent expensive vehicles to staff.

- **"What can we, the company, do better?"** It shows you value their opinion. This is so small a thing, but what a treasure trove of value you can get from this question. Don't ask if you don't want to hear a touch of criticism. Ask it with genuine interest and be open-minded.

- **"We are grateful to have you."** Recently, I was on a job site with an alpha dog. (I am talking about the guy who wears shorts in 25° F weather and swears he is not cold.) This team member is so talented as well. I stopped at a job and when leaving, I just shared how I genuinely appreciated that he works for our company. That I knew he probably got an offer a month to leave and that we were so lucky to have him. He paused and started to wipe his eyes. Yes, even alphas appreciate being wanted and recognized for their value and contribution.

- **"I was wrong."** "I was wrong" is so powerful in the arsenal of a leader. It shows humility. There are times when there's nothing else you can say that will be more effective than telling your staff, your partners, or customer that you were wrong. Be sincere, and this can be a well-timed plane dropping water over a forest fire.

INCORPORATE POWER PHRASES INTO YOUR LEADERSHIP DIALECT.

SEPTEMBER 3
PREEMPTIVE STRIKE

A preemptive strike means we're going to hit you first before you have the chance to hit us.

I want you to think of this regarding starting a business: I want you to take a preemptive strike on your competition with a bold, audacious branding position. As I said, my company's bold statement was, "We are the area's leader in home repairs and projects." That was a bold statement because we hadn't even been open for business. I can tell you that twenty years later, we've won every single magazine award that you could possibly win in our area. We have an A+ rating. We have 20,000 customers. We have eight divisions.

From day one, I grabbed the position that my competition didn't have. None of them dared to say they were going to be the leader, and I expanded that position: not just in home repairs, but in projects.

The point is this, make a preemptive strike. Strike your competition with a bold declaration of where you're going to be in the marketplace with your company. It will force your company to do great things.

***TAKE A PREEMPTIVE STRIKE ON YOUR
COMPETITION.***

SEPTEMBER 4
BOOKS AND PEOPLE

"In my whole life, I have known no wise people (over a broad subject matter area) who didn't read all the time—none, zero."
—Charlie Munger

Charlie Tremendous Jones came and spoke at my university, and I'll never forget what he said. "You are the same today as you will be in five years except for two things: the people you meet and the books you read." That was the most valuable information I would learn in those four years.

The problem was that it took me a decade to decipher the insight.

Reading seems to be the one common denominator high achievers who also happen to be very wealthy share. Billionaires love to read. Warren Buffet spends 80 percent of his day reading. Mark Cuban spends 2–3 hours per day doing the same. Why? Because they know the power of knowledge and it lubricates the mind for great ideas.

In my thirties, I became a convert to the value of reading, and in my forties, I became an evangelist.

Books have expanded my thoughts and given me post-collegiate knowledge that has superseded my paid education a hundredfold.

That's the argument for reading books, but what about when you meet people who change you? I have met people over the years who either inspired me or from whom I learned a lesson. I looked at what they did and thought, "Man, I don't want to do it that way." I witnessed bad decisions resulting in painful and expensive consequences. I have also met so many people that have life stories that inspire me to do more, give more, and be more.

Are you reading great books, and do you meet and spend time with people who make you better?

BOOKS AND PEOPLE PROVIDE INVALUABLE LESSONS.

SEPTEMBER 5
"PROOF OF LIFE"

What I constantly hear from people is, "How do I get the money I need to start a business?" This is what I know: sharp people attract money, and great ideas attract money. If you watch Shark Tank, I will give you their cheat sheet to the type of businesses they invest in: businesses with a proven concept and people who impress them.

Let me drill down on this further. If you can prove that your idea is a winner, you can find investors. First of all, how do you show it is profitable? It is not in a business plan. I would tell you if you wanted my money that I want "proof of life." This is a term the military uses when they kill a terrorist on their Top Ten list. To prove to the world and to their leaders that this person is without question dead, they provide pictures, a DNA test, and, if possible, dental records. They are trying to establish one thing: this person that we killed is who we say they are with no dispute or conspiracy theories.

This is what you need to do: have undeniable proof that this concept, idea, or model you have works. "Works" is defined as "is profitable." You can manufacture the product or provide a service at a cost that leaves an attractive margin of profit. Do you have a unique value proposition to customers? Do you have a proven market ready to buy your product? Investors want to know how many sales you have made so far. What was the profit? What is the potential for this business? How fast can you get it to scale? You need to take your idea off the computer screen and get it tested so you can show "Proof of Life."

Finally, people must like or trust you, since it is more than likely that the person investing in your business will be someone you already know—a family member or friend. You need to establish you are worth investing in, and that they can trust you. There are people I love but to whom I would not give a dime of start-up money. The one-two punch I look for is "Proof of Life" and "Proof of Character." I want a proven, profitable idea in the stewardship of a quality person.

PROVEN IDEAS IN THE HANDS OF A QUALITY PERSON ATTRACT MONEY.

SEPTEMBER 6
LOYALTY

I remember watching the movie Social Network about the founding of Facebook and how Mark Zuckerberg treated his cofounder and friend when he realized that he was onto a billion-dollar idea. I tell you that he was disloyal at every level. I would not have done it. Maybe at a billion dollars, you have no loyalty. Loyalty is my one nonnegotiable quality in someone close to me whether that is a friend or business partner.

Loyalty to me means that no matter what, you are on this ship with me, good or bad. I can count on you. I expect this with my business partners and key employees. I know it is a lot to hope for, but without loyalty, you have no foundation for your business. If I worry every day that I could lose a key person in my organization to a competitor or that they are going out on their own; that would be distracting at the very least.

I give loyalty at a two-for-one return to those who are my friends and business partners. What do I mean? I have a phrase I use, "You have a 'yes' in advance." This means if you are close to me, the answer is yes. Sometimes a close friend would say, "But you don't know what I am going to ask for," to which I would reply, "It does not matter."

My business partners, as I have shared, have check-writing privileges from day one. This was always intended to show them not only are they equal with me in the leadership structure, but also that I trust them. This formula has attracted some of the most talented and sought-after people to my organizations. Even more importantly, it has kept them there.

I also have a funny illustration that I share with my close friends. "I want people that are so loyal to me that if I call you and tell you I think I hit a deer, and you come to the scene of the accident, and tell me, 'Sean, the deer has a baseball hat on,' you would bury the body with me." Clearly a joke, but you get the point.

LOYALTY IS A SADLY RARE QUALITY, BUT IT IS THE GLUE OF ANY VALUABLE RELATIONSHIP.

SEPTEMBER 7
REFLECTIVE THINKING

"Reflective thinking is like a crock pot of the mind and encourages your thoughts to simmer until they're done, then you go back and keep looking at them."
—John Maxwell

This is when you reflect at the end of the week and ask, "What would I do differently? Had I known that what would I have done differently? What do-over would I like to have?" This is where sometimes you have to send some text apologies, for example. Reflective thinking makes you ask yourself, "Knowing what I now know, what did I learn? How can I apply it?" This is the learning part.

I like what Elon Musk says, "I think it's very important to have a feedback loop, where you're constantly thinking about what you've done and how you could be doing it better. I think that's the single best piece of advice — constantly think about how you could be doing things better and questioning yourself."

Reflective thinking allows mistakes to be one-time events. Failures become life lessons you now share with others. You have a wealth of axioms learned through your rearview mirror.

TAKE TIME EACH WEEK TO DO
REFLECTIVE THINKING.

SEPTEMBER 8
REINVENTING

There are times and situations where your business needs to make a shift; it needs to reinvent itself. Apple did that. It was a computer company, then it went into music with the iPod and iTunes and then reinvented the laptop computer with the iPad. Now it is the largest cell phone manufacturer in the world. That is what I call repositioning. Sometimes your company is positioned in a crowded lane where everybody has a similar value proposition. Like Apple, you may discover a new product line that has more potential than your current lead products.

Toyota reinvented themselves from their only position of offering a modestly-priced economy car that was in a tug of war year in and year out with Honda and Nissan for market share, to make the bold move into luxury cars with Lexus. I like both Apple and Toyota's strategy: you keep your original product and introduce something completely new to the marketplace. Amazon followed this same formula, starting with books as its sole product line, and now offering anything you could ever want.

Sometimes you have to stop, pause, look at the marketplace, look at what your competitors are doing, and really consider reinventing yourself. It's very effective if you think it through and have a long-term strategy. Sometimes it is your only choice for survival.

DECIDE IF YOU NEED TO REINVENT YOURSELF.

SEPTEMBER 9
WALKING ON WATER

I have heard it said, "The problem with walking on water is no one can follow you." The principle is that it is hard to follow or even relate to someone who seems to do no wrong. Often, we as leaders feel the need to share our endless victories—and yes, they can inspire confidence—but I have learned it is equally as important to share stories of failure, struggle, and inadequacy.

I am a big fan of stories. I believe they are a powerful tool to bring others to your way of thinking. Sharing your stories of struggle may often inspire your team. We are all aware of Nelson Mandela but only because of his twenty-seven years in prison. Many would love to have his legacy, but I think that few would want his lengthy stay in Robben Island prison. In our struggles, we gain something that cannot be taught by anything else. Struggle creates a resilience that success does not bestow.

My advice today is to add a few stories of struggle and failure in your motivational toolbox. Sometimes this is the perfect instrument to bring a team member alongside you. I have found older team members who see my current financial state as "luck" or even worse, think that I only achieved it because of their toil. Once an employee told me that it was he who provided what I had. I quickly had to let him know that my big house was built well before his arrival. Yes, I can be petty when pushed. I just wanted him to know there were endless struggles, failures, and a few all-in bets before his arrival.

STORIES OF STRUGGLE AND FAILURE ARE WELL-HONED TOOLS IN THE HANDS OF A LEADER.

SEPTEMBER 10
BIG IDEA MYTH

I recently spoke at a college business class where I asked, "Do you feel like you need to have a big idea to move forward with starting a business?" Nearly all of the class, which was fairly large, raised their hands. I have yet to have my "aha" moment in business. I do not have a nine-figure business yet, nor one on the New York Stock Exchange, but my radar for finding profitable businesses rarely fails me.

I see opportunities all the time because I see life through the lens of an entrepreneur. Once you have hit gold a few times, you know the soil to look in. This is the lens I look through every day that alerts me to viable businesses:

Is there a need that no one is filling?

I tried to hire someone to do something and it was like trying to hire a one-eyed leprechaun.

Is there a problem that I believe we can solve?

You experienced a problem and you solved it. Tommy John found problems with underwear; waistband rolled over, etc. Underwear has been around for a long time. They decided to improve it based on the problems they experienced. Now they have taken a three-pack of underwear for $10 to one pair at $32.

Is there a captive audience?

You have a large audience who love something, so feed them what they want. My wife loves her Jeep and received a catalog with over five hundred products to modify her Jeep.

Is there a successful model with no competition?

You copy what works with a new value proposition. Example: Target vs Walmart. Both are very similar. Target niches out the buyer who wants more higher-end selections.

Have I had a great experience I can offer where I live?

You go to visit someone in another city and experience something that is not offered in your area.

Have I had a poor experience that I can improve?

You have a poor buying experience and learn from it.

Is there a niche that is not being served?

Big and Tall is a great example —this became a gold mine.

LOOK THROUGH THE LENS OF AN ENTREPRENEUR.

SEPTEMBER 11
SACRIFICE

"You aren't going to find anybody that's going to be successful without making a sacrifice."
—Lou Holtz

What sacrifices would you make for your company? What did you give up initially when you started your business? Is there something you're willing to give up now if it would grow your organization again? Would you give back 25 percent of your income to invest in infrastructure to allow your business to provide better speed of delivery? Would you give up half your salary to bring on that one missing team member who can provide expertise and experience in an area your business lacks?

Sacrifice is what you are willing to give up. I'm surprised when I work with businesses and I see what the business owner is making, and then what everybody else is making, and then they're surprised that they don't have a great staff. They have no strong leaders and are surprised they cannot expand their business.

I remember year two of one of my businesses that I still own, and which now pays me more than a sitting president earns, and in which I now work less than five hours per week. That year I forfeited my profit to bring on a tremendous partner. This sacrifice paid me back a million. I knew we needed someone with expertise in our industry, as we were growing faster than my level of understanding. I have continued to forfeit my salary to bring on great team members or improve our customer experience with better infrastructure.

If you want to be a successful entrepreneur, what are you willing to sacrifice?

SUCCESSFUL ENTREPRENEURS SACRIFICE FOR THEIR BUSINESSES.

SEPTEMBER 12
SALES PITCH

I've been involved in a few start-ups over the last few months, and I like to be involved in the sales pitch because if it can't sell me, I don't think it's going to work on anybody else. Whoever is trying to get me to be involved in a start-up, is always asked, "Sell me the product, sell me the service," and they get nervous. There needs to be an organized sales pitch just like there needs to be an elevator pitch.

I'm just going to give you a couple of things to consider in your sales pitch. You need to create a need or want. You need something that makes the person say, "I wish I had this." There's got to be something that gets them interested.

Can you solve a problem? Did you experience a problem and it caused you to create a solution? People love personal triumphs. Listen to commercials. They are often based on a solution discovered. The radio is littered with tax resolution or timeshare cancellation companies. These are problems that many others face, for which their founders discovered a solution. Their pitch is personal. They create empathy by sharing that they know what you are going through, but good news—they have the answer.

Next, you need to create trust somewhere in this because trust makes people believe that your product or your service can deliver on what you promise. Finally, you need to overcome skepticism. This may be through your experience, credentials, or customer testimonies.

I've given you just a few things to build a good sales pitch around:

- Draw attention to a need or want.
- Solve a problem.
- Share a story.
- Create trust.
- Overcome skepticism.

WHAT'S YOUR SALES PITCH?

SEPTEMBER 13
OPPORTUNITY COSTS

I have spent countless hours illustrating this principle to my business partners when they first come aboard. I share with them that we have a finite amount of resources, staff, and days to work. I want every opportunity that we take to have the highest payoff. Because I have spent years creating dashboards, I know numbers I like and numbers I don't. When I am offered an opportunity that may seem good, I have to weigh it against every other possible opportunity.

In his book *Originals*, Adam Grant gives a telling story of opportunity costs when he recounts how in 2008, a few college students approached him about investing in their eyewear start-up. It was a simple concept; fashionable eyeglasses at a fraction of the price sold online. He failed to invest, and this company, Warby Parker, went on to be a billion-dollar company. Did Adam Grant lose any of his money? No, he didn't invest, but he could have made a fortune.

I don't agree to take on work just to keep people busy, and this is what too many young service businesses do. The argument is some work is better than no work. Or I just want to know we have work over the winter if it is a seasonal business. This is a big mistake. For one, you need to know your daily operating costs for your business and the desired profit you want to make each day your doors are open. You never compromise by doing work where you make no profit. When you lower your prices for a client, you can never get them to pay your preferred pricing. Once you give a child candy, they don't want vegetables.

Money that comes in but has no profit is like moving money from my right pocket to my left. It is all show and no go. I have the same thoughts toward my investments. I have limited resources, so I need my investments to pay the best rate of return for the level of risk I am willing to take.

In closing, you have a limited amount of resources and yet countless opportunities. With experience and discernment, you will learn which opportunities are best.

DEVELOP A NUMBER THAT EVERY OPPORTUNITY
NEEDS TO PAY OUT.

SEPTEMBER 14
SELF-CONFIDENCE IS A SECRET WEAPON

You've got to have self-confidence; there's no substitute for it. And yes, sometimes you have to fake it early on. Success and experience breed self-confidence. Don't ever let failures destroy your confidence; this is common. Remember, we learn from failures. They are only temporary; they do not define you. When you are around someone with confidence, you can tell. They give off an energy that says, "I can handle this."

Self-confidence:

- Will whisper in the ear of the entrepreneur and lets them do something big.

- Tells investors, "This person is going to build something great and I want to be a part of it."

- Tells potential team members, "We're going to build something great and you can be a part of it."

- Wins over customers, "We're going to offer something great, and you're not going to want to do business with anyone else."

- Must first start with you believing in yourself. It will then become contagious, attracting others who want to invest and participate in your vision. The result will be a great company that reflects the confidence of its founder. This confidence has resulted in delivering great products and services to its customers. Why? Because when you talk a good game, you have to deliver.

I really want to encourage you to ask yourself, "Do I have self-confidence?" Not arrogance, just an inner belief that you can accomplish what you have set out to do. That you give off an energy that makes others want to take this journey with you.

DO YOU HAVE SELF-CONFIDENCE?

PITCHING YOUR IDEA TO AN INVESTOR

First quality of your investor: do they have the money to invest? Not every family member or friend has disposable money to invest in your venture. I said disposable because any money put in a start-up can be lost. We need to be clear: the statistics for a start-up succeeding are not a good bet.

Second, do you have a relationship with this person that gives you the benefit of the doubt? They like you and have known you and your parents, etc. You probably have noticed I am assuming you will be pitching this to someone in your orbit: friend, family member, or acquaintance. As a seasoned entrepreneur, I would encourage you to practice your presentation. It needs to be concise and to the point.

Robert Herjavec lends advice for a pitch, "You have ninety seconds if you're lucky. If you can't make your point persuasively in that time, you've lost the chance for impact. Facts and figures are important, but it's not the only criteria, you must present in a manner that generates expertise and confidence."

Pitching Your Idea to Friends, Family, and Acquaintances:

- **Proof of Life:** Show them with valid support your idea has merit.

- **Proof of Character:** You are worth investing in.

- **Return on Investment:** Gives them a return worth the risk.

- **Sell Your Vision:** Inspire them to be a part of something great.

- **Cheer for You:** You need to be someone they want to root for.

If you're pitching your idea to a bank, you'd better have a business plan with questions answered. I would ask them in advance what they will want so you don't waste your time. In most cases, it's a personal loan that you will fully guarantee. And if you have any assets they can use as collateral, they will prefer that. They are loaning you money and honestly don't care whether the business works because they will get their money back.

WOULD I INVEST IN THE IDEA THAT
I JUST PITCHED?

SEPTEMBER 16
VALUE IN ASSOCIATIONS

A simple way to build credibility and to learn more about your industry is to join associations. These are also a great way to learn what is working for others within your industry. They may also offer discounts on products and professional services you may need.

Associations usually have a logo or a seal that can be used to show your affiliation, which is a good marketing bonus. Using these association logos in your advertising gives credibility. The more support you have when starting a business, the better, so being a part of an association offers no downsides.

Talk to other business owners in your area and industry. Find out what associations they are actively involved in. Ask which associations they find worthwhile and why.

General associations like the Chamber of Commerce may be good for networking and sharing local marketing tips. However, industry-specific associations might help with labor recruitment, training, getting involved in lobbying, and keeping up on changes to regulations and other important industry news.

Additionally, associations can provide a social network of like-minded people with similar experiences. As a boss and manager of employees, you may feel isolated—especially when you are just getting started. Keith Ashmus, the chairman of the National Small Business Association explains, "[Business owners] often can't talk to their employees about what concerns them, and they need to talk to a peer who is not a competitor. An association is a great way to find those connections."

Twenty years ago, our company joined the Better Business Bureau (BBB), and I would venture to say this one decision has paid for itself possibly a million times over. At the time, it just seemed like the thing to do since we were a service company and this association would tell customers we were committed to a higher standard. We have had an A+ rating for well over a decade, and there is not a week that goes by where someone does not tell us that this is why they used our company.

WHAT ASSOCIATIONS WOULD GIVE YOU
MORE CREDIBILITY?

SEPTEMBER 17
TASTE IT BEFORE YOU SERVE IT

Tesla unveiled its electric truck this week with what was to have been bulletproof windows as its example of durability. However, its well-attended launch, with cameras recording, did not go the way its founder had hoped. The person on stage next to founder Elon Musk during this well-hyped launch tossed a metal ball at the driver's side window only to have it shatter. He was caught on the live microphone expressing his surprise with a phrase that needed to be bleeped out. It was a priceless example of not tasting the food before you serve it. This is a billion-dollar company, and no one thought to shoot the glass with a gun prior to this demonstration? Yes, I said gun because the softball pitch I saw on TV did not have anything close to the force of a gun. I say this because even if this initial demonstration had withstood the projectile, my question would have been, "You are touting it as bulletproof, why did you not shoot a bullet at it?"

It was just a disaster at every level. To make it worse—and I did not think it could get worse—the announcer tossed a second object at the rear window to only have the same embarrassing thing happen. I am no Elon Musk, Tesla's billionaire genius founder, but I know this for sure: before I introduce a product—and well before I bring the press to my public event—I would have shot that glass with everything but a cannon, and for fun, I am sure I would have tried that once or twice.

I learned this simple point early on: before something is available for public consumption, you test every possible link in the chain. The week before a business launch I, personally—yes, me, not my staff—test everything. I go to the website and try every page, link, email, etc. I call the phone number and make sure it goes to who it should. I meet with my staff and ask them to go over how we have the first day planned. Is it staffed adequately? I confirm we can deliver what we intend to without a hiccup. I beg my team to let me know if there is anything we may have missed. If we have a marketing campaign, I speak with whoever we have advertising with to review the commercial—yes, I want to see it again. This is where you debunk Murphy's Law because if you do not, something will go wrong. My simple advice is to test every possible link of the chain.

TEST AND RETEST EVERY LINK OF THE CHAIN.

STAFFING UP

Your ability to build a team and create teamwork is critical as a leader, but specifically, **how do you build a team within your organization?**

Know the critical positions needed.

So, when I'm going to start a business, I always say, "What is it going to take to open the doors?" You start with just that. So, you start with the critical positions that you absolutely must have to open the doors for your business. This is the list of your mandatory positions.

Know exactly what their responsibilities are.

Define exactly what it is you want them to do.

Define your expectations.

Define what a win looks like. Give them a target that will exceed your expectations. You rarely get more than what you ask for.

Know the intangibles you like.

I want people with a can-do attitude. I want people who, if I ask them to sit on the corner of our building and count cars because I'm thinking about building a bridge over that road, will sit there and come back to me the next day and say, "There were 4,745 cars, boss."

Have a salary cap.

You need to have a position cap and a company cap.

Know how to locate and hire people.

I played golf the other morning and I watched the head professional mow the grass himself because they couldn't attract somebody who could perform this simple task. Sadly, I saw it repeat itself for months to follow. Finally, I offered to run an ad and interview for them.

STAFFING UP IS A CRITICAL AREA IN BUILDING YOUR BUSINESS.

STAY HUNGRY

"For me, life is continuously being hungry."
—Arnold Schwarzenegger

Steve Jobs said in a commencement address, "Stay hungry," and as we all know; Steve Jobs was never satisfied. He had a never-ending hunger to satisfy customers and to grow his products. It's been said, "A hungry dog runs faster." I have also heard this phrase a little differently when referring to how hard you work before becoming a champion. When you sleep on silk sheets, you're less likely to get up at 5 a.m. to train.

To keep your hunger for success:
- Always want to grow your bottom line.
- Always desire to add more customers.
- Always strive to grow your team.

The list is endless, but you need to have the hunger you had when you started the business. It was that desire that allowed you to do what was required to get it off the ground. That intensity needs to stay with you, or you become complacent and lazy. I tell my team "We start every Monday as if we have no customers and no money." We start over every week working to be the best company.

BE HUNGRY, STAY HUNGRY.

STRATEGY

"Without strategy, execution is aimless."
—Morris Chang

One of the more famous Saturday Night Live skits from the last few decades is arguably the portrayal of a supposed debate between presidential candidates George W. Bush and Al Gore. In the skit, each candidate is asked to "sum up, in a single word, the best argument for [his] candidacy." Riffing off Bush's reputation for mispronouncing words, the skit portrays him as saying that he's going to win because of "strategery."

Although that is a humorous example, *strategy* is, in fact, one of the most important skills for successful entrepreneurs. It is easy to say, and believe, that your idea will succeed, but creating the battle plan is a lot harder. As author Brian Tracy explains: "Your ability to plan well, in advance of acting, is a measure of your overall competency." He also cites the wise words of Alex MacKenzie: "Action without planning is the cause of every failure."

I have also learned that having a grand vision will excite people for a moment, but it is your strategy to make it a reality that will bring others alongside you. The simple way to create a strategy is first to determine the target. What is the outcome you want? What resources (capital, staff, expertise, etc.) will be required? What actions will need to be done? What is a realistic timeline? What obstacles do you need to plan for? You can modify your strategy to your objective, but don't go into battle without a plan.

STRATEGY IS WHAT MAKES BIG IDEAS A REALITY.

SEPTEMBER 21
WHY I PARTNER

I think partnerships are the easiest way to make money in business. There is something about the synergy and the exponential growth that partnerships can create. I have often said, "I would rather have 50 percent of a lot than 100 percent of a little."

I create brands, as marketing is my strength. I develop systems within our business, and finally, I have a very large high-end client base. These are the three pillars that I have most recently used to bring on partners. I have harnessed the power of six extraordinarily talented people who wanted to partner with me in one of my larger companies. They all make incredible money; six figures that they would never make doing what they were doing prior to partnering. I know what I bring to the table and I know what they bring to the table.

My strategy is basically to franchise my companies from the inside out. My core businesses are juggernauts with tremendous room for growth, but I cannot, nor do I want to, do this alone. I constantly saw all these opportunities where, with the right partner leading the charge, we could make our footprint.

As I have shared, a partnership requires each person to bring something critical for survival—and hopefully growth—to the table. I encourage you to embrace the power in partnerships. It allows you to seize opportunities that one person just does not have the time to effectively exploit.

When people ask me why I love to partner, recognizing their hesitations, I say, "When things are going great, it is so much more fun having somebody to share it with, and when things are awful, it is so much easier having somebody to share the burden with."

***CONSIDER ADDING A PARTNER IN YOUR
NEXT VENTURE.***

SEPTEMBER 22
TAKING ACTION

"Dreams don't work unless you take action."
—Roy T. Bennett

Taking action is the major difference between successful entrepreneurs and would-be entrepreneurs. I constantly hear people at seminars, or just in everyday life, who share with me a great idea they had. They say, "I had this amazing idea; it was such a profitable idea," and then when I press them and ask, "What did you do with it?" they say, "Well, I haven't done anything with it yet. I'm thinking about doing something with it, I'm not so sure it would work."

I have a weekly poker game where all the participants own a small business. When I look back over my entrepreneurial life and at my friends who now own successful businesses, I don't think any of our initial start-up ideas were guaranteed home runs. They were, in the mind of the person initiating the enterprise, good ideas that they each hoped, with some supporting reason, had a chance to be special. That is all you ever have: an idea you think might work. It is the taking action part that brings everything to life. Without action, it's just a talking point at a family reunion. My dad still believes he came up with the Jiffy Lube idea. This is a go-to conversation piece for him.

So, the biggest difference between being a successful entrepreneur and being somebody who just talks about it is that you need to take action. Take action on great ideas and watch your ideas turn into profit. I like what Eckhart Tolle said: "Any action is often better than no action, especially if you have been stuck."

SUCCESSFUL ENTREPRENEURS TAKE ACTION.

SEPTEMBER 23
JUSTIFY YOUR WORTH

My go-to business model is to bring on partners who do the heavy lifting once the start-up has been launched. When bringing a partner into one of my businesses, I don't usually ask for any capital, just their expertise and time. They will do the day-to-day heavy lifting once the start-up has been launched. I am very involved in the front end, and then become a shadow partner in most cases. I am always accessible and available to talk and do carry a few responsibilities moving forward.

I believe I still need to continue to bring value to my partners, as I take nothing less than 50 percent profit of anything in which I am involved. In twenty-five years, I have yet to have a partner tell me I am not worth what I receive. I joke like Liam Neeson in Taken, "I have a few unique skills." I consider my two unique skills to be my ability to see opportunities others don't see and getting ideas off the ground. Recruiting a team and marketing are the ongoing talents that I continue to bring to any of my ventures.

To continue to be worthwhile, you need to bring at least a few of the things listed below to the table.

- Capital
- Resources (real estate, credit, etc.)
- Experience
- Advice
- Encouragement
- Direction
- Leveraging relationships
- Leveraging your assets
- Being accessible and available

CONTINUE TO BRING VALUE TO THE TABLE.

SEPTEMBER 24
WHO WANTS TO BE A MILLIONAIRE?

There used to be a popular TV game show called *Who Wants to Be a Millionaire* that, at the time, offered contestants the chance to win a million dollars. It was wildly successful. Have you ever met someone who would not want to be a millionaire? Sadly, there are far too many people who believe this can only happen by winning it somehow, either on a game show or with a lottery ticket.

Growing up less than rich, I knew from very early on that I never wanted to lack money. I am not sure I had a set number, but I did not want to live "paycheck to paycheck." That was a popular term. Growing up I heard, "It takes money to make money," or "Only the rich can afford that." So, I decided to be rich. It is not as hard as you may think it is to accomplish.

As I shared, I speak quite often at colleges. There is always a question and answer period, and without fail, someone will ask me the secret or formula to being rich, successful or both. I quickly reply the two are very different, but I go on to share my formula for achieving financial security, which is what people want and just assume a million dollars is the base amount needed.

First, your income, your money earned, must exceed your expenditures. I encourage students from the very first paycheck they receive upon graduation to pay themselves a "wealth tax." This is 10 percent of every penny you make over your lifetime. This discipline will make you a millionaire. The average income in America is about $50,000 per year. If you put $5,000 in a retirement plan and never increase it—but also never touch it—receiving the stock market's average 9.8 percent annual return, you would have over $2 million when you retire.

The next secret: debt is not your friend. Learn to "live at the speed of cash," preaches Dave Ramsey, financial expert and the greatest evangelist of telling and showing people how to live debt-free. If you are in debt, work overtime and pay down one credit card at a time with your smallest debt being your initial target, and then apply that amount to the next, and so forth.

Finally, owning two homes is the secret to real estate. Buy your first home and do not sell it to buy your second home. If you own two homes at retirement age, you have in most cases another million dollars in assets, not to mention no mortgage payment and a rental income in retirement.

This is my bulletproof plan to be a millionaire and more:
- Pay yourself a Wealth Tax of 10 percent.
- Live at the speed of cash—avoid debt other than mortgage.
- Have two real estate purchases.

START BY PAYING YOURSELF A WEALTH TAX.

SEPTEMBER 25
THE LAW OF ATTRACTION

Jack Canfield gives a simple but accurate description of this law when he says, "The law of attraction states that whatever you focus on, think about, read about, talk about intensely, you're going to attract more of into your life."

Among many highly successful people over the years, there is a strong belief first made famous by Andrew Carnegie when he shared it with author Napoleon Hill, that says what you think about—your predominant thoughts—you will attract. Negative people attract negative things. So, think about it for a second: what are your predominant thoughts? Do you focus on good or bad?

We have seen the negative before when people will say, "Bad things happen in threes," or "I never have any good luck." We have experienced it when we purchase or have a desire for a certain car, and then we start seeing them everywhere. We become hyper-alert to this. I do believe in this law and have seen it work without fail. I will share one example, although I have countless more examples within my companies.

One of my core businesses is supposed to be a seasonal business, which means that over the winter, people are told work slows down dramatically, and they hold on for dear life. This never made sense to me, as I believed we could "attract" different work (interior) during the cold and snowy periods. I began this dramatic change in mindset over the summer, sharing with my team, "This winter is going to be great, as we have so much interior work coming in." I said this endlessly, and yes, last January, we had more work in the coldest month than we had during our peak months. I made more profit over the winter than at any other time in the history of the company. I changed my mindset and that of everyone around me to expect a great winter, and I then took action to make it happen by marketing interior work and getting clients to book ahead.

I slipped in the second part of the law of attraction that when you think about something and are talking about its positive outcome all the time, it should remind you to take massive action on what you want to happen.

YOU ATTRACT YOUR MOST DOMINANT THOUGHTS.

SEPTEMBER 26
THINKING LIKE A SMALL BUSINESS

Let me share with you what I have learned over the years about small-business owners who don't think big. They get trapped thinking and acting like a small business.

Hiring friends and family

You need people with certain skill sets and certain industry understandings. You need to hire the best people, not just people you can hire because they are available, such as friends and family.

Treating customers like family

The problem with treating customers like family is that you tend to be paid like family, and you know what that is like: you get little or nothing.

Having a survival mentality

Many small businesses are just glad to open their doors. At the end of another year, they share, "We did it again; we survived another year."

Having one bank account

This practice does not lend itself to good fiduciary responsibility. You need to have reserve accounts, tax accounts, etc. It is not a good idea to be treating your business' finances like a general household fund. At the very least, have reserve accounts.

Not having a system in place

There are no systems in place or processes by which you operate. I encourage you to run your business in such a way that if you had to leave for ninety days, your business could run without you.

Being a "word-of-mouth" business

Word-of-mouth customers should make up a portion—not all—of your business. Even the largest companies still advertise. They still want to attract new customers, protect their market share, and introduce new products.

Having a week-to-week mentality

Many small businesses don't set goals or have a vision for the company. They have a survival mentality instead of being forward-thinking.

STOP THINKING AND ACTING LIKE A
SMALL BUSINESS.

SEPTEMBER 27
PERSONAL SCOREBOARD

"Can't manage what you can't measure."
—Peter Drucker

Management expert Peter Drucker advises that you cannot know whether you are successful unless success is defined and tracked. I am competitive, and I know you cannot improve on things you do not measure. I want to set daily and weekly targets that lead to me being successful and accomplishing the big goals I have set.

Anyone who has ever run a marathon will tell you that in their training and on the day of the actual race, they have mile markers they wish to hit in a given time. I have learned to create a weekly personal scorecard. I have always believed that if you win the week, you will win the month and, of course, win the year. I share and teach this principle to all of my business partners.

When I score my week, these are the critical mile markers I want to hit:

· Did I generate income? (I do not work for free.)

· How much passive income did I generate?

· What major steps did I take toward accomplishing my big goals?

· What was the big domino I knocked down this week?

· Did I meet my savings/investment goals?

· Did I do the daily habits that make me successful?

Again, the principle is simple: you will be inclined to do the things you hold yourself accountable for. I have learned doing weekly not monthly scorecards works best for me. I can recover from a bad week, but a bad month? That is never acceptable.

HOLD YOURSELF ACCOUNTABLE
WITH A WEEKLY PERSONAL SCORECARD.

SEPTEMBER 28
THRIVING UNDER PRESSURE

"Winning comes down to who can execute under pressure."
—Billie Jean King

I once had a business partner who would go home and declare some random sickness that prevented him from coming back to work when we faced a difficult situation. With no exaggeration, I could count on him being a no-show during any challenging time our company faced. This cost him credibility with our team and because it forced me to take on the storm by myself, I quickly got my sea legs.

As I have said, I get paid the big money because I can make big decisions when faced with them, and they normally come under duress. The biggest decision I generally have to make is navigating our company out of a storm or one that might be brewing. What I have learned is your staff, if not the owner, will rarely deliver you from a battle. They will never have a battle plan. That is not their job. And I doubt they are making as much money as you are, so their motivation is limited.

Specifically, in the first couple of years of starting a business, this is where a lot of people fail. They just can't handle the pressure. They just crumble. This often forces them into a default setting that believes the smaller the company, the less stress. However, the smaller the company, the less revenue. Often, they are more fragile and have fewer people to share the burden. Loyal employees will help you scoop water out of the boat if you ask.

If you want to be a successful entrepreneur, you need to thrive under pressure. Yes, it is an acquired skill, but learn it. You need the pressure to make you better. Bryan Cranston lends support for my thoughts with this: "To me, character in a person is judged by the decisions that are made under pressure."

REMEMBER, IT IS PRESSURE THAT CREATES A DIAMOND.

SEPTEMBER 29
TIME MANAGEMENT

I am very selfish with my time. I know it is a limited resource, and I spend it based on:

- Tasks that must get done
- Access that I have granted (business partners, people I mentor, etc.)
- Goals that I have set
- Relationships that I treasure
- Priorities based on my values

I get so many demands for my time. One secret I learned years ago is to set all my meetings at a quarter till the hour, and why do I do this? I found that when I set a meeting at 3:00 p.m., the person just assumes that they have one hour of my time. But by making it at a quarter 'til the hour, they get the idea that they only have fifteen minutes of my time.

When the hour strikes 2:00 p.m., and I am in a 1:45 p.m. meeting, my secretary walks in and says, "You have something else scheduled." I then have the choice to extend the meeting or reschedule to discuss further.

Another secret I have used to eliminate—or at the very least shorten—meetings and keep them on target is that before the meeting, I ask the person to email me in three sentences or less what the main purpose of this meeting is. What do you want to cover or the outcome to be? After reviewing this, I often realize I am just going to be getting sold something I do not want or need. At the very least, I go in more prepared and able to bring more value to the other party.

**MANAGE YOUR TIME WELL; IT IS A
LIMITED RESOURCE.**

SPEED OF TRUST

"Trust is equal parts character and competence. You can look at any leadership failure, and it's always a failure of one or the other."
—Stephen Covey

The *Speed of Trust* by Stephen Covey is a must-read. What he's talking about in this book is how trustworthy people and trustworthy companies actually make so much more money because when somebody has great confidence in them, the deal goes at warp speed. It says, "if somebody doesn't trust you, and you don't give an air of confidence, they're not going to move forward with you." This book establishes the pillars of what every good business owner and company should make a priority building from day one.

You constantly need to evaluate if your company is trustworthy. Do you constantly deliver as the owner of the company? The whole concept is to be trustworthy, and it just means that people believe what you say and equally as important, that you have the competence to deliver on what you have promised.

Consider being trustworthy. Your clients, your customers, your staff, they'll all have great confidence that when you say you're going to do something, you're going to do it. What I have learned about trust is that it takes time and a few wins to earn, and far less to lose.

TRUST ATTRACTS CUSTOMERS.

OCTOBER 1
DEMAND URGENCY

"If I came in to recruit your son, I would tell you, your wife and your son that I will be the most demanding coach your son can play for."
—**Bobby Knight**

Have you ever met certain people that just don't have a high gear? They don't do anything faster than necessary? When you're starting a business or growing a business, there will be key periods where urgency is required, so urgency will need to be demanded.

You as the owner may be the only person right now who can create that urgency. It doesn't mean that everything runs at some crazy pace. It just means that you're aware that there are certain projects and certain times when things need to be done immediately, and you have the unique quality to create this momentum within your staff to get them to do that.

There are times when I make a demand, not a request. Some deadlines must be met no matter how challenging they are. In the start-up phase and in critical times throughout the life of the company, you will have to play the demand and urgency card. "I need this done, and I need it done by this date. Yes, I know it will take eighteen-hour days for a time, but I need us to step up to this challenge." You can't do this every week, but once or twice a year, it's not a bad idea to stretch your team. This is the only way you will know what their capacity is. You will also find out who your most valuable players are.

PERIODICALLY DEMAND URGENCY.

OCTOBER 2
POWER OF A TESTIMONY

I encourage you to collect customer testimonials like a child collects baseball cards. OK, in my day, collecting baseball cards was quite popular. Used well, testimonials from your customers will move potential customers to buy. When I become aware of a positive or unique customer experience through a comment they made, whether to my staff or me or in a survey, we reach out and get that comment memorialized. We now have a collection of testimonials from nearly every demographic as well nearly every "false belief" a customer may have that is preventing them from doing business.

Our average customer spends $2,000 and some over $100,000, so it is not surprising that they have skepticism. A testimonial that addresses their false belief is just what the doctor ordered.

I have over twenty radio or TV testimonials that we drop throughout the year, so at some point, we will have addressed every objection a potential customer may have. We will also include an applicable testimonial in an attachment with all our estimates. This overcomes what would normally be the follow-up email, "Can you give me some references?"

Some tips on collecting and using testimonials:

Create a system where you become aware of customer comments and experiences. When I started the company, we mailed out feedback surveys. Obviously now you can email or use social media, but the point is the same. We have a system to get feedback from our customers.

Identify your target customer so you know which testimonial will have the greatest impact. Example: older clients want to hear older clients' experiences. There is a reason why Pat Boone is doing twenty different product endorsements. I am joking, but you get the point.

What are the false beliefs that keep customers from buying from you? Every industry, product, or service has different false beliefs. You want your testimonials to identify with and overcome each potential false belief your customers have.

START STOCKPILING TESTIMONIALS.

OCTOBER 3
PERSONAL EXPERIENCE

"The best businesses come from people's bad personal experiences.
If you just keep your eyes open, you're going to find something that
frustrates you, and then you think, 'well I could maybe do it better than
it's being done,' and there you have a business."
—Richard Branson

The common denominator 90 percent of my start-ups have had is that they come from having had a poor experience trying either to locate a company to do something I need done or finding one that does it as well as I require or they have led me to believe that they can produce. If you just stay alert to your personal experiences—good or bad—you will bump into a potential start-up every year.

You may go on vacation, or visit a friend, and experience a restaurant, concept, or service experience that takes you by storm. I felt this way the first time I had Sweet Frogs frozen yogurt and Panera Bread. At the time, they were unique concepts, and I knew immediately that owning one of these franchises would be a hit. Years later, my suspicions were spot on. I look to start a franchise—not buy one—but purchasing a franchise is a very safe way to begin your entrepreneurial journey.

My frustrations with finding a handyman started me on an obsession with service companies as they fit my comfort zone: no more than $10,000 to get in; no inventory; and easy to carve out a niche against the competition. Build a brand with great marketing and overdeliver. That is a foolproof plan for any service company and will be a day's lesson in the pages to come. I have rinsed and repeated this formula more than a handful of times.

My newest start-up I am plotting grows from my frustration in trying to find a company that not only launches a book but monetizes the words, image, and influence of its author. Wasn't that a good tagline? You will see that coming soon as another business in the stable that resulted from experiencing a personal frustration.

KEEP YOUR ANTENNA UP FOR GREAT AND
BAD EXPERIENCES.

OCTOBER 4
VISIONEERING

We are constantly told that entrepreneurs need to have a big vision. They must be able to cast a vision that gets others excited. This is all true, but I would encourage you to master visioneering. Wiktionary defines *visioneering* as "the process of making a vision or a dream a reality, building a concept into a workable application." Pastor and leadership expert Andy Stanley titled one of his early books *Visioneering* and went through the process of discerning a vision worth chasing and the process of bringing it to reality.

A vision without a plan is a wish, so how do we become proficient at visioneering?

- We start with a goal or dream that seems almost impossible.
- We create a plan for how to accomplish this.
- We identify who we will need to help us.
- We list the resources that will be required.
- We create a timeline that makes real sense.

It begins to look like a treasure map. If we follow it, there is a good chance that we will, in fact, achieve the nearly impossible. I have learned that every great vision will have some help that will come from places I could never have planned for. Visioneering values the "how we are going to do this" as much as the aspirational vision itself.

BE AS PASSIONATE ABOUT HOW WE WILL DO IT.

OCTOBER 5
BETTER THAN YESTERDAY

I was recently listening to a college football player who shared this phrase that one of his coaches used to motivate the team. It is the mindset of anyone who desires a great achievement. "Better than yesterday" should be our goal: to be personally better than we were yesterday, and for our organizations to be better than yesterday. Let me list some companies that failed to become better than they were yesterday: Blockbuster Video, Countrywide Mortgage, Circuit City, Toys R Us, and Sears. Are you seeing a pattern? If you are not improving your business, start preparing to be extinct.

Wake up each day with a desire to improve even just a little. Incremental improvements made every day for years result in a life well lived as well as a company that continues to innovate and to lead their industry. Being complacent and content is the other option. What habits can you instill that will force you to improve daily? What goals can you set for your company that will require constant improvement?

YESTERDAY IS OVER; LET'S BE GREAT TODAY.

OCTOBER 6
TEAMWORK

"The best teamwork comes from men who are working independently toward one goal in unison."
—J.C. Penney

"Talent wins games, but teamwork and intelligence win championships," says the great Michael Jordan. You're the business owner; you set the culture of your company. What you don't want is individual people working toward individual goals. If you can get your staff to work together on big projects in unison as a team, that's teamwork, and when you have more than one person working together toward a goal, anything can happen. That's why I'm such a big fan of partnerships. I know what I'm capable of doing, but if you give me one or two people beside me, well, we're going to do something exponentially better than I can do as an individual.

Teamwork is getting everyone to row the boat in the same direction. As I have shared, I am rarely passionate about the actual business I choose to start, and I know that is contrary to many of my peers. I look for profitable ideas, and then my passion takes shape. My passion is building teams and getting them to do something remarkable with my idea. That is what excites me: to win another person over to help build something unique, to make someone feel valuable within my organization, to put the right people in the right positions, and to train and motivate them to be their best.

So, I encourage you today to consider building more teamwork within your company. No one person can create the force of many.

THERE'S STRENGTH IN NUMBERS.

OCTOBER 7
PLAY TO YOUR STRENGTHS

"Play to your strengths."
—J.K. Rowling

I've learned as I've gotten older. I'm not as good at everything as I thought I was. When I got out of college, I foolishly thought I was pretty broadly skilled. Now, as I get older, I know I'm good at about two or three things. What I can tell is that what I am good at, I am really good at. You should feel the same way. I am fully aware of my weaknesses, but I never play that position on the team, so I am never exposed. As I have shared before, it is critical to know what you don't know. But it's equally as important not only to know your strengths but play to your strengths. Too many owners play too many positions, and we are all limited.

You need to know what your strengths are. You should be able to do things easier and better than other people in your organization. What comes easy to you? What do you like to do?

What do you do extremely well? This is a simple way of identifying your strengths. Sadly, too many owners have other people playing their position because for whatever reason they have handcuffed themselves to a "need." This is when you are doing something out of default. You have picked up a responsibility that you at best should have done in the short term. Start removing these from your job description.

I would encourage you to identify the two or three things that you love to do and do better than anyone in the building. Build your responsibilities and schedule around these. Spend 80 percent of your time playing the position you are the most talented at. When Steve Jobs immersed himself in new-product development on his second go-round with Apple, this was his area of genius. This decision will not only increase your love of your business, it will put a better team on the field.

PLAY THE POSITION YOU ARE MEANT TO PLAY.

OCTOBER 8
LEVERAGE

"When you combine ignorance and leverage, you get
some pretty interesting results."
—*Warren Buffett*

In business, we often think of leverage only in regard to an investment strategy where you use borrowed money for something that you believe will give you a better return than what you are paying for this loaned capital. A simple example is real estate. I am confident Donald Trump has a certain figure he knows he can both build a hotel for and what it will be worth at completion. He is happy to borrow the needed capital (leveraging) if the profit is well above the cost to borrow.

I have learned as a small-business owner to leverage every asset I have. I think more in the general definition of leverage: to use something to gain the maximum advantage. Have you ever tried to open a jar and could not? Then, you take a thin piece of rubber (often with advertising on it)—and you drape this simple contraption over the lid of your jar, and, with your newfound grip, it comes off effortlessly. This is using leverage.

For example, let's say I buy a piece of machinery for my company so that I can increase productivity. So, I'm leveraging some of my money to be able to produce more. That's really what we do in business. We have so many assets, but with our assets, we need to get the greatest return on our assets, whether that's machinery, real estate, our dollar, or maybe we leverage our staff. We have to get the maximum amount of leverage for all the assets we have within our company today. I recently leveraged my contacts, reputation, and years of business experience to be a partner in a company. They knew that I could get them in front of people they could not reach themselves. They recognized that I had a reputation that would provide instant credibility and finally, my experience could help navigate shark-infested waters.

ARE YOU EFFECTIVELY LEVERAGING YOUR ASSETS?

OCTOBER 9
HOW TO TIP THE SCALE OF A SALE

"Leadership must be likable."
—*Vicente del Bosque*

People do business with people they like and trust. What this means is, assuming you're competent in the area that you portray, you need also to have personal qualities that make others like you. The longer I am in business, the more I am convinced that likeability makes the difference. The combination of competence and likability is a formidable one-two punch. Often, we meet likable people, but when we press them, they simply do not have the experience or the skill to do what we need. But assuming we have two competent people or two reputable companies to choose from, it will be the one who has likeability on their side that will win.

What you will learn is that every person has their own personality type and by extension, has certain personalities that naturally clash with theirs. Learning how to discern who you are speaking to and how to come across as likable to them is an art form. It is like Judo, in that you take what they give you and use it to your advantage.

I have learned over the years to discern quickly who makes the decisions. You can spend an hour pitching to the wrong person no matter what their title is. Some people like high-energy people, while others like a slower-spoken, more detailed plan. You will never sell a big idea with little details to an engineering mindset. They want to know how the sausage is made. Other people you will pitch in a grand way that excites them, and they are all-in. I could go on and on, but you need to connect and win over buyers as well as people of influence.

BECOME MORE LIKABLE TO MORE PERSONALITY TYPES.

OCTOBER 10
THE LIFE CYCLE OF A CUSTOMER

Three companies I have founded have now reached their twenty-year milestone. Two of the companies I no longer own, but because one is a magazine, I can browse through it and see how many of the advertisers were my original clients. I remember how each of these small-business owners originally came on board, and it is great to see them advertising twenty years later and about ten years since I last had the publication. It also shows I like durable business models. But let's move on to what I want to share with you; customers have a life cycle. This means you understand that like all relationships, a customer relationship is a relationship that grows in depth over time.

Let me share with you what I have found to be the life cycle of a customer:

- **They express interest:** Not a buyer yet, but they respond to your advertising or come into your store to see what you offer.

- **They buy:** This can start at a minimal level or at a grand level, but they make their first purchase from you.

- **They tell others:** They share their experience, good or bad.

- **They buy from you again:** This transaction should be easier; quantity may be greater, or for a higher ticket item.

- **You have your first breakup:** It is not a fight, but they return something or require customer service. It is how you respond to this that determines whether the relationship continues. If you handle it well, they move to the next phase.

- **They become your advocate:** They not only tell others how great you are, but they will fight for you and defend you if needed.

- **They are a lifetime buyer:** They begin their buying process with you. If you offer it, they buy it.

- **You express appreciation:** This is where you treat them specially. They get offered discounts and privileges others don't get. Your motivation has changed from profit-motivated to appreciation-motivated.

A GOOD BUSINESS MODEL TAKES A CUSTOMER
THROUGH THE COMPLETE LIFE CYCLE.

OCTOBER 11
REBRANDING—PART I

Rebranding is somewhat self-explanatory in that it is a change in the company image. I recently had to rebrand one of my companies that was in its seventeenth year with a well-identified name, tagline, and logo. However, our services over the years had expanded greatly, and our existing name reflected our original offering and not the bevy of services we could now provide.

I had also brought on a partner who had made a profit in these new services and felt like our old name limited their profit potential. All of which, under careful review, I believed to be true. However, my default position for a time was, "Everyone knows us and knows we do that now." True, everyone did know us, but I was spending a lot of money educating people because our name was limited.

When to Rebrand:

- Recent merger or acquisition
- Introducing a new product or service
- Outdated language or image
- Demographics of customers changing
- Losing market share to competition
- Moving into a new market or demographic area
- Overcoming a poor reputation

Finally, be all-in with no reservations, knowing why you have chosen to rebrand and recognizing this is not a quick fix but a marriage that will require work and commitment. To make this work, you will need to provide the financial resources to make it a success. You'll need to make sure your high-level leaders and managers are aware of why you are doing this.

IF YOUR BRAND IS TOO RESTRICTIVE,
CONSIDER REBRANDING.

OCTOBER 12
REBRANDING—PART II

Now that you have decided a rebrand might be a good long-term strategy, let me show you how to do it.

How do you rebrand?

- Know why you are doing it.
- Have your team on board.
- Don't do it halfway, go all-in.
- Recognizing this is not a quick fix.
- Have a long-term strategy in place including a launch period.
- Have the budget needed to effectively promote this new brand.
- Don't backslide, because you will be tempted to.

The Key Components of Your New Brand:

- **Brand promise**—who you are and what are you doing or offering that makes your company different and attractive to customers.
- **Visual identity**—name, colors, logo, tagline, signage, vehicles, uniforms, etc.
- **Attitude**—traditional, modern, stoic, cutting edge, rebellious, comedic, etc.

THE TEMPTATION WILL BE TO SWITCH BACK.
DON'T DO IT!

OCTOBER 13
SUSTAINABILITY

When I am approached about a new opportunity or I have a start-up in mind, I remember the importance of sustainability. There is a difference between getting something off the ground and keeping it going. I have learned that there are many businesses that I can get off the ground, but some of them do not convince me that they have sustainability.

There are cost differences between a pup tent and a home. You can advise not spending any more than needed to see if you have a viable business idea, but taking it to the next level may require a significant financial commitment.

Often, my staff will present me with a service they want to add and the number one thing I ask is, "Is it sustainable?"

- Will the market have a long-term need for this?

- Is it seasonal or is it just a fad?

- Is it in a dying industry?

- Can we staff this? Hiring ease is critical to me.

- When will this new venture stand on its own?

- What resources will it take from an existing business, if any?

I look at it this way. It is easy to have a child, but then you have to raise it. I look at businesses the same way; it's never a short-term commitment. Once you birth this child, you have another mouth to feed.

THERE IS A DIFFERENCE BETWEEN LAUNCHING
AND SUSTAINING A BUSINESS.

OCTOBER 14
THE CURE FOR RETIREMENT

A 2010 study from Barclays Wealth found that 54 percent of millionaires say they want to continue working in retirement. Globally, 60 percent of those with a net worth of $15 million or more plan to stay involved with work "no matter what their age." Spectrum Group had a similar study and found that the highest earners—and those who can best afford to retire—are actually working the longest. George Walper, president of Spectrum, added that even among top earners who say they're "retired," many continue to serve on boards, advise, or do business from a more pleasant spot. The point is, why retire when you can do what you want, wherever you want, and finally, whenever you want?

This is one of the biggest reasons I became an entrepreneur in the first place. I had one overriding goal: to be financially independent, which I achieved in my late thirties. I wanted to do only what I do well and enjoy doing within my businesses and finally, only when I want to do it. With this achieved, why would I retire? My wife said I have been retired for more than ten years. However, I own more companies, make more money, and am having more fun than ever in business.

Warren Buffet is nearing ninety years old and doesn't seem to be slowing down. The 2020 US presidential election is likely to pit against eachother two candidates in their seventies. Two Democratic candidates would have been into their eighties in their first term if they had won. Two Democratic candidates would be into their eighties in their first term if they win. People don't stop doing things they love, things that give them fulfillment. In fact, it is in doing these that we get our energy. I just wanted to encourage you today with why you want to grow a tremendously successful company where you can put a team around you that does the heavy lifting.

BUILD A WILDLY SUCCESSFUL COMPANY

OCTOBER 15
CREATE FORCE MULTIPLIERS

"Perpetual optimism is a force multiplier."
—General Colin Powell

In relation to military science, according to Wikipedia, force multipliers refer to a factor or a combination of factors that gives personnel or weapons (or other hardware) the ability to accomplish greater feats than without it. I want you as a business owner to start thinking like a general commanding troops for a battle where losing is not an option. I am always trying to create force multipliers within my businesses. This is where a combination of resources (staff, automation, or systems) brings a greater return or result than each could alone. The simplest illustration is when I put two workers together, I want the result of three. I apply this principle from my office staff to workers in the field. Anyone can get the production of two people, but when a company can create the right combination of skills, experience, and personality, it results in a force multiplier.

Where can you take 1 + 1, add energy, and get 3? That, my friend, is a force multiplier.

Ways That I Create Force Multipliers:

- Systems
- Automation (technology)
- Right process or order
- Planning and origination (most direct path of least resistance)
- Best timing
- Best combination of talent
- Efficiency
- Attitude
- Culture

You must maximize every resource available, getting premium results, so consider different mixtures of the above list to create force multipliers.

HOW CAN I GET 1 + 1 TO EQUAL 3 IN MY ORGANIZATION?

OCTOBER 16
CREATE A SALES MACHINE

Many companies go out of business for only one reason: they've stopped selling enough of their products or services at an acceptable price to sustain the business.

If you're not selling enough of your products and services, you will be out of business. And if you're not selling enough of your products and services at a profit margin that's worthy of being in business, you're going to be out of business. Your margin must be enough to pay your overhead, your employees, and make it worth it for you, the business owner.

Your sales engine needs to be the most important priority in a small business. Nothing solves more problems than revenue, and nothing creates more revenue than robust sales. My advice to any business: Once you have your product or service you plan to offer, create a sales machine.

Sales comes down to a few basics:

- Offer a product or service that has an attractive value proposition.
- Create a demand for what you offer via consistent, effective marketing.
- The people selling your product or service need to be superstars.
- Make buying from you fast and easy.
- Offer them more of what you have.

Do not be sidetracked by anything that does not increase sales. Everything else is just window dressing.

INCREASING SALES IS JOB NUMBER ONE.

MESSENGERS

I recently traveled over Thanksgiving weekend, and I must have heard fifty radio and TV commercials pitching products and services. What began to stand out to me was the number of messages being pitched by people I did not believe actually used the product being pitched. It reminds me of when Tiger Woods was the frontman for Buick with their logo emblazoned on his golf bag. Does anybody actually believe Tiger Woods was driving a Buick? I never did. When he had his infamous Thanksgiving golf club mishap with the wife, she struck the back window of his Cadillac Escalade. *I knew it!*

I believe your message, as well as who is pitching that message to your customers, is an important component of good advertising. Your message needs to compel potential buyers to either like your company more or remind or encourage them to buy from you. Your message needs to be shared by someone your buyers believe is genuine. Someone who actually uses your products or services—and the first time they use them is not the week before pitching them.

I was approached by a radio station about one of their very popular on-air personalities doing a commercial for us—a testimonial sharing their experience. I went to meet with this person and found out that they rented their home. This was a disconnect, as renters do not spend big money on any of the many renovation services we offer. The message would have been inauthentic, even if I was the only one who knew it. I chose another popular voice and asked her if we could perform services for one of our divisions at her house so that she could share her genuine experience. This commercial brought customers in droves. It worked because she was the perfect messenger for our target market.

If you are a new start-up, if you as the owner don't want to pitch your company (some owners cannot do this well), my advice is to find a personality that speaks the language of your target market. There is a reason Pat Boone is on Fox News as the face of multiple products to the over-sixty-five market. They recognize and trust him, and he speaks their language. When I was launching my company, I asked my neighbor who was very photogenic with an upbeat, mom-next-door image to pitch our company. She was fantastic, and the launch exceeded my expectations. To this day, twenty years later I thank her for doing that commercial.

HAVE SOMEONE AUTHENTIC PITCHING YOUR OFFERING TO YOUR IDEAL CUSTOMER.

OCTOBER 18
OUTLIERS

What is an outlier? It is a very rare product, event, or person. Basically, it's anything that came along, and it's just so completely rare that you can't count on it happening again. You'll hire this one person who is so talented that you may never get anybody like them again, but don't you dare build a division around this person. That would be like trying to replace a unicorn. In sports, quarterback Russell Wilson is an outlier, and using his measurables for your next quarterback would be a mistake. He is inches under six feet tall, and that is very troubling, as, over the last twenty-five years, only he and Drew Brees have been successful at this limited height. So, you would not begin looking for shorter quarterbacks because of this outlier experience. (When in doubt, six feet, three inches is the ideal height for a quarterback).

Outliers are random and I'm encouraging you not to bet your money on them. The point is this, you may have a service that works in a unique area. What works down south may not work up north. Sometimes lightning does come in a bottle, and you can just be glad you have it, but don't bet the farm you will catch it again. I have seen people start businesses on outliers that can also be called a fad, and what was popular for a short season never became wanted again. Do you remember Cabbage Patch dolls?

This again is why sustainability is one of my pillars when vetting a start-up idea. Can this business be sustained, and will there be a sustained interest in what I am offering? I have had employees with incredible talents that I was able to make money with, but I would not start a company based on this one unique person.

NEVER BET ON AN OUTLIER.

OCTOBER 19
MASTERMIND GROUP

Success Alliance shares, "Mastermind groups offer a combination of masterminding, peer brainstorming, accountability and support in a group setting." Henry Ford and Thomas Edison had a mastermind group. Famed authors J.R.R. Tolkien and C.S. Lewis met at Oxford and had a friendship that would last a lifetime, and their creative fruits would become *The Lord of the Rings* and *The Chronicles of Narnia.*

In the classic book *Think and Grow Rich*, it was the world's richest man at the time—Andrew Carnegie—who attributed his success to the power of a mastermind group. And finally, President Theodore Roosevelt started a mastermind group during his presidency to help him work with other politicians.

So why would you want to start a mastermind group?

- **Support**—As a business owner, there will be times when you will need the encouragement of someone who has been in your situation.

- **Learning**—Others in your group may lend insight into a situation you are experiencing or a new opportunity you are considering.

- **Ideas**—Not only will this group improve your ideas, but they will often share new thoughts you had never considered.

- **Accountability**—This group will hold you to the lofty goals you speak of.

- **Networking**—They will help you network with others who can assist you.

I have used partnerships within my companies to create my mastermind groups, as my in-house peers have improved ideas and extinguished truly horrible plans I thought might work. In times of struggle, they have given me encouragement that the sun was on the horizon. They have encouraged my grand visions and have just made the business journey so much more enjoyable. Consider starting a monthly lunch group of a few business owners you know or do business with.

A MASTERMIND GROUP MIGHT BE JUST WHAT YOU ARE MISSING.

OCTOBER 20
CREDIT IS YOUR LIFEBLOOD

Credit is the lifeblood of your business, as it keeps all the vital organs of your business functioning. Get credit, then get more credit, and when you are done getting that credit, get a touch more. The Small Business Network advises, "The best time to apply for a credit line is when you don't need it. Lenders are most likely to grant a LOC when your business' cash flow is strong and your balance sheet is clean."

If you are averse to debt, good luck owning a business. I am not a fan of debt, but you need it to operate your business. For example, I have a good friend who owns a sign company. A new crane costs $250,000. Few small businesses can afford that kind of capital expense without obtaining a loan to help pay for it.

If you are giving customers thirty days to pay their invoices, you will need credit to operate while you are waiting for these payments to come in. The basic credit you need to seek is overdraft protection on checking accounts. This can come in handy if a large check written by a customer is returned or if a payment you are waiting to receive does not arrive.

You may also get a line of credit from your bank, which is very common for established businesses and even new businesses where the owner has personal assets to secure the loan.

These credit lines usually range from $25,000 and up.

A word of caution with lines of credit: They can be called in each year by the lender. This means at the end of the term, which is usually one year, they can ask you to pay the outstanding balance in full. They also do not have to renew the loan. I have had banks call this loan in and it creates a panic. They will also request your financial statement at the end of each year and decide if they want to continue this line of credit.

It never hurts to have a few credit cards hidden in your desk drawer for emergencies. Be very careful using business credit cards, as you can easily abuse them. I've had an experience where a monthly credit card statement came and no one in the business could adequately explain what the charges were for.

GET CREDIT BEFORE YOU NEED IT.

OCTOBER 21
LEARN FROM YOUR CUSTOMERS

What you can learn from every customer?
Gain customer service experience.

When you deal with a warranty or a complaint, this is an opportunity for you to learn. For one, do you have a system in place that can fulfill warranties? Are you getting complaints on the same issue? On the same person? Always be on the alert for patterns. I don't want issues to become systemic.

Ask your customers what they want and what they need.

I started one of my companies nearly twenty years ago, and it was a simple handyman company, but yet I own a multimillion-dollar construction company with eight divisions. Each division operated with a partner much like a separate company. And how did it grow to eight divisions?

Because I've been asking people what they need or want every year. To which I would hear, "Can you paint our house?" Added a painting division. They said, "Can you do our kitchen?" You kind of get where it went.

You want to find out their overall experience dealing with your company. You want to find out if it was a good experience. Was it effortless? Was your staff helpful, courteous, and professional? Did they present themselves well? Learn from your customers, talk to your customers. You should have a survey in place. You need to have something in place that allows you to follow up with your customers and find out what their experience is.

I strongly recommend establishing a systematic survey of your customers, asking a few critical questions that can allow you to improve their experience as well as to understand their current and future needs.

UNHAPPY CUSTOMERS ARE A GREAT
SOURCE OF LEARNING.

OCTOBER 22
OPTIONS

Successful entrepreneurs and seasoned business owners love options. When I'm starting a business, a new division, or a deal, one of the key things I look at is, do I have options for it? Is this venture a one-trick pony that I don't want to ride? Can I diversify this company? Can we possibly move in a different direction?

I ask my team what safety ramps we have with this idea. If you have ever driven down a mountain road, they have truck ramps built into the shoulder of the road in strategic places, so that if a truck goes out of control, it can safely wreck, avoiding horror for other travelers. I think the same way. I am an optimist and expect my business to succeed beyond my expectations, but I want options. Not only do I want options, but I also want a safety ramp built into this deal or business so that there are few to no casualties.

I would strongly encourage you to think the same way. What options does this new business have? What options does your current business have? What capabilities do you have that could be used for something else? Spend some time actually thinking through these questions. Pose these questions to your team and listen to their ideas.

I have a friend who owns a multimillion-dollar roofing company, and he makes a fortune, but he knows his team can work on roofs anywhere, doing almost anything. That seems fairly obvious, but how has he used it? He has contracts to remove the snow off Walmart stores during the winter. He understands that commercial roofs have a weight limit, so it is wise to not let heavy snow sit on the roof, not to mention the need to prevent the melting effect that could rain down on customers for days on end when the temperature changes. Nowadays, if his team could not install a roof, they actually have quite lucrative work waiting for them. This is just taking your expertise and creating options.

When you're looking at a deal, something you're going to get involved in, make sure you have a lot of options available to you.

DO YOU HAVE OPTIONS AND SAFETY RAMPS?

OCTOBER 23
THE LION KING

Ijust watched the remake of *The Lion King*, and the strength and roar of a lion is jaw-dropping. You should have a lion in your partnership group. There needs to be somebody who can confront that difficult client and say, "No, we didn't promise that; we can't give you that." There needs to be somebody who can have hard discussions with employees, someone who can articulate an intelligent debate or negotiation when needed.

Over the last two years, I have watched Mark Zuckerberg of Facebook get pounded into dust during congressional hearings because he is far from being a lion. He comes across like a slow stuffed animal. Personally, I think he is brilliant, but being the front person in certain situations is not his area of strength. He may have been wise to have brought on an extremely adept individual with experience in congressional hearings, possibly someone with courtroom experience, to be his mouthpiece.

I encourage you, if confrontations are not in your comfort zone, you may need to expand your comfort zone. If this will never be your strength, you may want to recruit a lion. This doesn't mean that they're on top of you—remember that you're the owner—but maybe you take their unique strength and allow it to be beneficial to you. Some small businesses will never require this, but remember, I am trying to help you develop into a great entrepreneur who can lead the largest of organizations.

OCCASIONALLY SOMEONE NEEDS TO ROAR.

OCTOBER 24
MANAGING MONEY

"We are moving at the speed of cash."
—Dave Ramsey

I find that too many business owners manage their business accounts similar to their personal accounts, week-to-week, with no strategy. If you struggle with managing money personally, you will struggle to handle your business income as well. The good news is the same rules for personal money management apply to small business money management. Jeff Haden lends good advice, "Never forget that your business needs to take in more money than it spends. I know that sounds too simple, but so many people lose sight of that."

Simple Steps to Managing Money:

· **Generate more income than expenses.**

· **Create a budget.**

· **Establish a reserve fund for emergencies and down periods.**

· **Reduce debt until you become debt-free.**

· **Take the money you were spending on debt and begin investing.**

Let me go through the steps quickly with the plan. You first need to make more money than you have expenses. Everyone including business needs a budget so you can see where you are wasting money. You create an emergency fund as well as enough reserves to take you through a downturn. Start paying down debt, beginning with the smallest debt first. When this is paid off, you apply this to the next smallest debt. This is a debt snowball. At some point, all debt will be paid off, and you can then begin investing money in technology, real estate—always own the land under your business— and infrastructure. You invest in items that increase your revenue or value of the company. This is a simple plan that I have used, and it works.

MASTER MONEY OR IT WILL BE YOUR MASTER.

CONTRACTS AND AGREEMENTS

This one lesson will, I hope, save you not only a great deal of money but also aggravation.

Early on in business, I was excited to bid on a large commercial job. It would have been quite lucrative, so I let excitement blind me. I signed a ten-page agreement—actually, not sure how many pages, but it was long enough that I know I did not read all of it. I assumed it was pretty standard, and in reflection it was. However, it was written by the other party, so it had none of our best interests in mind.

As you can imagine, this project went south even prior to beginning, and in hindsight, that may have been a blessing in disguise. The agreement I signed made me fight with one hand tied behind my back. As I do with any mistake, I mined the experience for gold. I decided then I would never have someone other than our company provide or make any major modifications to our contracts. I don't mind a suggestion here and there, but it is like a text: you have a limited amount of characters.

A contract protects both parties: you the company as well as the customer. You should want contracts and good, paying customers want contracts. But again, your contracts should protect you and your company first. They need to be written by your attorney, never someone else's. They should clearly spell out what it is you're agreeing to. I believe in most cases a twelve-year-old should be able to tell you what is being provided. A very important section is how disputes will be resolved, and I have learned to be a fan of mediation prior to courtrooms.

DO YOUR CONTRACTS BENEFIT YOUR COMPANY?

OCTOBER 26
MODELING A FRANCHISE

I don't always think it's a great idea to buy a franchise, but you can't go wrong with modeling one.

Pick a name that has a national or at least a regional feel to it.

Stay away from local names if you ever plan to expand. Think big with regard to your name. Do not pick a name for which you can't get the domain. You've got to own that path of entry to the internet.

Keep your business focused on what it does well.

One of the core fundamentals of a franchise is to specialize. They don't try to do one hundred different things. They do one thing extremely well. Find something that you and only you can do better than everybody else in your marketplace.

Create systems.

Go inside a McDonald's, place an order, and look at how they have all the stations lined up: people doing one specific task over and over all day. They create systems. Systems allow average people to excel. You don't need great talent because they break the tasks into very simple portions. This also allows a new hire to be an asset from day one.

Advertise a consistent message.

Come up with a message that is a promise to your customer that you can fulfill, and that makes them absolutely want to do business with you. Now beat this message over their head for years.

Create and commit to an image.

Create and commit to an image from day one. This is uniforms, vehicles with logos, website, stationery, forms, everything that represents your business to your customers every possible way they can see you. It makes you look credible, and you'll be able to get paid well for it.

Seek to duplicate your business.

When you start your business, have a goal to duplicate it in three years or less. If you know you're going to duplicate it, it's going to force you to do all the things I just mentioned.

IF YOU DON'T BUY A FRANCHISE, CONSIDER COPYING THE MODEL.

OCTOBER 27
EMPOWERING OTHERS

Empowering others means that you give people the power to act on your behalf. What you want is staff who can solve problems at the lowest level and not need to bring that problem back to you because you've empowered them to make the decision. They can act as if they're you. They have your authority.

There's a big difference between delegating something and empowering someone, so I encourage you, if you want to have a staff who can keep problems away from you, if you want to build the morale of your staff, consider empowering them. Give them the right to handle some financial decisions or give them some hiring decisions. If you want to bring your staff up to the highest level of your leadership team, you need to constantly empower them with more and more responsibility and more and more power to act on your behalf.

I empower my partners to make most unilateral decisions and complete power up to $10,000 annually to solve any customer service issues. By empowering them (and the secret is giving a budget), this has allowed me not to be involved in approving solutions to problems they can solve with a monetary credit or even return a deposit if they sense a customer will be a problem. They appreciate that I have empowered them and given them the resources to handle problems. Now when they tell me about a situation, it is in the past tense; just sharing how they solved it where before, I was involved in the resolution.

Empowering your team members accomplishes many things:

- It gets you out of being involved in every decision.
- Your staff can grow their leadership and problem-solving skills.
- It increases speed because you are no longer a cog in the wheel.
- You get to work on your business and not in it.
- It allows you to start other businesses and not be chained to one.

LEARN TO EMPOWER OTHERS.

OCTOBER 28
ALL-IN OR DIE

There are times when you have to go all-in or, if you prefer, "bet the farm." When do you know when to go all-in? When what you are currently doing is not working and you know that you are going to run out of money? When you see sales consistently drop year after year? Do you sometimes feel like you are holding a hand grenade? These are all signals that something needs to change, and usually, that change needs to be seismic.

I was recently speaking with a business owner who was sharing the life story of his business, a large commercial sign company, which is now about thirty years old. I always encourage business owners to tell me their stories. "What made you choose the business you are in? What one decision was the game-changer?"

To answer that question, he began a lengthy story of how at one time, he had three small retail stores in shopping centers. He began noticing just how small his average sale was. He said emphatically, "Small store, small sales," as this clearly became the aha moment which he went on to share. "I decided to have one big store and go for big sales." He moved away from selling yard and door signs to homeowners and toward selling large scoreboards for major universities and stadiums as well as large contracts to do signage for an entire building. He said, "When I went big, it changed everything." He was convinced they would have gone under had he not gone all-in.

I don't wish an all-in situation on anyone, but to be in business for any length of time, you will need to at the very least recognize times where change is needed and yes, there will be a time where you will "bet the farm" to survive.

DO YOU NEED TO GO ALL-IN?

OCTOBER 29
FREE ALWAYS COSTS ME MONEY

If there is one thing I have learned over the years, it's free always costs me money. What do I mean? Whenever someone offers to do something for me at no charge, I get exactly what I paid for—nothing—and quite often, I have to pay someone to come behind them and fix what they did or complete it. I know when you are starting a business you try to keep costs down, so you have a stable of freebies. Your neighbor offers to do your bookkeeping at no charge. Your friend's dad has agreed to help with your IT needs at no charge. There is a small window of time where this can be helpful, I would say the first three to six months of a business, and then you have to take the training wheels off and start pedaling.

This brief window of "Freebie Euphoria" will crash if extended past the window I gave you and that is because free is never forever. It will give you a false sense of the actual costs necessary to sustain your business. Finally, what I have learned is "free services" means that I cannot hold them accountable for the quality of their work and the timeline for it. And to me, these two things keep me from wanting free services.

So now when I get someone—yes, even in my church—who offers to do something for me for free, I quickly reply, "I am happy to pay you because I want to define the job, what I consider a successful outcome and the deadline. And for all these reasons, I am glad to write a check."

I have a close friend whose counseling practice is made up of freebies and trades, to which I tell him this is not how you run a business. When currency does not change hands, it's a hobby.

When I press him on critical services and professionals his company should have as this is a decade-old business, he lists a roster of hodgepodge volunteers providing legal advice and makeshift accounting.

IT IS TIME TO TAKE OFF THE TRAINING WHEELS.

OCTOBER 30
TIMING

"A year from now you may wish you had started today."
—Karen Lam

Timing is so critical. A lot of times you can have a great idea, but it's the wrong time. When great companies are launched: everything comes together at one time and the timing is just right. The marketplace is panting like a dog for whatever is being offered. Some people call it luck, but I have learned that a great idea needs the soil of good timing as well. When in doubt, always take action and make today your most opportune time, but clearly some ventures need to be placed in fertile soil. Surprisingly, being first is not always the best time to bring something to the market. Consider that there were more than ten search engines in the market prior to Google's entry.

If you are launching a small business, consider that 99 percent of all start-ups are fragile.

Your timing has value, as poor timing often results in burning through cash. Your business might be either a business that has a better season than others to begin or there may be a couple of foundation blocks that still need improvement. Simply put, you don't rush into war, you count the costs and put together the best time to attack. Timing is critical.

I heard this story about a mentor of Mark Zuckerberg and during one of their meetings he said to Mark, "You're going to have an offer for a billion dollars to buy Facebook *from* you and you're going to really think about selling it because you're going to think that you could cash out and you can duplicate what you're doing right now." He continued, "Mark, it never happens again. You never have the idea and the timing together again, never at the magnitude of Facebook." Timing is critical for making great decisions. Timing is critical in the success of a company. You want to ask yourself, is the timing right today to go forward with anything that you're thinking about.

TIMING IS CRITICAL: MAKE SURE YOU GET IT RIGHT.

OCTOBER 31
GETTING ON THE SAME PAGE

My least favorite team, the Dallas Cowboys, are once again in turmoil; sadly, my Redskins are equally struggling, so I revel in the misery of my foe. Dallas owner Jerry Jones, who never met a microphone he did not like, shared, after another defeat, how he was focused on winning the Super Bowl. It was a fairly obvious target for anyone who knows professional football. However, their coach, Jason Garrett, took a different view in an interview, saying that his focus was on Tuesday. He explained, "That's all we're worried about is having the best practice today that we can possibly have." Let me share the disconnect between the two. Jerry is a big goal, specific target guy, "Win the Superbowl." His coach is a micro thinker, focus on today. Sure, you want every day to be a good practice, but as the coach, you need to mirror and echo the goal of the organization which was stated by owner Jones.

I find this problem more often than I would like to admit within my companies. It can seem like we are all going in a different direction and even playing tug of war against ourselves. I found myself meeting with my partners in two of my organizations just to confirm they understand the script I have set and that we are all reading from this same script. They looked at me oddly, but I asked, "Tell me what you understand the script to be." Simply asking them to describe our main focus as I laid it out three months ago made it clear that my version had been watered down, and the definitive objectives it contained now seemed to be optional.

This happens within any leadership structure and in all organizations. You, the leader, set a goal or initiative, and you allow high-level teammates to work toward it in their own way. It begins to become their initiative or project and it no longer reflects exactly what you wanted in the first place. What I experienced was that we were attacking the problem from too many directions and wasting money. After re-sharing the page I wanted everyone on, I also needed to narrow our focus and re-explain our key objective. The team was all over the place, the goal had morphed into more than what mattered to me, so the budget had ballooned, and that was the alarm that alerted me to the problem.

My advice is that if you have high-level leaders who you allow to work on big projects, regularly meet with them and ask the very simple question, "Tell me what you understand the script to be." Very similar to the game telephone we played in elementary school where you whisper in someone's ear and five kids later the sentence has no resemblance to the one initially shared. Keep everybody on the same page.

IS EVERYBODY READING FROM THE SAME SCRIPT?

NOVEMBER 1
GET FEEDBACK

"Don't build your product behind closed doors.
Get feedback and validate your idea."
—Cody Lister

One of the advantages of starting a business today as opposed to twenty years ago is that the internet and social media allow you to not only test the interest level of a new product or service but to also get instant feedback. Remember, feedback is your friend. Don't be so married to your idea that you don't allow for improvement and adjustments. Don't launch your venture in a vacuum where the only feedback you are getting is from a limited group of supporters. I could launch anything, and I have a fan club of friends and family that would let me believe it was the best idea since the wheel. I, however, know better and prefer real data.

Feedback costs little to nothing with today's technology. I would encourage you to use it. You absolutely should consider ways to introduce your idea to people and hear what they like and what they would like or want to be done differently.

I live in a town with a major university and its medical center. This is a world-renowned hospital and they are constantly offering test studies for medication and the like. This is pretty standard in the medical community and they would never allow, nor would the FDA allow, an unproven product to be in the marketplace. You would be wise to follow the same rule.

You can test a product at a county fair or home show and get instant feedback. You can test your marketing campaign online with small samples to make sure that what you think is the big hook that gets customers' attention actually works.

I just recently launched a product online—and I am so glad we did it with limited expense—to test our marketing campaign. We learned that it was lacking. What we thought would attract buyers needed to be reworded. Our call to action was not strong enough. The good news is that we paid a minimal amount of money to obtain this feedback before our major launch. I would advise you to do the same. It never hurts to ask, What did you like? What would you like to see changed?

Even if these were the only two questions you asked, you would benefit immensely from the answers.

FEEDBACK IS YOUR FRIEND.

NOVEMBER 2
PSYCHIC POWERS

You may laugh or be cynical about what I am getting ready to share, but any seasoned entrepreneur will tell you it's the gospel. Veteran business owners and high-level leaders or organizations have "psychic powers." I am joking, as I have never had a palm reading in my life or paid much attention to my astrological sign, but I see the future in a business before my staff. They see only today. I see problems that will surface a month or year from now. It's a gift!

I would not be exaggerating if I told you that I have said to my partners and high-level employees over one hundred times in the past twenty-five years, "This is going to be a problem," well in advance of it surfacing. I will sense something is off and ask my accountant to do some financial forensic work to put my mind at ease only to have my suspicions confirmed.

I have sat in on countless interviews with new employees and will share my opinion that this employee will start strong and fade quickly and is not as advertised on their resume. I don't want to be right, but this is how it will play out. I shake my head and tell them, "I want to be wrong." But guess what? I rarely am.

Truth is that I am not a psychic, but I pay attention to trends and numbers and have mined past mistakes and experiences like a seasoned archaeologist goes through dirt at a dig site. This exercise has allowed me to learn endless warning signs and "beware of crap soon to come." And the funny part is, I am one of the most optimistic people you will ever meet, but, as I share with my team, this is one of my unique skills: to see problems before they actually come. It is my job. I also see potential and opportunities before anyone else as well. My "psychic powers" are a two-sided coin.

CULTIVATE YOUR "PSYCHIC POWERS."

NOVEMBER 3
LESS IS MORE

I can remember years ago when I would create a to-do list that looked more like a grocery list. I would have my A, B, and C tasks, as I once took a time-management class that taught me how to categorize tasks. A is something that must get done, B is something that should get done and C is something that could get done. This works well when you have a large list of anything and everything you could be working on completing. My list (and day) twenty years later looks more like a military attack with a clearly defined target, and not like my shotgun approach years ago, when more shot hitting various targets was my objective.

Let me share with you how I decide what my target for each day looks like now. Yes, you read that correctly: singular target. On Sunday, I lay out my week with every important meeting I may have so I have a snapshot of my schedule. As I have gotten older, I recognize I can handle one or two draining events in a day and no more. If I have a high-level meeting or project that requires my focus, I do not want to be distracted or exhausted going into it. So, I schedule my week allowing for large windows of time for each major meeting, allowing me to have the preparation as well as the energy required.

The next thing I list when organizing my week is what must get done. These are items that only I can do. These are commitments I have made to others that are not optional. I will then decide which day I will handle these on my schedule. So quickly, I have what must get done clearly scheduled in my weekly blueprint. Each morning when I get up, I will look at this snapshot of my schedule which has my main events and must-do items clearly listed. My goal now is never to have more than five items on my to-do list on any given day. I will begin each day listing everything I think needs to be done and will also delegate everything that has arisen that I do not have to do personally. Again, I want my day to be able to be put on a 3 x 5 notecard that I will carry with me everywhere for that given day. I have found that this card forces me to keep my day limited and focused.

IT'S NOT HOW MANY THINGS ARE ON YOUR TO DO LIST THAT MAKES YOU SUCCESSFUL.

NOVEMBER 4
MONEY DOES MAKE YOU HAPPY

I just Googled the search term, "What causes most stress in marriages," and the first sentence at top of the page said, "Money problems are the leading cause of stress in American marriages." So, with this fact as our tickler, let's discuss what seems to make people unhappy. In general, according to an American Psychological Association study, 72 percent of people surveyed were stressed over money. In fact, money was the leading cause of problems and, sadly, divorce in marriages. In my hunt for why people were so unhappy, I found that 75 percent of people are exhausted, according to the Virgin Pulse Institute. And finally, because if I did much more research on this subject, I might have become unhappy myself, I found that 85 percent of people hate their jobs, based on a recent Gallup Poll.

I have concluded that lack of money, being exhausted, and having a job makes most people unhappy, and I have found that being a successful entrepreneur solves every one of these problems. I can tell you that my wife and I have never had one argument over money, never. And for one reason: from the day we got married, I hustled and always had a side business going. Now owning countless businesses where I work on my businesses and not a daily grind in them, I work a very limited schedule. I am rarely, if ever, exhausted because I plan my schedule in a way that prevents that from ever happening. So, I *love* my job and do not fall into the 85 percent who don't.

In conclusion, the remedy for all the leading factors of unhappiness is owning a successful business. Let's quickly list its benefits:

- **Money**—Entrepreneurs are the wealthiest people in America.

- **Fatigue**—You make your own schedule.

- **Job**—You create the job description that fits your strengths and passion. Yes, I have said it, "Money does make you happy."

HOW MANY WEALTHY BUSINESS OWNERS HAVE YOU MET THAT WERE GENUINELY UNHAPPY?

NOVEMBER 5
BE A COACH

I don't know of one skill that could serve you better as an entrepreneur than being a coach.

At this point in the book, I am sure you have concluded that I love sports, and my participation in athletics has formulated much of my thought processes as well as the habits that I believe have helped me achieve at a high level. I have also had a few coaches along the way that I believe have given me the model for how to recruit, lead, motivate, and retain talent. All of these skills would serve you well as an entrepreneur.

Let's quickly summarize what great coaches do:

- Recruit talent
- See the potential in players
- Develop talent
- Motivate
- Encourage
- Set big goals
- Create winning strategies
- Develop a healthy winning culture

These are also the qualities of a great entrepreneur. So, you might want to think about being a good coach today. I would encourage you to add a book or two on coaching or books written by great coaches to your reading list. The list of iconic coaches who have shared their thoughts in print is endless, but you can start with John Wooden, Pat Riley, Urban Meyer, Phil Jackson, Bill Walsh, Mike Kryxewski, Joe Gibbs, and Pete Carroll, to name just a few.

BE A GREAT COACH.

NOVEMBER 6
FUNDAMENTALS

I am fully aware of how many start-up and business books are available, as I am always on the lookout for valuable insights, but I rarely hear something genuinely new. The author puts a new take on something that is what I call a fundamental. These are very simple and often obvious foundations that any business needs to be successful. There is very little new under the sun, I have heard it said, and it is also true in business.

I have narrowed business down to four fundamentals such that if any of these is not strong, your business will struggle and never grow to its potential. Let's take a brief look at each and see if I am wrong. I believe a company will only go as far as the person leading it. This person needs to set a vision that inspires others to want to be a part of it. This person needs to display confidence that others believe the vision will happen. In challenging times, the leader will set and navigate the correct course to take.

Marketing

If you cannot sell your products or services, you will be out of business. Nothing is more important than developing a message and strategy to attract buyers. Your ability to convert customers into fans who buy more and more from you will be what makes the difference.

Staffing

Your company will only be as good as those who toil with you. No resource is more valuable than human resources. Your ability to attract, grow, and retain talent will provide the fuel needed to become a great company. Fail at this, and your company will never reach beyond a struggling small business.

Innovation

You would be wise to be alert for changes that need to be made in order to stay ahead of your competition. The innovative company leads its industry with transformational ideas and ways of doing things that others thought impossible. Companies that do not change, die. Simple as that.

You would be smart to stick to these four building blocks as everything else is just a distraction from what matters most. If you cannot do these, everything else is just a waste of time and resources.

LET'S GET BACK TO THE BASICS.

NOVEMBER 7
BUILD CONFIDENCE

I have shared that self-confidence is a must-have quality in your journey to success. There will be times when you, and only you, will believe that you can accomplish what you set out to achieve. As a leader, I can smell weakness in others. I test their confidence level just to get a feel for what their potential is. Their level of confidence will often become their ceiling of how far I can take them.

Confidence is important and one thing I have learned in leadership is that my job is to build confidence in others, not tear it down. My minor in college was psychology and I have come to believe that it has helped me more than any business class could have. I know the value of self-esteem and how easily people lose it and struggle their whole lifetime to improve it. With all that said, I want to build people, not diminish them.

So how do you do this? For one, you express to people under you from the day you hire them that you saw potential in them. I plant a seed from the interview process onward. I will share, "I have interviewed hundreds of people over the years and I could just tell you are a winner." It is the truth, or we would not have hired them, but how often do they hear that?

Like a football coach, I also like to script a few easy plays when they come on board where they will get an easy win. I put them in their strengths and let them flourish before I stretch their capacity in areas that will challenge them. This allows me to remind them how well they have done for us on other projects, and it is because of their potential that we want to begin to stretch them. Stretching them will often require some degree of criticism.

Too often, leaders put down their staff, and then they are surprised when they can never get them to achieve greatness in the future. You can share needed criticism and adjustments that need to be made (always in private), but never let them walk away feeling disrespected.

WHEN YOU BUILD OTHERS UP,
THEY CAN DO SO MUCH MORE.

NOVEMBER 8
BE A GENERAL

I've found that very few people want to work for a passive, weak leader. They want to work for somebody who can create plans to make everything that they're excited about happen. There's nothing worse than working for a leader who brings out all these ideas, but you know they're never going to happen. They're a leader in name only.

And let me be clear: there is a difference between tactics and strategy. A tactic is an individual element or activity you may use to achieve your strategy. An example would be using a tank to implement an attack, which is just one element in the strategy to win the war. To have an effective strategy, you first need to understand all your options based on every resource and tactic you have available. Legendary CEO of General Electric Jack Welch explains, "Strategy is simply resource allocation."

If your goal is to grow your company by 20 percent per year, that is an ambitious goal, but what is your strategy to make it happen? There are a few you could employ, from a more aggressive marketing campaign that increases advertising, to updating software to offer add-on purchases at checkout, or make suggestions of other items you may want. These are tactics you could use. Being strategic is also deciding what to discontinue doing.

You want to be a strategic leader. You want to be somebody that makes everybody think, "Yes, that is a good idea. I think that person can make it happen." Strategy means that you have a game plan that your team believes in.

When you're strategic, you're able to outmaneuver your competition. You see openings in the marketplace, and you beat your competition to them because you have a strategy. You put together an offensive plan. Richard Koch wraps it up succinctly: "To be strategic is to concentrate on what is important, on those few objectives that can give us a competitive advantage. On what is important to us rather than others, and to plan and execute the resulting plan with determination and steadfastness."

BE STRATEGIC; MAXIMIZE YOUR RESOURCES.

NOVEMBER 9
NICHE

"If everybody is doing it one way, there's a good chance you can find your niche by going exactly in the opposite direction."
—Sam Walton

This means that instead of doing a broad range of services or offering a wide variety of products, you specialize. You have an individual focus you just keep narrowing down. Look at Untuckit. They sell one type of shirt, a shirt that you wear untucked. I would never think you could make a business out of just one type of shirt, but they're doing it. Kane11 has socks with sizes ranging in seventeen different fits. DXL Menswear is only for larger men. ThirdLove has bras in half sizes, something Victoria's Secret and others do not. I can go on and on, but I know I have a sharp audience, so I will let the point rest.

It is possible your business is offering too much and maybe you need to specialize a little bit more. One test I like to use is what generates 80 percent of your company revenue. This is usually earned from only 20 percent of what you offer. Finally, like in the illustrations I shared above, what is not being offered yet? (ThirdLove) What solves a unique problem? (Untuckit) What is a business within a business? (DXL) What is a very common item that could use some specialization? (Kane11)

The one thing to keep in mind is to make sure there's a big enough marketplace there to serve it. You don't want to have something so esoteric that trying to find a customer for it is like trying to find a needle in a haystack.

WHAT ONE UNIQUE CHANGE COULD ALLOW YOU TO HAVE A NICHE IN THE MARKET?

NOVEMBER 10
SPEAK THE NATIVE LANGUAGE

I hope the title got your attention as I don't personally curse, but on occasion, I have found a need to speak the native language. When first entering home remodeling, which I knew little about, I felt as if I could offer very little practical experience. I had the business ability and keen marketing skills but could not tell you the difference between two screwdrivers and still can't. I do, however, represent our ideal customer: an affluent buyer who wants a turnkey project done exceptionally well with no budget surprises. If we can touch these buttons in our sales pitch and commercials, we will have customers lined up like in a soup kitchen.

Back to my story. I would go by a job site on the occasion of having a very high-end project and notice something that I thought looked, let's say not great. I would politely, in my educated vernacular, share with the worker, "It just does not look that good." To which I would get a smart look back with no sense that anything was going to be done about it. I would then go further with, "Is this the best we can get it to look?" To which I would get an excuse, leading me to believe this unacceptable (in my opinion) finished product was going to be the final outcome. Knowing we had reached a stalemate, I would finally say, "John, it looks like shit!" to which I would get a "Sorry, boss. I will fix it even if I need to redo it on my time." That is why I have learned when necessary to speak the native language.

SPEAK IN A LANGUAGE THAT CREATES ACTION.

PROFILE EMPLOYEE

The New England Patriots get a lot of credit for building great teams and, in a previous lesson, I shared how they choose the person over talent. They want a quality individual with character, knowing that talent only goes so far when opposition faces you. Great managers and leaders have a profile player that fits their system and organization.

The Patriots, for example, have a profile player—an ideal player—that they are looking for.

When drafting someone, the qualities they value are obvious, and you would think other teams would have caught on by now. For one, they want someone smart and versatile. To be clear, these are not the two most common qualities discussed in the April draft. Talent, measurables, and statistics are at the forefront of every player's biography. The NFL Combine tests players — how fast they can run, how high they can jump, and other physical attributes.

On the other hand, the New England Patriots want someone smart, someone who will study the playbook instead of watching TV at night. Second, they want someone who is versatile. This year, they had a guy on the team who actually played rugby in college. They had a lacrosse player as well. Their best wide receiver was a college quarterback. It is no different when building a team in a small business. You need to know the kind of player that fits your organization. I start with being smart, because you can't hide stupid. There is a lot you can do with smart. I define a smart person as someone who has competency in the area that I am hiring them for, whether that is sales, management, or marketing. I want them to have the competency and a proven track record in that area.

I also love capacity, the ability to do another person's job if needed. They may not want to, but I know that they are smart and versatile enough that I can move them somewhere else. This is critical for small businesses.

WHAT TWO OR THREE QUALITIES
ARE THE MOST VALUABLE TO YOU?

UNDERPROMISE, OVERDELIVER

"Always deliver more than expected."
—Larry Page, cofounder of Google

My experience in life has been people and companies overpromise and underdeliver. In their effort to win your business, they promise the moon and deliver something far less. I have learned that when someone is spreading it on a little thick to snap them back into reality. Don't BS me; just tell me what I can actually count on you doing in the time frame you have promised for the cost we have agreed on. Yes, at this point I know to have a few qualifiers, so they don't wiggle out of a commitment with one of these as their excuse. My final vetting question is, "What are you willing to bet your life on that you can actually deliver?" You would be shocked how many sales proposals and job interviews get scaled back to reality when I give them my no-BS approach.

Overpromising is so common in business, especially in start-ups who feel like they need to give so much to gain someone's trust and business. For one to gain their trust, which is what you really want, you need to deliver repeatedly on promises. It is having a track record of consistent excellence. I have learned and taught my staff to actually "underpromise." Set their expectations on reality. I tell them customers know when you are over your skis.

I assure customers the difference between our proposal and others is that we will actually deliver on our commitments and in the time frame given. It is not fancy, but let me tell you it works. I want to build a touch of margin in both time and money into my jobs. I most importantly want to deliver a "WOW" effect on everything we do which is impossible if we promised a "WOW" from the beginning. Leave room for something with which you can exceed their expectations. Customers will only remember one of two things; most importantly, did you deliver what you promised, and if that was achieved, did you exceed their expectations?

IF YOU PROMISE THE MOON, YOU CAN NEVER OVERDELIVER.

NOVEMBER 13
LANGUAGE OF LEADERS—PART I

It's so true that when trying to communicate with our staff, I hear people use the same language to motivate everybody. Have you heard the phrase "to a hammer, everything is a nail"? You have probably worked for someone whose only arrow in the quiver of motivating employees was threats. They threaten to fire or threaten to give a pay cut. They're constantly threatening. So, the language they use is a hammer; they just hit people. They beat them down and threaten them. And that's just not an effective language. Some people actually think this motivates. It may get a young team member to move a little faster early on, but it will quickly get old.

I think I'm a pretty good motivator, but if that is the only seasoning I bring to the dish, it will not be anything close to how good it could be within the entire dish. So even though motivation is helpful, it's not enough. Having built many companies with many diverse staff, diverse skills, and diverse partnership groups, I have learned over twenty years that I've got to speak different languages to everyone. Not everyone will respond to every language. Some of your communication will fall on deaf ears if it is not the dialect they understand. Can you motivate in a way that they not only understand but that also creates an emotional buy-in? Yes, it sounds kind of gooey, but you need to reach the brain and the heart to effectively communicate and, most importantly, get results from your team.

What I need to speak to my partners to get them excited may be different from what I have to use to motivate my office staff. How I talk to construction workers is different than how I speak to my digital marketing company teammates. The point is, there are a lot of languages in which you need to be very fluent.

This is the only lesson in the book that consumes three days, and I want to warn you, there is nothing in this book more valuable. Your ability to recruit, motivate, and retain talent as an entrepreneur will set the ceiling height of your success and your organization. If you cannot speak all the languages that allow you to retain and motivate people, you will fail mightily.

RECOGNIZE THAT NOT EVERY PLAYER RESPONDS TO THE SAME LANGUAGE.

NOVEMBER 14
LANGUAGE OF LEADERS—PART II

Let me now share the languages I use to get the most out of my team:

Affirmation and Appreciation

There is no substitute for telling someone they did a great job or that you appreciate their contribution. This is an easy one, as you can tell when you compliment them, they just light up.

Security

You have an employee that has five children, or you have someone who's maybe a single parent. Security may be the language they need to hear. You don't ever threaten to fire this person. You constantly stress the strength of the company and how secure their place in it is.

A Seat at the Table

This is how they feel: "Hey, if you want me to be involved in leading and managing the company, then I want to be involved in setting the direction." They would like to have some input about the direction that they are being asked to manage, so you need to get them involved in some of the meetings. This gets them on board.

Money Talks

There's no substitute for money to this person. There are employees that I treat like I'm running a bingo hall. I'm constantly offering spiffs: "A hundred dollars if you finish this, two hundred if you finish this. Hey, I'll give you two extra days of paid vacation." Money makes them perk up.

Ownership

There are certain people, who, if you don't bring them in, will never be loyal and you are going to be competing against them at some point. You have to pick up on people who are constantly asking, "How did you set this up?" or "What did it take?" These are buzzwords you need to keep your ears attentive to. Ask yourself, Would you rather have them on your team or your competition? If the answer is obvious, then you need to bring them in the ownership group.

*ARE YOU BEGINNING TO EXPAND
YOUR LANGUAGES?*

LANGUAGE OF LEADERS—PART III

The languages we are going to cover today are not the obvious ones, but if you lack them, you will lose these star players every time. The other languages speak more to the obvious. These tickle the heart of the contributors. Grab their heart, and you will have a journeyman who will go to hell and back for you. Mastering all ten of these languages will give you an unfair advantage when it comes to recruiting, motivating, and retaining team members.

Culture

Some people are very motivated to be on a team. They are drawn to the group dynamic. Culture is very important to them. They want to be a part of a team. They want to help others on the team and feel the support of their mates.

Mission

Some employees want to be a part of a mission. They want to know that the profits of their company are going toward something that they believe in. Simply put, they understand that they need to work for a living, but they want there to be an ancillary benefit to their hard work. They are in search of being a part of something greater than just a job.

Flexibility

Some people need flexibility. Period. That is their language. When you negotiate a salary with them, they want to hear that they don't have to come in on Fridays if all their work is done. They want to hear that on certain days of the week, they can work from home. They've shown that they can produce, whatever it is. They want flexibility. They want to be able to attend all their kids' activities.

Opportunity

Don't read this wrong, as this is not so much financial as it is about growth. They want to know they will be better because they work for you. This may require providing an educational subsidy or internship. They want to know that working for you will open other opportunities. I love launching employees. Yes, I know they will not be with me forever, and I am fine with them making an impact somewhere else.

BECOME FLUENT IN THESE LANGUAGES.

SET OF SKILLS

"If you are looking for ransom, I can tell you I don't have money.
But what I do have are a very particular set of skills;
skills I have acquired over a very long career.
Skills that make me a nightmare for people like you."
—Liam Neeson, from the movie Taken

My success in business is based on a "particular set of skills" that alone has helped me achieve any success I have had in business: first is my ability to identify, recruit, and retain talent. Next is my confidence that I will persevere and accomplish whatever it is I have set out to achieve. Finally, the area within business that I have passion for, and have been successful at, is marketing. These three skills have allowed me to navigate through shark-infested waters and climb some very high ambitions in business.

There are countless skills that would serve you well as an entrepreneur:

- Team building
- Culture building
- Marketing
- Management
- Financial management
- Leadership
- Imagination
- Execution
- Big thinking
- Strategic planning
- Messenger (frontman of the company)
- Goal-Driven
- Deal maker
- Business acumen

DEVELOP YOUR "PARTICULAR SET OF SKILLS."

NOVEMBER 17
LEARNING PLAN

"The minute that you're not learning, I believe you're dead."
—Actor Jack Nicholson

You have heard me say that if your business is not growing, it's dying, and I share that same philosophy to you as a person. Each year, I strategically plan to learn. I focus on areas I am already strong in and try to become even better. Sometimes I need to update my learning as well as tactics. What worked five years ago may not, and probably does not, work now. How I would reach my target market five years ago has changed dramatically. The vehicles are different, and the messaging I use now is different. So, each year, I make sure marketing and sales is one area I will improve on.

This year, I wanted to improve my ability to teach selling. I brought on four new partners, and each of them needed help in selling, so I made a goal to read four sales books. I would then share what I was learning with them and even pass a book along as I like to share the doctrine of learning to all my high-level team members.

Finally, since I read so much, I am also trying to learn speed reading through a couple of online courses. These are just a couple of my areas that I am seeking to learn and be more proficient at. In years past, it was time management, leadership, and basic accounting. Learning is not optional for me, and I encourage you to think the same. Most importantly, put a plan in place.

I AM COMMITTED TO LEARNING AND IMPROVING EVERY YEAR.

CLONE YOURSELF

I just recently had a year-end review with one of my business partners where he wanted to discuss how the year went and, more importantly, how we could continue the amazing growth we were experiencing. He began sharing ideas he had. They were good, but they all required the one resource which he did not have to give: his time. The fact is that he had maxed out his day and week. He was doing a fabulous job, but there are only so many hours in a given week, and his quota had been reached.

As the CEO, it is my job to be like a UFC referee and step in when the fight is over, and he was finished in regard to any more work or fights he could take on. This observation I made was met with a frown and a look of skepticism, to which I replied, "Show me how you do this," to which he tried to fit things into a schedule that already had little to no margin. On each attempt, I would debunk his plan. It is my job to protect my team members from themselves as I bring them on because I love their ambition and energy, but these same sought-after qualities do have a maximum capacity, and again, his was reached. I politely reminded him of how much money he made last year, which was more than the vice president, and that it would be OK to be content.

Of course, I knew he would never be content as this was like throwing red meat to a lion. We adjourned the meeting, and it was less than an hour before he began texting new proposals, to which I had to finally reply, "Do you want the real secret to taking your income to a new level?"

He salivated for my answer, so I called him on the phone and said, "The reason I make the money I do is because I have learned how to find other Seans." I then started reciting the roster of talented partners I had recruited to my team over the last twenty years. He had worked with or had met many of them at my Christmas dinner party, so he knew it was the truth.

Most undeniable was the fact that I interviewed him for a salaried $850 a week job originally but saw a diamond dressed up as a handyman. I repeated in a slightly different version, "You need to clone Tony." I said, "You have no more time available other than enough time to recruit and mentor someone to duplicate you."

He finally conceded, "You are right. I am going to find another me." I smiled and agreed to help him with this project. In my revised version of this book in five years, I will share our progress in my lesson titled "How I Cloned Myself and Made a Million Dollars."

FIND ANOTHER YOU, AND REAL WEALTH BEGINS.

NOVEMBER 19
OUTGROWING YOUR GROUP

My core group of friends have been with me since college, as I have five buddies I have had the privilege of doing life with. However, it is not the same group I went to high school with. It was obvious after a few weekend trips home that my plans for the future were much bigger than my classmates.

My friendship and its accompanying loyalty come at a price, and it is not given without thought. I want people that have ambition so when I share my audacious goals, they will fuel them. My family is second only to my faith, so if your core values don't align with mine, our friendship will max out at being acquaintances. Why would I spend time around someone who does not have the same core values as I do? What we each would consider fun entertainment might be dramatically different. How I want to spend my time is probably different.

In business, I don't spend a great deal of time with strugglers. I will assist them and offer advice but will limit my exposure. My goals are big, and I want to spend my time with high achievers, as I have found we feed off of each other's energy.

I have also found that there are certain people who, because of their financial situation, will never be in my close orbit. I have found that I am the first person they want to get a loan from. I also find I have to be secretive about the things I want, as this year, NetJets is on the list. It's hard to share that you are excited about flying private when the other person is barely making a car payment.

Finally, I want people who live optimistically. I want to be clear: I am just telling you my inner circle is small and protective. I want people who reflect my ambitious nature and core values and share my positive view of life. Look around and ask yourself if the group you have surrounded yourself with is helping you or holding you back.

DO YOU NEED TO MAKE AN UPGRADE?

NOVEMBER 20
STRETCH GOAL

I am a big believer in having goals and, in particular, goals that stretch you past your current comfort level, talent, and capacity. I think if a goal accomplishes those three items, then when you accomplish it, you are so much further then when you began. What I find when talking with someone about their goals is either that they have none, or the goals that they do have don't require enough effort or sacrifice. Stretch goals don't just apply to your personal goals; they also are critical for growing a business. A business with no ambitious goals will stay average and eventually fight for its life to survive.

Let's begin setting some stretch goals today. I am going to stretch your stretch goals with something I also try to include in my goal setting, an ambitious *only God* goal. If your faith doesn't recognize a Creator, call it whatever you wish, but my faith allows me to set a goal that is beyond anything I can do myself, and this is my *only God* goal. This is way past a stretch goal as that just requires great effort and sacrifice, which is still enough to discourage the average participant.

I have found setting these two types of goals has pushed me beyond average and has not only allowed me to achieve personally beyond my capacity but also my companies to achieve. And my *only God* goals, while not all have been achieved And while not all my only God goals have been achieved, a few have shocked me by how they have been reached. Someone I have never met seems to come into my life for a short period that provides a resource I did not have. When I look back over my twenty-five years in business, I can see a few mammoth goals that were above my talent and resources.

So in conclusion, I want to encourage you not only to have goals but to have some that stretch you beyond who you presently are, and because I am a believer and a "more than you can ask or imagine" follower, consider an *only God* goal.

WE DON'T JUST SET GOALS. WE SET GOALS THAT STRETCH US AND A FEW THAT REQUIRE FAITH.

340

NOVEMBER 21
BEING DECISIVE

"It's better to be boldly decisive and risk being wrong
than to agonize at length and be right too late."
—Marilyn Kennedy

There are times when you just have to make a decision. One of the biggest problems I've always had with partnerships is that I'll have some partners who cannot make a decision. I'll know the answer within thirty seconds, and I have to watch them agonize about making a decision.

Why can I make a decision so fast? Because for one, I am deciding to be decisive, as leadership demands it. This does not mean I can and do make all decisions in thirty seconds. Some require a day or possibly longer. But being decisive means that I can and will make what I believe is the correct decision before I miss out on an opportunity or advantage over my competition. It is recognizing that there is often a time limit to your final decision, or you will be too late.

I have worked with people who torture themselves trying to get every piece of information before pulling the trigger. I don't need every piece of information, as I know that no matter how much due diligence I do—and I will gather what information I believe is relevant—there will still be unknowns.

When I do make a firm decision, my standard answer to anyone who asks why I made this move is, "based on the information I had at the time along with my gut feeling" that it was the right decision. Now if that decision ends up not being right, I will change course or abandon the idea quickly and with no remorse. There is no certainty in some decisions. The very foundation of leadership is moving your team into the unknown. If every road had no forks in it, travel would not require leadership. And may I also add, there are times when I make a decision, and I beat that decision into submission. Yes, I fit a square peg into a round hole.

THERE ARE TIMES YOU SIMPLY HAVE TO BE
DECISIVE AND MOVE FORWARD.

NOVEMBER 22
LET'S KEEP IT CONCISE

We all have the ability to express an idea in a brief summary, and it's so important. I heard Donald Trump say that when somebody starts a sentence, within four words, he believes he knows the entire rest of the paragraph. I also heard him say that he once met with a Brazilian businessman, and he gave the guy three minutes to express his business idea. The guy did it, and they became partners. Billion-dollar deals done in minutes. I recently just read a book on sales pitches that confirmed three minutes is the optimum amount of time you have someone's attention for, so make your pitch concise.

I have also heard President George W. Bush did not like long-winded explanations on nearly any subject and requested them to be less than fifteen minutes long. Most high-level leaders have very little patience and have an innate skill of reading your mind, or at least believe they can. I am similar.

A staff member once began to share with me what I could tell was going to be a doctoral presentation on what I believed required not much more than a yes or no answer. I said, "Send me this entire conversation and the decision you want me to make in three sentences, no more."

I came from a sales background and initially worked for a CEO who said, "Don't bring me a problem without a solution," and he wanted that solution in two minutes or less, so I learned the value of making my pitches brief yet effective.

How To Be More Concise

- What is the one thing you are trying to tell your listener?
- What one opening sentence or two will get their attention?
- What is the one action or response you want them to make?
- What one supporting piece of information can you give to support your argument?
- What one thing can you share to win them over to your way of thinking?
- What closing remark, no more than five sentences long, can cement your point?

Why so brief? Because most audiences have a limited attention span and at the end, you can always ask them if they have any further questions.

EFFECTIVE COMMUNICATION DOES NOT REQUIRE MORE COMMUNICATION.

NOVEMBER 23
IMPLEMENTATION

"Ideas are easy, implementation is hard."
—Guy Kawasaki

Everybody has ideas, but my ability to implement an idea, to take it from just a thought in my head to something that's actually functioning and creating profit, something that's actually employing somebody, gives me greater satisfaction than any other thing I do. My thoughts align with Sue Grafton's: "Ideas are easy. It's the execution of ideas that really separates the sheep from the goats."

This is the effective execution of an idea, strategy, or high-level initiative. I get proposals for many business ventures by many different people, but the one thing I have to be confident of is their ability to implement the idea into reality. And it is this qualifier that makes me ask any would-be entrepreneur, "What have you ever started from scratch? I don't care if it is a neighborhood watch program or a small group at your church. Have you ever taken something from nothing more than a wish and brought it into a functioning organization?"

My whole life has small implementation victories that gave me the confidence to start my first business. Whether it was starting numerous intramural teams in college or starting a sports program. I then moved to a new city where within a year, not knowing one single soul before arriving, not only did I start a softball team, but it won our city championship. These just kept building my confidence, so when I decided to start a business, I had a track record of successful implementation.

My advice to anyone who has yet to start a successful business is to initiate something from scratch. No other victory will pay a higher dividend than the skill of taking something from a mere wish to reality.

A business plan is thoughts and strategies on paper, nothing more. You can give me a five-point business plan written with a sharpie marker on toilet paper, and I will make it a thriving company.

WHAT MAKES THE DIFFERENCE IS
IMPLEMENTATION.

NOVEMBER 24
SYNERGY

"The secret to success in business is synergy."
—Fah Jarod Sai

In business, you must have synergy. Often when considering adding something to your business, you don't consider synergy. You don't consider how they're going to complement each other, and you really need to. The opposite is opposing forces pulling against each other. I have been white water rafting when everyone is rowing but not in unison, and the boat just stays in the same location, turning in circles in one dominant direction. There is plenty of action but no progress, and this is why more is not always better.

Synergy is critical to consider when adding new divisions or businesses to your organization. The ventures all need to cooperate. Amazon does a great job of purchasing businesses that have perfect synergy with what they do. The Ring doorbell with monthly subscribers and Pill Pack bringing medication users to its monthly auto-shipment business are examples of this. This business model started early for Amazon with the purchase of Audible, which expand its book delivery platform. The list is endless, but the one common theme is synergy.

A perfect example of not having synergy and two forces cannibalizing the resources and focus of a company was when Circuit City added CarMax. Please, someone, tell me how they go together.

Too many business owners grow by adding new things for the sake of growth with no clear strategy and, more importantly, no clear idea of how the companies will complement each other.

Small businesses by nature do not have the cash reserves or overflow staffing to waste critical resources, and if there is no synergy, these assets get exhausted quickly.

So, synergy is when two things create something even better than each of them would be by themselves. So, I encourage you when considering adding something to your company, determine if they might have synergy because if they don't, it's a bad idea.

MORE IS NOT ALWAYS BETTER.

JUST A FEW NEW WAYS

In your effort to find new ways of growing your business, just go visit your grocery store for effective ideas. Do you have a product that has maxed out its potential? Let's take a trip together through the aisles to spark how many different ways you can fix your fledgling product sales.

Supersize it—It takes one trip to Sam's Club (where you can see peanut butter jars large enough to feed a starving village year) for you to know how effective providing larger portions of something works.

Mini-size it—How many of you now pack lunches with single-serving chip bags?

Narrow or simplify the uses—John Maxwell recently has made a fortune publishing smaller versions of his larger popular books with a more abbreviated single topic theme. This strategy not only delivers a more affordable cost to buyers but allows for new readers who want to try a bite-sized version of a book. I see these in the boutique book aisle. Merchandisers love small books as a wider variety can be carried in the limited space available.

Targeted market—Now grocery stores have sections for vegans, organic food lovers, and those who have sworn off gluten. Whole Foods made billions on this idea.

Combine it—Cereal has mastered this with adding yogurt to Special K, not to mention Honey Nuts to that bland Cheerios making Honey Nut Cheerios—now a favorite of mine.

Add something to it—Advil and Tylenol now come in PM form as well as in nearly every cold or cough medicine. PM means of course that it will help you sleep at night.

Create more uses—A good example of this is OxiClean, which was once a stand-alone stain remover and now is in laundry detergent, carpet cleaner, and dishwasher detergent, just to name a few of their now exhaustive cleaning products.

Expand your demographics—There is no greater example of this than Chicken Soup for the Soul. Note the series titles with brand, followed by demographically-targeted words for everything from pet owners to teenagers.

THESE WILL GIVE YOU SOMETHING TO GET
STARTED BRAINSTORMING ON.

NOVEMBER 26
CURIOSITY

"We keep moving forward, opening new doors, and doing new things because we're curious and curiosity keeps us leading down new paths." —Walt Disney

Curiosity is just a fascination with what could be. Something you don't presently see, yet you wonder where you can take it. That's what an entrepreneur does. They'll see a business idea, and they know it's not been maximized. They'll see a product, and they see where they can take it to.

A great example of what could be is the Star Wars movie franchise and the curiosity of its creator and now billionaire George Lucas. In the early 1970s, he directed American Graffiti, which he won an Oscar for, the movie industry's highest honor. In his late twenties, he was already an Oscar-winning director, and his curiosity said, "Let's do a science fiction movie where we will need technology that has never been used before." He was told it could not be done the way he wanted. It would require him to establish his own special effects company (Industrial Light and Magic) to make this happen. It started with curiosity about what could be, which led to a relentless pursuit of making it happen, which would bear the fruit of one of the most valuable movie franchises ever to be conceived.

Sheryl Sandberg, author and COO of Facebook shares, "Innovation and disruptive thinking stem from a common trait: curiosity." As a child, we could take a box and come up with twenty ways to have fun with it. It was a fort, maybe a dollhouse, a car, a tank, a sled that could ride down the steps, and anything else we wanted it to be because we had a curious mind. Anything was possible, and everything we touched had more than one use. The entrepreneur would be wise to keep this youthful approach.

Brian Grazer, the great movie producer and author of *A Curious Mind*, opines, "Curiosity—asking questions—isn't just a way of understanding the world. It's a way of changing it." And to beat the nail just a little deeper, Albert Einstein advised "to not stop questioning." So, I ask, are you still curious? Do you have a curious mind that continues to ask, "What if? Can it be done that way? What else can we do with this?" The list is endless, but the point is obvious—don't lose your curiosity.

BUILD YOUR SENSE OF CURIOSITY.

ANNUITY

I want you to think a little differently about why you want to start and build a successful company. I want to lower the bar a little, maybe even a lot, to show you how valuable even a small successful, durable venture can be. I began this new way of thinking about a decade ago when I had a few smaller ventures that I realized would never become juggernauts. I had to lower my expectations.

It was during some financial planning and looking at what I would want financially in retirement. To be clear, I don't want or plan to retire, but as I share, you plan for options, and in my senior years, anything I choose to do will be done because I want to, not have to. With that said, it was proposed that I create an annuity, which is a financial tool that in retirement will pay a fixed sum of money (normally each month) until you die. That is the typical way it works. Because it has the potential to pay out over a lengthy period of time, the annual return on investment is low, something on average of 3.5 percent. It was when I saw the payout on a substantial amount of money that I had my aha moment.

Let me see if I can jar your motivation. If I had $1,000,000 that I had amassed into my annuity, then at retirement, it would be $35,000 before taxes. After taxes and capital gains of about 20% on a moderate income, my annual income would be about $28,000. So, after I sacrificed and amassed $1,000,000, my annual reward for this would be around $28,000 with a monthly income of $2,350. The monthly payout of less than $2,500 on a million dollars changed my paradigm in business.

I always felt like every company I started needed to be big and great; that is just my way of thinking. If you are going to do it, do it better and bigger! I have since learned that some companies, no matter what you do, have a ceiling. I realized that even a low ceiling would net me a nice return. I could accomplish making the $2,500 per month profit that I would make as an owner with one hand tied behind my back. So instead of being disappointed about a few struggling ventures I had in my portfolio, I changed my strategy.

CREATE A FEW ANNUITIES.

NOVEMBER 28
PACK MULE OR RACEHORSE

I had a meeting this week with one of my partners regarding a new venture we started. It was doing very well, but I still wanted to touch base on cash flow and staffing. My partner shared that cash flow was good, to which I asked if there was any waste. He responded, "I hope not." We then moved on to staff, and I asked him to play the hit TV show Survivor with me for a moment. He had three new hires, and I asked him if he could only have two of them, who would they be? In under ten seconds, he shared the winners. I asked what the difference between them is, and he made some comparisons. I replied, "She is not a racehorse or a pack mule, so we need to put her down."

My analysis was this person was not fast at anything, so our profit margins on her work were not as great as they could be, and finally, she is fragile in that under pressure or heavy assignments, she collapses. Again, one is a racehorse and one a pack mule. In a start-up, you better have one or the other. Anything else is costing you money. It is a simple game with only two lines. The only person that gets an immunity idol, which in the show is an item that allows you to be exempt from being voted out of the game, is a highly productive salesperson. When putting your start-up team on the field, you need these three. Anyone else is a luxury you cannot afford.

I ask myself toward the end of each year, if I had to start my company over again, who would I want on the team? I naturally cut the roster in half, forcing me to make tough choices. I don't have to let anyone go, but I do become reminded of whom I value the most. As your company grows, you can have many players that can play ancillary roles, but a start-up must have instant contributors, or they are costing you money.

ANYBODY NEED TO GET VOTED OFF THE ISLAND?

348

NOVEMBER 29
NEVER STOP, NEVER QUIT

One thing about championship teams is that they're resilient. No matter what is thrown at them, no matter how deep the hole, they find a way to bounce back and overcome adversity."
—*Nick Saban, Legendary College Football Coach*

As a former Division 1 wrestler, I had my hesitations when my son was recruited to wrestle in eighth grade. I told him that unlike other sports in which he had participated, wrestling was unique. It is a one-on-one sport with no timeouts, nowhere to hide, and no one else to blame. And that is why I loved it and believe it prepared me for life's journey. It taught me to never give up! I also had a choice of how much effort I would give. Someone could be better than me, more skilled, but they would never outwork me, and this would quite often be the weapon even the more skilled combatant could not handle.

With all this said, recently my son participated in an event with multiple matches, and I could tell he was not putting forth the effort required to be great. His final match was a loss resulting from a lack of effort. I shared with him, "You quit in that match." He confided that he, in fact, did not give it everything he could. I suggested he resign as team captain until that could be overcome. "I can live with you losing, as that happens, but your quitting is not acceptable. Not in wrestling or anything else." He would go on to apologize to his team, and a new wrestler was born. His new motto: never stop, never quit.

Do you want to be an entrepreneur? Well, how many businesses are you going to start? Do you honestly think they're all going to work out perfectly? I'm as optimistic as anybody, but your ability to be resilient, to get back up, not to let things knock you down, that's going to be the difference. You have to be able to adapt, to overcome. That's what successful people do.

MAKE A CHOICE TO NEVER QUIT, TO NEVER GIVE LESS THAN YOUR BEST EFFORT.

NOVEMBER 30
WHOM DO YOU SERVE?

"Every decision in your business should flow from two questions;
whom do you serve and how can you better serve them?"
—Sean Castrina

Think about it just for a second: your business has one job to do that if you fail, you are out of business, and if you are successful, the money will take care of itself. That one job is to have a product or service that serves the needs, wants, or desires of a customer. So, whom do you serve? The answer is a target customer and their needs, wants, and desires. As an example of meeting the desire of a customer, Sandals vacations has a target market—couples who want a romantic vacation. Nothing else. This is accomplished through childfree visits to the most beautiful places in the world with endless ways to be entertained as well as relax. They serve that one audience with the best possible vacation.

I can go on and on, but your business has an audience that you must feel privileged to serve. Continually ask how you can better meet their needs. Nothing you can do is more paramount.

Who is your target customer, and how can you better serve them? This should be your ongoing North Star for your business. There are countless ways to achieve this objective.

- Can we make a better project?
- Can we create a better experience?
- Can we make buying easier?
- Can we give them more value for their dollar?
- Can we provide more information?
- Can we remove skepticism?
- Can we build more confidence in our company?
- Can we make returns effortless?
- Can we provide more customer support?
- Can we better reward their patronage of our business?
- Can we better reward their referrals?
- Are we providing the best shopping experience possible?

The list is endless.

WHO DO YOU SERVE AND HOW CAN YOU DO IT BETTER?

DECEMBER 1
HOW TO MAXIMIZE AN INTERVIEW

You will find that any high-level position within a company will have to do staffing, and as I am sure you already know, your ability to amass talent will make the difference. When I bring on a partner, they often have had interviews for a job but have never yet been the interviewer. I shared a lesson earlier about interviewing Benjamin Button. Within three minutes, I knew this person was not a good fit by any of the countless qualifiers I use. However, even though I thought the candidate's grand claims were not factual, and that I saw little to no value in this person, my new partner still thought there might be potential. I, of course, shared that we are a start-up; we don't hire for what we hope might happen with this person. We hire someone we both would almost bet our lives on would be a superstar. "We cannot afford to miss on this hire," to which he agreed this would not be a bet he would be willing to make.

My partner would then ask me to be a part of another interview in the upcoming week. Now that he understood that missing was not an option, he liked that I had a keen BS detector. He shared a time and date, and I gave him a few of my rules for interviewing.

Never do one interview in a day; always schedule back-to-back interviews. This keeps interviews from going unnecessarily long as well as creates natural competition as the contestants see others coming and going. This method will reveal the contrasts in the two that will allow for easier determination of what you like and don't like. Finally, this maximizes your time as you get two interviews done for what would normally be one long interview.

Bonus: I also would advise making an effort to involve staff in your hires. Have them rate each candidate with a number from one through ten, of course, ten being earned by a superstar. You will be surprised by the different number you will have as a leader and what they will have, which will nearly always be higher. But let me give you the real secret: tell them that no one is allowed a seven. Seven does not exist, as it's easy to give this average, no-commitment score. This one exercise will force them to be committed to an eight or six, which is two different categories of talent: one below average, and one above it.

MAKE EVERY HIRE COUNT.

DECEMBER 2
THIRTY-DAY CEO—PART I

"Everything rises and falls on leadership."
—John Maxwell

Your company will only go as far as your leadership, so if you are young or have never held a position of leadership before, this can be intimidating, but you can develop this area. If I had thirty days to train you to be a CEO, the list to follow is where I would spend my time getting you to focus on and commit to improving daily in each of these areas over the lifetime of your organization.

Decide from day one to be an effective leader.

Everything starts with your decision to recognize that you want to be an effective leader. Can you remember a strong leader you admire? Why do you admire that person?

Have a vision.

You need to have a vivid picture of what you want for this company. Create a vision for your company that not only excites you but everyone around you.

Communicate the vision to others.

When you tell others your dream for the company, they get excited and want to be a part of what is to come.

Recruit and retain needed talent.

If you cannot build a team, you will never grow a great company. Start becoming a talent scout.

Have the motivational skill to bring out the best in others.

If you cannot bring out the best in people, they will never reach their potential and thus will fail to be the assets they could be for your organization.

Place people in their areas of strength.

Leaders are coaches and know where people will flourish. You adeptly identify where best to place people in their strength.

Push people to expand their capacity and increase their productivity.

You have the ability to maximize not only people's talent but also their capacity. They do more for the organization than one person would normally do.

BECOMING A GREAT LEADER IS NOT OPTIONAL.

DECEMBER 3
THIRTY DAY CEO—PART II

Create strategies to achieve major goals and initiatives. Ideas are worthless without a strategy to achieve them. You have the confidence of your team not because your vision is grand but because you have created a plan to achieve it that others believe is possible.

Hire managers and others so the day-to-day needs do not strangle you.

Do not allow yourself to be tangled up in tasks that can be delegated. You work on your company, not in your company. You hover above so you can see ahead and what will be needed to get you there.

Stay focused on high-level objectives and goals.

Recognize the value of accomplishing high-payoff tasks and goals. You will decide what one goal, if accomplished, will take the organization further. What one initiative, when achieved, will have the highest payoff?

Create a culture.

If you do not create the culture, someone else will. Decide what attitude and behavior you want the organization to display.

Problem-solve.

Not only do you see problems before others, you solve them when they arise. Big problems don't get solved by accident or time and rarely by others.

Manage money and other valuable resources.

No one will manage resources like the owner. Keep your eyes on every dime. Maximize and leverage every asset you have.

Value other leaders.

One leader on the team will end up being a very small, ineffective team. Knowing the value of a leader, you will be in an ongoing search to hire them as well as to develop them on your team.

Grow your leadership skills.

Knowing the value of leadership, you will strengthen this area indefinitely. Spend time reading leadership books, listening to podcasts, and attending seminars on this subject.

I HAVE DETERMINED TO BE A GREAT LEADER.

DECEMBER 4
SOME THINGS JUST COME TO AN END

*"Endings don't have to be failures, especially when you choose
to end a project or shut down a business."*
—Samin Nosrat

Samin would go on to say, "Even the best gigs don't last forever. Nor should they." To which I give a hearty "Amen." I spend plenty of time talking about persistence, determination, and a never-quit attitude as traits you would be lucky to have as an entrepreneur, but do not let these also allow you to make the mistake of putting a business on life support. There are some businesses, projects, and investments that need to come to an end.

These are my Big Three for knowing when to put an end to a project, business, or initiative:

The return (financial payoff) is no longer worth the amount of time, energy, focus, and resources I am giving it.

I have lost interest, and this is not for the person who loses interest in everything. But some initiatives no longer pull at me. It just starts becoming all work and no fun. I have other projects that I do not have the time to start because I am shackled to this venture.

Finally, I do not have the resources to do other things that I either want to do or feel could be very profitable because they are getting sapped up in what I am currently involved in.

Your motivators to bring something to a close may be different, but what I shared will more often than not give you a warning signal that it may be time.

NOT EVERY VENTURE IS A LIFE SENTENCE.

DECEMBER 5
PERSONAL RESPONSIBILITY

"The buck stops here."
—President Harry S. Truman

President Truman had this quote made into a sign that was on his desk in the Oval Office. It would be a daily reminder that he had the final word and responsibility for the decisions he made.

If you want to be a leader, you've got to be able to take personal responsibility for things. You cannot constantly throw your team members under the bus when things go wrong, especially if you either did not step up to the plate, abdicating your leadership, or you were involved in the decision in any way. There are times when I have to throw myself under the bus if I have had anything to do with the choices made because I want to shield my staff. There are countless situations where I will ask for input, but I made it clear that I will render the final verdict and be responsible for the results.

There are times I may choose to take the road my partners have warned against taking. I don't do this often, but on occasion, I see an opportunity that may have a grand payoff and be worth the risk or accompanying resources required. It may turn out to be a total loser, to which I say, "This one is totally on me." I have actually led my partner into a venture that turned out to be an expensive loss. I absorbed the financial hit because I knew I was the primary cheerleader that got us into it. For the record, it was no small amount, as it took five years to pay this back, but it was the right thing to do.

Stephen Covey talked about personal responsibility in *Seven Habits of Highly Effective People*, where he says, "You just can't blame people for your situations in life. You've got to take responsibility for where you're at in life." Take personal responsibility for the wins and the failures.

Let me ask, "Does the buck stop with you?" It should.

GREAT LEADERS TAKE PERSONAL RESPONSIBILITY.

DECEMBER 6
MANAGING PERSONALITIES

You need to learn how to manage personalities. As a small-business owner, you may have only five people on your staff, but they may all have different personalities, and I hope they do. Your goal is to have a series of ingredients that when combined create a great dish. I always share the value of great hiring even if, and more importantly when, you only have a smaller team.

This lesson should alert you to the fact that every candidate you interview not only has a skill set that may be valuable but that you should also be trying to get a quick read on their personality type. Are they quiet, loud, easygoing, confrontational, or non-confrontational? Are they a leader or a follower? They each lend themselves to strengths and weaknesses.

Your team should be made up of a nice combination of personalities. Having all hard-charging, loud personalities can wear a team out quickly. I have found seasoning the dish with some quieter, less confrontational members is a great salt additive. A touch of a happy-go-lucky personality provides a nice addition to any culture. I have learned over the years to put contrasting personalities together by design, as two high-energy, loud people together more often than not will combust sooner rather than later.

In my hiring, I am creating duets and ensembles, and I consider which notes they can all sing because I don't want four baritones. So, in my effort to have varying personalities, I also have learned to manage them all differently. How I talk to a loud, confrontational person I can mirror in approach is very different from the way I talk to a quiet, non-confrontational personality.

A great culture involves different personalities, and you need to be the conductor who creates an amazing symphony. I want to encourage you today to learn to hire and manage diverse personalities.

MANAGING PERSONALITIES WILL BRING OUT THE BEST IN YOUR TEAM.

DECEMBER 7
DON'T BECOME DEPENDENT

There are very few pieces of advice I can give you more valuable than this: Do not allow yourself to be too dependent on others. For instance, if you are not computer savvy, and all of your business reports and financial information are housed on a computer, then you are in trouble. If you don't have the passcodes to all computer accounts and voicemail systems, then you are not in control of your business.

I am passive in many of my businesses, but I have mechanisms in place that always allow me to know what is going on. Here are two ideas that worked for me to allow me to maintain control of my businesses without relying too much on others:

- In my service companies, I have a spiral-bound notebook with fifty-two pages, one for each week. An abbreviated view of customer contact information and money received is entered here before being logged in the computer. I can scan this book and know the call volume, how calls were generated, what was contracted for, and how much was received. This is like my car's dashboard instruments. I can easily tell if I am low on oil or need emergency servicing.

- I once owned a retail business where I received a text message every night at closing with sales for the day. I also had all the business mail go to my personal office so I could be aware of the bills. If your staff knows you have no idea what's going on, you've lost control of your company.

To some degree, you are dependent on your employees, vendors, and contractors. The way you don't become too dependent is having a plan in place for when the unexpected happens.

Susan Payton, a marketing communications instructor, has a plan in place: "When an employee quits, it can be a shock, especially if you don't have a contingency plan to replace them. Become independent and prevent this by 1.) Having processes in place to make it easy to train a replacement and 2.) Ensure you have enough employees to get the work done, rather than having extra strain on one person who will soon quit from the pressure."

Using the same logic, have alternate vendors you can depend upon when your regular vendor drops the ball.

DELEGATION AND BEING DEPENDENT ARE DIFFERENT: NEVER BE DEPENDENT.

DECEMBER 8
MY TAKE ON CULTURE

It seems like company culture is the current buzzword like management was in the 1980s, led by people like Peter Drucker. Leadership was paramount in the 1990s, and innovation led the internet and tech era. All have tremendous value, and a massive deficiency in any could without question affect a company, but culture is the seasoning to a great steak.

When a company is struggling, it seems like the first go-to move is to fix the culture. Guess what? If your company is struggling, your team knows it, and your culture will reflect a struggling, uncertain environment. When things are great and profitable, and everyone is getting raises and bonuses, the flock is happy.

The steak is what you offer to your customers. Do they still want it, and are you able to charge enough to have an attractive margin? That is a simplification of the complicated. If you lack any of what I just listed, culture will not fix it. These are the foundations of your home, and culture is the landscaping. It makes it look a lot better and welcoming, but it does not hold up the house.

Let me share what I think culture can and cannot do. Culture is the attitude of your company. Do you have positive or negative energy? To put it more simply, do you get the idea that most people want to come to work for your company each day? They like the team and the direction it is moving. If the chemistry of employees is bad or they don't believe in what you are offering customers, they will not have a positive view of their workplace. Do they feel appreciated by owners and their leadership? Feeling appreciated and valuable will affect whether someone likes where they work, and this will permeate the culture.

Do you have a customer-centric approach to how you do business? This means you genuinely want to do right by the customer, and it is obvious in your handling of problems, warranties, returns, etc. Team members want to feel like you care about whom they are serving and selling to, so if they sense the customer is not valued or is being taken advantage of, this will disconnect them from a full buy-in of your company. The result is a negative culture.

CULTURE IS A GREAT SEASONING
TO ADD TO A GREAT STEAK.

DECEMBER 9
STOP AND PAUSE

I am a go-go-go kind of person, which at times has served me well. If you wanted something done, I was the guy you gave it to or wanted on your team. I have learned as I have gotten older that inactivity has value as well. Actually, I have learned to not run into a fire without first pausing and considering all my options.

Why stop and pause? It will improve every decision you make. At a minimum, it will confirm your initial decision, giving you greater confidence.

Stop and pause:

- Think.
- Consider your best option.
- Confirm that this is your only option.
- Consider the consequences.
- Contemplate the collateral damage.
- Count the costs.
- Maximize your resources.
- Ask questions of others.
- Gain peace of mind.
- Get over emotions.

If you're a person of faith, do as I do and consider stopping and praying first. When I do, I gain insight my human brain does not have. Praying gives me a peace that surpasses my normal understanding.

TO HAVE CLARITY, OFTEN TIMES YOU NEED A MOMENT OF SILENCE.

DECEMBER 10
NOBODY WANTS WHAT YOU ARE SELLING

"Life's too short to build something nobody wants."
—Ash Maurya

Bram Krommenhook shares in an article, "*Why 90 percent of start-ups fail and what to do about it,*" "A founder gets an idea, builds the solution, tries to sell it, nobody buys the solution. The founder runs out of money, the start-up dies." I have heard that no business plan survives its first contact with the market. The reality is that you present to the world what you think they want, and they quickly give you feedback. It is your ability to adapt to this feedback that will determine if your start-up survives. Steve Blank, an entrepreneurial expert, advises, "The only way you'll be able to grow your start-up is by combining building with research. By embracing feedback, you open yourself up to enormous success you've never seen before."

I am always surprised by what my start-up business is actually selling three years from its inception. Without fail, we are offering something I never intended in my original strategy, and we are no longer offering something I believed at inception to be critical. And it is because of this that I developed the "pup tent" philosophy. You believe with every ounce of data that you have something the marketplace wants and needs, so you start a business with just enough resources to breathe. It is then that you begin making adjustments as they present themselves.

The law of survival in the start-up phase is this: Your ability to get feedback from your customers as quickly as possible and your openness to accept it, followed by your ability to implement adjustments, will determine your survival. Smart founders begin getting feedback from friends, family, and neighbors even prior to launch, knowing the value of others' opinions outside of their overly optimistic and limited view as the founder. We tend to have blinders on, not seeing the obvious. My advice is to get feedback by any and all means available, and be open to making changes, no matter how much you love your original idea.

NEXT ONLY TO CASH, FEEDBACK IS YOUR
NEXT BEST ASSET AS A START-UP.

DECEMBER 11
SWING FOR THE FENCE

"I was a better builder than a manager. I'd rather focus on maximizing the opportunities swinging for the fences than minimizing the risk with bunts and singles." —Steve Case, AOL Founder

I have just recently had to "swing for the fence." This just means I needed a home run to get my initiative off the ground. It had been struggling with no real progress, so I needed to stop playing it safe and go for the home run—an all-out swing, hoping for contact. To be frank with you, in business, I am more like Tony Gwynn, a Hall of Fame player, known for just getting on base with singles. Singles are the easiest hit you can make, but what made Tony an outlier was that he hit them with ease. He did it at a rate of one in three times at the plate, which I'll say for those not familiar with hitting 100 miles-per-hour pitches, is a feat not many can do.

I have learned there are times when you or your team need a home run. It is the bottom of the ninth, and there are two outs, no one on base, and you are tied or down by a run, and you need a long-ball hitter. That one guy who swings for the fence; when they make contact, it just sounds different. They hit the ball with bad intentions, trying to crush its core. In business, there are moments when you need to swing much harder.

My current project is just on a treadmill, so I needed to bring on someone who has tremendous experience and a proven track record for accomplishing what my team and I have been trying to accomplish. This player does not even live in the United States, and the amount of money I wire-transferred to bring them on the team was so large my bank representative literally looked at me like a family member was being held hostage. The banker repeated the amount with skepticism, reminding me the receiving bank was seven thousand miles away. I confirmed all was accurate and "Yes," I said firmly, "please make the transfer." That was me swinging for the fence.

This one decision brought me exponentially closer to my main goal of the past four years than any one thing we have done in all that time. Yes, it cost a fortune, and sure, I had second thoughts at the time, but "Insanity is doing the same thing over and over again and expecting different results" (Einstein). So, I decided it was time to "swing for the fence."

IS IT TIME FOR YOU TO SWING FOR THE FENCE?

VALUE ADDED

My wife and I have found a new restaurant we love, and it is the perfect example of value-added and a payoff. One thing it does that is quite smart and unique for a restaurant is to be open for breakfast and lunch only. I have finally picked up on what seems to be the reason, and it's brilliant. If you serve all three meals, your staffing is much more of a challenge because you have multiple shifts. This abbreviated schedule allows your servers to make more money because they are not working only one meal rush.

What I am also fairly confident of is that their net profit for only two meals equals the revenue of three average meals served. The secret is the value added to what they serve and the elevated pricing the customer pays. My normal breakfast at my usual hotspot runs me about $7–8, and at my new eating parlor, I pay $10 at a minimum and closer to $12 per plate. I gladly pay it because everything is better there.

The interior is decorated perfectly, giving it a great local feel, but the high-end accent pieces are obvious to me. The food is plated perfectly and on robust kitchenware. The plates are large and square, and they fill every inch of it with organic eggs that are simply huge. These healthy monster eggs are surrounded with bacon that is twice as thick as standard bacon with very little fat. The potatoes are not your standard hash browns or tater tots—heck no, these could be served with a dinner steak. Because you have been hypnotized by the folksy manner of the highly-skilled wait staff, you don't pay attention to the $3 price tag on the coffee being served.

Everything you experience is a value add, not what you expect—so much more than just average. The payoff is loyal customers waiting thirty minutes to be seated for a meal that they have told their friends about. You will gladly pay a bill that is 50 percent more than your customary breakfast or lunch spot.

FIND SOMETHING OF VALUE YOU CAN ADD TO YOUR CUSTOMERS.

DECEMBER 13
HOW DECLINE HAPPENS

I am surprised when I talk to business owners who don't recognize they are in decline. I often get asked to help prevent a company from going out of business. Oftentimes, they are too far gone and cannot be resuscitated. If you look at the demise of any stalwart company, you will see a combination of the reasons listed below for their extinction.

Twelve Reasons For Decline and Possible Extinction

1. Became overconfident

2. Grew too fast (size)

3. Expanded geographically

4. Got distracted by the new shiny object

5. Forgot their core business (what made them the money to start with)

6. Wasted money on non-core business

7. Forgot the fundamentals of business

8. Changed for the sake of changing

9. Exhausted reserves

10. Had no clear focus (goal, objective, strategy, etc.)

11. Ignored small threats (Redbox, Netflix)

12. Had poor leadership

My simple advice: be alert to the warning signs I have shared. It tends to be a subtle combination of the above that leads to a consistent decline in revenue and customer acquisition, which eventually leads to being out of business.

A DECLINE IS YOUR ALERT SIGNAL.

DECEMBER 14
INTUITION, IMAGINATION, AND IMPLEMENTATION

I call these the Big Three *Is* of truly exceptional entrepreneurs. I have shared a lesson on each but wanted to put them all together so you can see their combined effect. The example I would share is that you may want a quarterback to have a strong throwing arm, as that is one valuable quality. They may also have a quick release, allowing them to get the ball out of their hand faster, preventing being sacked. Having both of these makes them even more sought after, but if this unicorn could also run the ball, giving them a dual threat, you have a superstar. I believe if you can develop the Big Three *Is*, you will be at the next level as a business owner.

Intuition just means that you have a keen gut instinct. I believe that I am a psychic at times and can sense problems coming before they actually do. I sense downturns in the market before anyone on my team—and remember, I am an optimist. I pay attention to trends and downturns and know they are the predictors of the future. Top-level business leaders just predict the future and have a plan for these challenging seasons. They are rarely caught off guard.

Next, imagination, the innate quality entrepreneurs all share that allows us to spend a little time in la-la land just wondering *what if?* We believe in the unseen. There is no such thing as *can't* in the mind of a gifted creator. President John F. Kennedy said it best: "Some men see things as they are and ask why. I dream of things that never were and ask why not." This should be the battle cry of entrepreneurs across the globe. Begin the daily habit of just thinking outside the box, or maybe you need to begin thinking big with no limits.

Finally, ideas are like belly buttons in nearly all cases; we all have one. It is the ability to take that idea from a mere thought to a breathing organization that gives us our credibility. We have ideas every day because we are idea machines, but we know how to discern the best idea—the one with the greatest payoff—and focus relentlessly on making it happen. Your ability to have big goals, initiatives, or even that initial start-up idea is worthless if you cannot make any of this happen.

BEGIN DEVELOPING THE BIG THREE.

DECEMBER 15
ACCOUNTING 101

Caron Beesley shares a great Fundbox article identifying accounting terms every small-business owner should know. I have shared that I believe that it is a big mistake for business owners to be completely dependent on their accountants for knowing the financial status of their business. So, with that said, I will draw most of my technical definitions from her article and lend my personal experience to it as well. To be clear, her article does the heavy lifting for me.

Eight Accounting Terms Every Business Owner Needs To Know and Understand:

Accounts Receivable is money owed to your company.

Accounts Payable is money the business owes.

Balance Sheet gives a snapshot of your company's financial health. It is a summary of your key financial data (assets, liabilities, and the owner's equity).

Expenses are the costs to keep your business running. You need to know what your daily, weekly, and monthly expenses are.

Break Even is the point where your income meets your expenses and profit begins.

Cash Flow is the money coming in and going out. Your ability to have enough cash on hand to meet accounts payable will determine if you survive. Think of cash flow like oxygen.

Profit is what is left over after expenses, the part you get to keep. I always say to the CPA who works in my office, "How much of what I am looking at (bank accounts with nice balances) is mine?"

Profit and Loss Statement (P/L) will provide an overview of how your business is performing over a given time period. It will break down revenue generated and expenses incurred.

DON'T BE FINANCIALLY IGNORANT.

DECEMBER 16
FINDING A NEEDLE IN A HAYSTACK

As I have shared, I am always on the lookout for talent, but one method that consistently puts people in front of me is simply running employment ads that have a few lines that will always catch the attention of the "needle in a haystack." I will litter our ads with statements like ownership possibility for the right person. "We are looking for those with an entrepreneurial mindset, not just someone just wanting to be an employee." Or "Tremendous compensation and flexibility of schedule for the right person, and that person is a superstar." We will only use one of these in any ad. I will run standard ads often, but once a month, I go "needle" hunting. This is when I don't want any employee, just a superstar. My searches will often build my employee depth charge if we need to make a hire.

So how does the interview flow? I start by asking them to give me a brief summary, (three minutes or less) of their employment history. Then, I ask what they are great at. Superstars will tell you they are a superstar. Assuming this person (whom I qualify prior to the interview with a review of their resume and often a quick phone call) meets the criteria I need, I then go on to my patented line, "Tell me which person you are." I present to them these four options:

Person One—Good, solid, reliable employee seeks, needs, and wants security—salary, fixed hours, etc.

Person Two—High achiever who because of their achievements earns the right to manage others. This person wants security and is not a natural-born leader but can lead.

Person Three—Has everything Person Two has but also is a natural leader. This person can initiate and oversee projects, divisions, and companies. They have great ambition but need to be told how to direct it. Needs motivation and financial security. Would rather make less with no risk.

Person Four—They can take something from nothing and make it into something special. This person can take a mere plan or even an idea and get it off the ground. This person has high-level ambition, initiative, and problem-solving skills. This person wants to make as much as possible and is willing to bet on themselves.

Bonus:

Person Five—This is the person who is smart enough to be able to recruit Person Four, and it'd better be you.

START FINDING THE NEEDLE IN THE HAYSTACK.

DECEMBER 17
ANNUAL COMPANY PHYSICAL

I give my companies a general physical. Each industry may have a variation on this, but you should understand the basics. Spending time at the close of each year analyzing the well-being of your company will allow you to address problems before they become unfixable.

- Do we still have a competitive advantage? If so, what is it?
- Do we have new competition? Where do they cause the greatest threat to us?
- What are our greatest threats to survival?
- Is our customer base growing or declining?
- What new opportunity or profit stream should we consider?
- How is our balance sheet? How do our cash reserves and debt look?
- Where are our staffing weaknesses and deficiencies?
- What infrastructure investments do we need to make? (software, machinery, vehicles, uniforms, etc.)
- What 1–3 things do we need to improve on?
- What is our core business, and are we still prioritizing it?
- Where are we leaking money (waste)?
- What expenses can we save on or costs we can renegotiate?
- Where do we need more or better leadership?
- What one change would make the biggest difference?
  Can we see where our industry is moving? Are we prepared?

HOW HEALTHY IS YOUR COMPANY?

DECEMBER 18
THE BERMUDA TRIANGLE OF START-UPS

According to a Fractyl study of why start-ups didn't survive, it confirmed the Big Three that I have cautioned founders about. They run out of money, they have a product or service but an uninterested market (not enough customers want what they are offering) and they have a business model that just cannot successfully and sustainably deliver on what they are offering. It is a model that cannot reach scale. The fact is, no matter how brilliant the idea, if you can't make it profitable or scalable, you won't have a successful business.

Let's take a glance at the three corners of our triangle that cause start-up failure. Running out of cash provides the death blow to a quarter of all start-ups, so let's examine this closer. Businesses are too fragile initially to be able to accommodate any waste of capital. Cash is like oxygen, and when you have a start-up, you need to think like a scuba diver who has one tank and it's already on low.

Reason two for meeting a fatal demise is no traction in the marketplace, which I blame for half of why businesses run out of cash. Businesses go out of business for one reason 99 percent of the time: they run out of money. The reasons for this can vary, but the final diagnosis is nearly always no more oxygen (cash). What is traction? It is your product finding a place in the marketplace. Customers want what you are selling—as simple as that.

The final boundary that brings start-ups to a spiraling death is a bad business model. You have something people may want, but you cannot consistently deliver it. Either product is bad, actual delivery is bad, follow-up service is poor, or you cannot ever get the initial model to scale. These create a fragile business that will not survive. Again, there are varying reasons why a model is weak, but that is a lesson for another day.

If you want to avoid the Bermuda Triangle that causes the statistical majority of all start-up failures, avoid:

- Running out of cash
- Having no traction in the market
- Having a bad business model

BE ALERT TO THE
BERMUDA TRIANGLE OF START-UPS.

DECEMBER 19
HOW TO FUND YOUR START-UP

Once you have your business plan and the amount you need, you can begin deciding the best ways to fund this. One thing to consider is whether you have time to work and save the money required. I call this going at the speed of cash. If you can launch in a year, that may give you the time to get all your ducks in a row, polish your plan, and even recruit a partner or team member. I do not think that waiting six months would have made the difference between success and failure to any one of the more than twenty businesses I started.

My plan for funding is starting from the top and working back. Remember if you can get off the ground and show potential, your chances of getting investors on board are much greater.

Work and put money away so you can personally fund your startup.

Use credit you already have (credit cards, lines of credit, etc.).

Borrow. Yes, borrow. Don't give equity unless it is the only choice available from family and friends. Create an attractive loan for them instead.

Go to your local bank, who may help with a SBA loan or personal loan.

Seek online lending institutions that specialize in these types of loans.

Seek venture capital—if you have a strong business plan and a "big-time" idea that has huge payoff potential.

Find an Angel investor—somewhat like a venture capital firm, these are individuals who just have a reputation and interest in being in on the ground floor of a start-up with potential. They can also serve as a good mentor, as they have skin in the game.

Crowdfunding is becoming more and more popular and is something to consider.

I HAVE LEARNED PROFITABLE IDEAS ALWAYS ATTRACT THE NEEDED MONEY TO LAUNCH.

DECEMBER 20
BEING DECISIVE DOESN'T MEAN BEING STUBBORN

*"If I need to change my mind, I might as well
do it sooner rather than later."*
—Al Pittampalli

I used to think that when I made a decision, it was final as if I were a judge delivering a verdict. What I have learned (and have read in support of this idea) is that it is OK for me to change my mind. I used to think this was being weak, indecisive, or "flippy floppy." It is not; it's just called being smart.

Fortunately, this characteristic is supported by others such as Al Pittampalli, author of *Persuadable: How Great Leaders Change Their Minds to Change the World,* who is a consultant who has worked with leaders at NASA, Boeing, and IBM. In an interview with *Canadian Business,* he argues that the smartest people "don't wait for that negative feedback to come to them, they hurry up and try to actually say, 'If I need to change my mind, I might as well do it sooner rather than later.'"

I read in a *Make It* article what Apple's CEO shared at a 2012 conference: "Steve would flip on something so fast that you would forget that he was the one taking the 180-degree polar opposite position the day before," he told the audience. "I saw it daily. This is a gift because things do change, and it takes courage to change. It takes courage to say, 'I was wrong.' I think he had that."

According to Jason Fried, cofounder of Basecamp and author of *Rework,* Amazon founder Jeff Bezos said, "People who were right a lot of the time were people who often changed their minds ... It's perfectly healthy—encouraged, even—to have an idea tomorrow that contradicted your idea today." Bezos went on to explain that the smartest people he's observed were always "revising their understanding, reconsidering a problem they thought they'd already solved. They're open to new points of view, new information, new ideas, contradictions, and challenges to their own way of thinking."

I WOULD RATHER BE RIGHT THAN STUBBORN.

DECEMBER 21
YOU MAY BE A TEAM OF ONE

Owning your own business, especially during the first few start-up years, can be a lonely time. Some of you will have left your full-time employment to start your own company. Previously, your coworkers were people you've known and socialized with for years. Those days could well be over.

In a start-up business, you will have many people that I call must-hires. You hire them because you need them to perform certain tasks. There is no guarantee that you will ever have a personal relationship with them. You shouldn't expect to, in fact.

As a corollary, I would warn you to think long and hard before you hire a friend or family member to work in your business. Noam Wasserman, a Harvard Business School professor, says that business partnerships with friends and family are one of the most common decisions, "But that type of team is the least stable. It's the most likely to end up in disaster." There is a great potential for misunderstanding, as the boundary lines and mutual expectations of your relationship start to change—as well they must.

I have a good friend who ended up having to fire his brother-in-law. To say that their last family reunion was awkward is an understatement. Letting a family member go—even more than a friend—can rebound in unpleasant ways.

There are reasons to hire people who are close to you. They can be loyal and trustworthy partners and employees. However, hiring them contains inherent risks. As a rule, you might not want to depend on these relationships to operate your business.

I encourage you to find a social network such as a sports league, church group, or poker night where you will have weekly interactions on a social level. Be prepared to look outside of your business for friendships. In general, family and friends and business relationships should be kept separate.

IT CAN BE LONELY AT THE TOP.

DECEMBER 22
ASK QUESTIONS

"Successful people ask better questions, and as a result, they get better answers."
—Tony Robbins

Why do you ask questions? Because when you ask questions, you find a better way to do things. Do you keep probing an idea and asking, "Can we do it better?" Or are you the type of person who just accepts that what is currently being done is the best way to do things? If you do that, the industry will change, and you'll be outdated soon enough. Percy Ross, a self-made millionaire and philanthropist offers, "You've got to ask! Asking is, in my opinion, the world's most powerful—and neglected—secret to success."

So again, start asking questions. Ask your employees, "Can we do it better? Is there a more efficient way to do it? Can we save costs?" You'll be surprised if you just add asking questions to your list of skills. How would it improve your company, make it more efficient, make it better, and make it more innovative? Authors Jack Canfield and Kent Healy put it, "There are so many answers, hints, techniques, benefits, and opportunities available ... if we just have the courage to ask for them."

I schedule lunches and Zoom calls, some where I pay crazy money, to just ask smart, experienced people questions about issues or problems that I have. Anytime I can, I gain insight from someone. When you make it a habit to spend time with sharp people and you have learned the value of asking great questions, you will do as I do and come prepared whenever I am going to be in the presence of someone I can learn from.

I have learned a powerful set of questions when considering an ambitious goal or initiative I want our company to achieve. The two questions are: Why do I want to achieve this? How will I (or we, if it is company-related) make this happen? What am I willing to sacrifice? I have learned anything worth getting has a correlating sacrifice that needs to be made.

IF YOU WANT TO LEARN, BE BOLD ENOUGH TO ASK QUESTIONS.

DECEMBER 23
BUDGET A, BUDGET B

I would love to be able to say that all my companies make so much money I don't have to worry about the weekly budget, but that would be a lie. Each has a budget that varies depending on the age and health of that company. Some of my companies are like a barge, and unless they hit an island or iceberg, nothing gets in their way. Some of my companies are like kayaks and can be turned over with a few mistakes. This is why I have learned to have a Budget A, which reflects how I want things to go and expect things to go. This is what should happen and is the *forty-four weeks out of fifty-two* scenario. Again, depending on the strength of a company, the consistency of my ideal weekly budget is reflected in Budget A. However, starting a company is like flying a kite. I have some companies whose budget is affected by every gust of wind. This is why I have my Plan B budget.

Plan A is my ideal budget where I am putting money in reserves and everything is how I planned the week to go. Plan B happens when I can detect a cash shortfall. I have found that in most of our businesses (we do not have any retail companies), the weeks we struggle are holiday weeks because of the shortened workweek (less money comes in) and many employees taking time off during this week. Again, most of my companies are service-oriented. I have owned retail and the holidays, because of sales, are usually stronger weeks. We still had periods of the year that were slower and we could plan on it.

I would encourage you to have two weekly budgets as I have detailed. I would also like to share one other thing I do. Each year, I try to have fewer Plan B weeks. I start the year off with eight empty bullet points on my big whiteboard. The bullets reflect the eight weeks I have predicted we may need our Plan B. My hopes are to need fewer and I absolutely don't want to need more than eight. I hope this gives you a new approach to how to handle short cash-flow weeks.

BUDGET FOR REALITY.

DECEMBER 24
MITIGATING RISK

"The best entrepreneurs don't seek risk. They seek to mitigate risk."
—Rick Desai

I believe there is an idea that has been cemented in people's minds that being an entrepreneur means you love risk. You are somehow this financial daredevil that is constantly looking for an adrenaline rush. I often share that you calculate the risk before moving into a start-up, and this determines whether the level of risk you are exposing yourself to is worth the risk.

Mitigating risk is a touch different. Normally you decide to move forward with something, but the last step before the leap is strategizing how to lessen the actual risk. What can you do to move the likelihood of success in your favor?

Great entrepreneurs first calculate the risk, determining if it is a potential windfall for them and finally, they do everything within their power to mitigate (lessen) the risk. As you can tell by both of these steps, entrepreneurs are far from adrenaline junkies who go all-in at every opportunity.

The Steps I Recommend for Mitigating Risk

- First uncover, identify, and assess all the potential risks facing you.
- Identify the consequences, as this may make you reconsider.
- Reduce risk by adding more knowledge and expertise to your team.
- Hold a strong cash position to be able to withstand unknowns.
- Have a Plan B.
- Keep potential losses to a fixed amount predetermined before starting.
- Have periodic reviews of progress.

You cannot avoid all risk, and generally, the more risk, the higher the reward. I would first begin by calculating whether the risk you are exposing yourself to equals the payoff. I would then do everything I could to mitigate my risk.

IT IS OK TO JUMP WITH A PARACHUTE ON.

DECEMBER 25
THE SYMPTOMS THAT LEAD TO DEATH

Over the last decade, most of America has watched shopping centers and malls become a shadow of what we once remembered, as the internet has wreaked havoc on traditional retail. But the death spiral is still the same as it has been for all once-great companies. There is a decline that has many symptoms that I have shared, but a death spiral is the next level. This is a plane falling straight to the ground and it is not a case *if* it is going to crash, but *when*.

I often get asked by owners who are piloting one of these planes what to do, and more often than not, the spiral is in motion and the crash inevitable without a massive course change. The death spiral goes in this order: sales decline (this is the result of competition), the industry changes, and you have not adapted to those changes or customers are just not drawn to what you are offering. The reasons can vary, but normally you cannot compete with current pricing, quality, service, and reputation.

A death spiral can be avoided if you create a dashboard (shared in previous lesson), take annual company physicals, and adapt without delay to the information these provide. However, what usually happens is that before companies reach the spiral, they have made only minor changes or what I call "quick fixes" year after year with no strategic plan. Companies will start setting new revenue goals, never addressing or even knowing why their income is down in the first place. This will sometimes create some enthusiasm, and minor improvement may be seen, but at year's end, the decline is still obvious. Sometimes companies change leadership, but bringing in an outsider in the middle of a death spiral is rarely a good idea, as they have no idea where all the bodies have been buried.

Another common move that will never fix this level of an issue is culture change. I love and value culture, but it is a seasoning, not a pillar.

BE ALERT TO DECLINING NUMBERS, STAFF EXITS,
AND INDUSTRY CHANGES.

DECEMBER 26
THERE IS NO FOUR-HOUR WORK WEEK

"A dream doesn't become reality through magic; it takes sweat, determination, and hard work."
—Colin Powell

I love the book by Tim Ferris, *The 4-Hour Work Week*, but let's remember that he took a sabbatical from his company that created the context of the book, which was already up and running at a sustainable level. I do not think Tim would have walked away if it was fragile and required his involvement for survival.

I constantly share with soon-to-be business owners and those new to the journey that success in business and, for that matter, in most things, tends to follow the same path as a roller coaster. The initial part of the ride is straight up (steady climb), and for every venture or dream, this will be the effort and hard work required to make it happen. Without this climb, there will be no hairpin turns and loops that create the amazing ride and experience you share with others. In every story I hear about luck having a role in someone's success, it seems to be wrapped in a story of five to twenty years of sacrifice and endless hours working when no one was looking.

Thomas Edison lends support to this notion with, "The reason a lot of people do not recognize opportunity is because it usually goes around wearing overalls looking like hard work." What I have always liked about the fact that effort is the qualifier for something great to happen is that I can control my effort level. My intelligence has limits, and there are countless other shortfalls I may have, but I will outwork you.

What are you willing to sacrifice to get your business off the ground? How hard are you willing to work? Yes, that might mean your current full-time job plus eight hours a day on your new start-up. The good news is just like the roller coaster illustration, the hard work is not forever. It gets the ride going, and at some point, you do get to just enjoy the ride.

ARE YOU WILLING TO OUTWORK EVERYONE?

DECEMBER 27
MEMBERSHIPS

L ately, memberships have become the golden goose of businesses with their monthly autopay cash infusions to companies.

In an article in *Money* magazine titled "Costco Doesn't Make Any Money Selling You Groceries—Here's How It Actually Rakes in Billions of Dollars Every Year," the article states, "There are more than 53 million paid members as of this year, according to the Twitter thread. That means Costco is on track to make $4.3 billion from memberships in 2019, which is around 110 percent of its net income for the year, the thread says." "Groceries are a commodity in that Costco has figured out how to make billions offering but not in the traditional; profit is made by marking up the actual items for sale."

Another great example is Harry's Shave Club, again taking common items—razors and shaving accessories—and turning it into a membership giant that would be purchased by Edgewater Personal Care Product (Schick) for $1.37 billion.

One more that I have personally experienced is Peloton. I did not even catch on to the gold mine until they gladly received my credit card information so that I could receive their streaming classes that would be displayed on the large monitor (that I now view as a cash register), attached to the handlebars of my Peloton bike.

Purchasing this bike—that I must admit has some of the best marketing I have seen in years—was pricey to begin with, but the monthly membership fee that is higher than most gyms is a corporate gold mine. You basically buy the gym equipment and pay to be a member. It is simply genius. They took a stationary bike, a common item, and morphed it into must-have exercise equipment that is now linked to your bank account. Kudos, Peloton!

Now it seems everybody is in on the game—Amazon, Disney, the list goes on and on.

CREATE A CULT OF AUTO PAYEES.

DECEMBER 28
STANDING STAFF MEETINGS

In my efforts to try to be always available to my team, I have learned to master the standing staff meeting. I am surprised by how many problems I can resolve within one minute of my time.

Well, now that I think about it, I have had twenty-five years of making some of the dumbest mistakes possible, so I hope I can shed light on some better solutions and save them the aggravation I put myself through. What I like about the standing meeting is that my staff members know they can have one at any time if there is something I can help with. They know that I am accessible if they have a problem they cannot solve, are in situations they cannot get out of, or there is something I can do in a minute that will take them thirty.

Not only can my staff approach me, but I have a standard routine when I enter the office to go through four questions that prompted the standing meeting. I begin the cadence with these three questions:

- **Is there anything that needs my attention immediately?** This is for problems and crisis issues that I not only need to know about but need to solve.

- **Is there anything I need to be concerned with?** This means something is going to fall on my lap anyway or become a problem that I am going to find out about, so tell me now.

- **Is there anything I need to handle or get involved in?** This again is where I have told them that if I can make one phone call to the highest level of a company, or I have an existing relationship with someone, then tell me, and I will make the call. There is no reason for them to waste thirty minutes when I can call someone I know and resolve or access something effortlessly. Then, fourth, my favorite:

- **Is there anything I can get excited about?** I love it when one of my business partners has something they are excited to share with me. You would be surprised by how grown adults share the good news with me like a child bragging about their report card.

This brief style of meeting allows me to be accessible to my team and allows me to remind them that I do not want to be in the dark about critical items or things I can help with. When you ask, "Is there anything I can get excited about" as often as I ask this question, they plan to achieve highly so they have something to share.

NOT EVERY MEETING NEEDS TO LAST AN HOUR OR BE FORMAL TO BE EFFECTIVE.

DECEMBER 29
RECORD OF ACHIEVEMENT

At this point in this book, and also if you have ever heard me speak, you know that I am a sports fan and former college wrestler. The most exciting thing in our sport was when you earned your way to the finals of a tournament. This is when they would turn down the lights and introduce the finalists in each weight class to the cheering crowd. But what I liked hearing was the part where they would tell the screaming crowd what your prior achievements were so you can decide who is most likely to win. Looking back over sports, there was no greater introduction to an athlete than boxer Mike Tyson, who was simply introduced as World Heavyweight Champion and, my favorite part, "The Baddest Man on Planet Earth."

Let me share a secret to success with you. I wrote the previous paragraph because you need to have your own record of achievement of your lifetime accomplishments that you can read off or recite from memory. This is not for the purpose of bragging, but it will serve you well every time you set out to accomplish another big milestone.

Each of our introductions will sound different, and that is fine. At the beginning of your entrepreneurial journey, you will probably not have any business accolades, so you will draw from previous achievements that reflect the traits needed to be a successful entrepreneur.

When I begin going after another business or personal Mount Everest, I have a page I keep in the back of all my journals as my Hall of Fame Introduction: state champion, quit painkillers cold turkey, started more than twenty businesses, wrote books, etc. Each of these gives me confidence that no matter what I want to achieve, I have what it takes. And just like each of these previous items seemed impossible prior to being achieved, somehow, I figured it out, and I will also do the same with my new target.

BEGIN CREATING YOUR HALL OF FAME
INTRODUCTION.

DECEMBER 30
VALUATION OF A BUSINESS

Businesses are rarely similar, so there are a variety of ways to determine the value. But like art, it is worth what you are willing to pay if you are a buyer.

Let me share a few of the most common ways to determine a company's value. Let's begin with assets minus liabilities, which should be reflected on the balance sheet. For example, equipment, machinery, and inventory minus whatever the outstanding liabilities are. This does not take into account profit or cash flow but just what the company would be worth if you sold off the assets and paid off the debts.

What is the annual revenue of the business? It is common, depending on the industry, to pay a multiple of the annual revenue. Earnings per year is more indicative, in my opinion, of what a company is actually worth.

This method reflects what you are likely to put in your pocket each year, assuming you operate it in an identical manner to the existing owner. You can also look at the books and determine a great deal of waste as well as inefficient operations and see where the profit can be improved under your ownership. This method at least shows you what the profit stream is, and has been over the most recent years, assuming the books are correct and match corporate tax returns. A warning: if the books are messed up and don't match tax returns, everything I have shared does not apply.

Let me share a method I have used, as I assume most small-business financial records, are sketchy at best and open to interpretation. I want to see the owner's tax returns. Yes, what he or she put in his or her pocket. And finally, I have what I believe (based on our existing track records as I would not buy a business outside of my core business) a customer is worth. I would look at how many customers reach out to the business each year and the amount of total customer information they have on record to determine the worth of the business. Since we have a very robust marketing budget for my companies, I can take money from this budget to use to buy their customers.

KNOW THE VALUE OF YOUR BUSINESS.

DECEMBER 31
BUSINESS IS A RELATIONSHIP

The longer I am in business, the more I realize business is a relationship—nothing more. Let me share why I take this position: an effective business model does one thing better than its competition—serve the needs, wants, and desires of its customers. This is what every relationship has at its core: understanding and meeting the needs of someone else. If you do it well, you become part of a valuable relationship.

The engine of your business plan is what are you offering to the marketplace that they want.

You know what your customers want because you engage in a relationship with them. As I have shared, the lifecycle of my customers in my core businesses is now close to twenty years. Our relationship, like all relationships, has evolved, but I am always asking one critical question to myself, my customers, and my team: What do our customers want most? What more can we give them? How can we better communicate with them? How can we provide better service? How can we meet their needs faster and more effortlessly?

It's simple. I want our company to be a valuable relationship for our customers in regard to what we offer. We provide a valuable service, and we want to be their first choice every time. We want to get their feedback to better know their needs. We want to think five years ahead, discerning what they are going to want and need. It has been this strategic effort, from day one, to build a relationship with our customers that has fed our expansion over the years to where we are now offering eight divisions to meet their evolving needs.

I have reaped the fruits of creating outstanding relationships with our clients over the years, and now I encourage new business owners to just build relationships with your customers. I will warn you this does not mean every relationship is meant to last a lifetime. I still part ways with customers I cannot make happy or making them happy makes me broke or drives my staff crazy.

Create a chain of feedback so you stay aware of your customers' current and future needs.

DO YOU HAVE A RELATIONSHIP WITH YOUR CUSTOMERS?

ABOUT THE AUTHOR

**EQUIPPING
ENTREPRENEURS
FOR SUCCESS**

SEAN CASTRINA is the bestselling author of *World's Greatest Business Plan*, *The Greatest Entrepreneur in the World* and *8 Unbreakable Rules for Business Startup Success*. He has contributed to some of the most recognized media outlets including *Forbes, Inc., Money,* as well as guest lectured at some of America's finest colleges.

He is a serial entrepreneur having started more than 20 companies and currently is an active C.E.O. He is the host of one of iTunes most listened to business podcasts, The Ten Minute Entrepreneur.

Visit SeanCastrina.com for more essential business tips!

www.ingramcontent.com/pod-product-compliance
Lightning Source LLC
LaVergne TN
LVHW051448080426
835509LV00017B/1696